Academe Demarcated
No More: Disciplines
and Interdisciplinarity

Academe Demarcated No More: Disciplines and Interdisciplinarity

Multiple Case Study of Collaborative Teaching in Higher Education

Andrzej Wlodarczyk, Ph.D.

authorHOUSE®

AuthorHouse™ LLC
1663 Liberty Drive
Bloomington, IN 47403
www.authorhouse.com
Phone: 1-800-839-8640

Published by AuthorHouse   07/09/2014

ISBN: 978-1-4969-2455-1 (sc)
ISBN: 978-1-4969-2454-4 (e)

CONTENTS

PART I
COLLABORATIVE TEACHING IN HIGHER EDUCATION

PART II
PROCESS OF COLLABORATIVE TEACHING
IN HIGHER EDUCATION

PART I

COLLABORATIVE TEACHING IN HIGHER EDUCATION

CHAPTER 1

COLLABORATION

Not all activity that involves a group of individuals can be deemed collaboration. Maienschein (1993) provides the example of museum collection development, where collectors who work together to build the museum's collection co-labor, but as they do not participate in defining the task, the activity cannot be considered 'collaboration.' Thus, to be considered a collaborator, one must, at some point in the activity, 'participate in articulating the goal' (Maienschein, 1993, p. 170). (Gunawardena et al., 2010, p. 212)

Sperling (1994) defined collaboration as a term that implies "a conscious mutuality by which individuals of somewhat equal standing work in conjunction with one another toward a unified purpose" (Sperling, 1994, p. 227). The "'collaborative' practices…carry implications from a root term, 'community.' This now privileged term suggests terms such as 'conversation,' 'dialectic,' 'sharing,' and 'respecting many voices,' in what are imagined to be face-to-face encounters" (Miller, 1994, p. 284). Freed et al. (1997) defined collaboration as involving "learning new behaviors and changing the way people perceive their work" (p. 112). According to Flower et al. (1994), collaborative planning "is about people making meaning together and about providing a supportive social context for students or other writers to develop their ideas" (p. XI). Donaldson et al. (1996) perceive collaboration as a state as well as process, "Collaborative work, though complex, has two fundamental components: a respectful

3

relationship among the collaborators and a productive process that assists the collaborators to do their work" (p. 9). A number of theorists attempted to compare, or rather contrast, the concept of collaboration with that of a team. However, the elements that distinguish collaboration from team structure are not clear and in many instances overlapping, "The elements that define a team and the relationship among team members are very similar to those of collaboration because the element of collaboration is what distinguishes a team from a group or committee" (Hewit et al., p. 130).

Austin et al. (1991) identified a number of theories that create theoretical dimensions for collaboration:

> The theories and research on small group interaction and team development all emphasize that a team—or collaborative group— is constantly changing and evolving. Conclusions about stages of development are a dominant term throughout much of the theoretical work on small groups and teams....While each theory is distinctive, they share an emphasis on the dual challenges that confront collaborative groups, however: that is both interpersonal and task issues must be handled if collaboration is to be successful and productive. (Austin et al., 1991, p. 65)

Austin et al. (1991) identified, in their view, single most practical theory for analyzing collaborative work in higher education, "While various organizational and group theories elucidate aspects of academic collaboration...the single theory that is most useful for analyzing and understanding these team efforts among faculty is the theory of negotiated order" (p. 62). The theory of negotiated order conceptualizes collaboration:

> as a mechanism by which a new negotiated order emerges among a set of stakeholders....Negotiated order refers to a social context in which relationships are negotiated and renegotiated. The social order is shaped through the self-conscious interactions of participants. (Gray, 1989, p. 228)

Day et al. (1977) postulates that the negotiated order theory changes the concept of organizations from rigid, constrained by strict rules system, to a vastly fluid and organic network of interdependent components, "Organizations are thus viewed as complex and highly fragile social constructions of reality which are subject to the numerous temporal, spatial, and situational events occurring both internally and externally" (p. 132). Within that system, stakeholders "can collectively negotiate agreements to govern their interactions…, collectively establishing an agreement that satisfies multiple stakeholders and involves considerable negotiation" (Gray, 1989, p. 229). The negotiated order involves the process of "joint appreciation" (Trist, 1983). "Building a joint appreciation, then means sharing these appraisals of the domain and trading individual and collective perceptions of what is and what is not possible" (Gray, 1989, p. 229). The stakeholders build agreements regulating their future interactions within the framework of the joint appreciation concept, "Essentially, these agreements constitute a normative framework through which members correlate their activities with respect to the problem. In so doing they establish a temporary order for the domain" (Gray, 1989, p. 230). Ramirez (1983) conceptualized collaborations as negotiated orders revolving around several key concepts. First, stakeholders collaboratively construct strategies to deal with the external environment. Second, the arrangements among stakeholders are emergent and developmental in nature. Third, collaborations serve as quasi-institutional mechanisms for coordinating relations and interests within a society. Fourth, collaborations serve as vehicles for action learning (Ramirez, 1983, qtd. in Gray, 1989, p. 230). Gray (1989) defined collaboration as "a process through which parties who see different aspects of a problem can constructively explore their differences and search for solutions that go beyond their own limited vision of what is possible" (p. 5). Gray (1989) identified further five dimensions that accompany the process:

> (1) The stakeholders are interdependent, (2) Solutions emerge by dealing constructively with differences, (3) Joint ownership of decisions is involved, (4) Stakeholders assume collective responsibility for the future direction of the domain, and (5) Collaboration is an emergent process. (p. 11)

Austin et al. (1991) insisted that dimensions identified by Gray (1989) are applicable to collaboration among faculty members:

> First, collaboration involves interdependence among the participants. Individuals are motivated to collaborate to work toward goals

that are not possible or feasible for one person alone to achieve. Second, through collaboration, partners encounter new views and approaches, and, by grappling with the differences between their views, participants find new understanding, ideas, or solutions. Third, joint ownership of decisions is necessary for successful collaboration; that is, collaborators must all agree on the direction of the joint work. The fourth key dynamic is closely related to the third. If collaborative relationships are to be productive, participants (or "stake holders") must share responsibility for decisions about the team members' relationships and roles. Finally, negotiated order theory emphasizes that 'collaboration is an emergent process' and their goals and agreements evolve over time. (p. 63)

Bennis et al. (1956) put forward a theory which addressed team development as a process including both interpersonal and task issues, "Dependence and interdependence–power and love, authority and intimacy–are regarded as the central problems of group life" (p. 435). "The evolution from Phase I to Phase II represents not only a change in emphasis from power to affection, but also from role to personality" (p. 436). In the analysis of Bennis et al.'s (1956) theory, Baldwin et al. (1991) issued the following rejoinder:

In the first phase labeled 'dependence,' members deal with the leader's authority, perhaps coping with dependence on the leader by discussing issues external to the group's work and sometimes revolting against the leader. During the second phase, 'interdependence,' group members grapple with conflicts around identity and intimacy, and perhaps form subgroups. By passing through these two phases, a group becomes mature, capable of resolving internal tensions, and able to act as a team. (p. 66)

Group interaction is a cyclical process, somewhat akin to changing a tire in which the bolts are tightened in sequence and then the sequence is repeated (Schutz, 1958, qtd. in Austin et al., 1991, p. 65). According to Austin et al. (1991), "this theory posits three phases: "the inclusion phase," "the control phase," and "the affection phase" (p. 65):

During inclusion, members often discuss small issues or their biographies as a route to become acquainted. Critical issues to be handled at this phase are interpersonal boundaries and members' commitment to the group. In the control phase, members deal with the issues of sharing responsibility, and distributing power and control. Elements of this task oriented phase are establishing rules and procedures, structuring decision making, discussing the group's orientation to its work, and dealing with competition and struggles for leadership. The emphasis of the affection phase is on the group's socio-emotional issues and needs and how they relate to the decisions made about the group's structure, decision making processes, and tasks. During this phase, group members might express hostility, jealousy, or positive feelings toward each other. As these issues are resolved, the group cycles back to the concerns of the first phase. (p. 66)

Over a decade later, another two-dimensional theory was proposed by Schein (1969):

Early studies of organization were dominated by the 'scientific management' school of thought leading to an almost exclusive preoccupation with the 'structural' or static elements of organization. (p. 10)

The problem with this approach is not that it is wrong but that it is incomplete. The network of positions and roles which define the formal organizational structure is occupied by people, and those people in varying degrees put their own personalities into getting their job done....People's personalities, perceptions, and experiences also determine how they will behave in their roles and how they will relate to others. (p. 11)

Schein (1969) formulated a theory in which clear distinction has been made between interpersonal issues–"self-oriented behavior," and task issue–"task functions" as two fundamental phases of group process development (p. 45). Schein (1969) proposed that "The problems which a person faces when he enters a new group stem from certain underlying emotional issues which must be resolved before he can feel comfortable in the new situation" (p. 32). Several issues have been identified in relation to the first interpersonal phase. Members of the team have to deal with issues like identity, control, power, influence, acceptance, intimacy, goal, and role identification. Various responses may accompany this phase such as mutual support, denial, withdrawal, or even aggression. With time, however, members of the group move beyond interpersonal to the task issues. Within that phase, members of the group move to dealing with task functions such as giving or seeking opinions, clarifying or elaborating on maintenance functions like encouraging, harmonizing, compromising (Schein, 1969).

Srivastva et al. (1977) analyzed previous findings on nature of group development and concluded that most researchers simplified their process to only two or three stages. Although those theories may have captured critical dimensions of the life of the group, they omitted other essential nuances that shape group processes, "While the small group has been extensively studied, there is a theoretical gap which prevents this knowledge from being optimally useful to the field of organization development" (p. 84). Even though prior models focused on the critical dimensions of group life, they created a theoretical gap by not recognizing group's external environment in which it is embedded, "Insufficient conceptual work has been done to describe the relationship between the small group and the larger organization that surrounds it, and thus forms its immediate environment" (p. 84). Srivastva et al. (1977) emphasized the complexity of group development by positing that:

> a group grows along six dimensions: members' relations to one another; members' relations to authority; the group's relation to its organizational environment; the group's task orientation; the group's orientation to learning; and the group's mode of reacting to its larger environment. In each of these dimensions, the group moves through five stages, shifting from individualistic and dependent modes of interacting, through stages of competition and conflict, to a stage of cooperative independence [that] allows for task concentration and performance. (Srivastva et al., p. 84; Obert, 1983)

This perspective on group development reflects both the interpersonal and task demands a group experiences as well as the group's changing interaction with the environment within which it works. (Oja et al., 1989, qtd. in Austin et al., 1991, p. 67)

Tuckman et al. (1977) modified Tuckman's (1965) model of group development. The original two-stage model included "An essential correspondence between the group structure [the interpersonal realm] and the task-activity [the task-activity realm]" (Tuckman et al., 1965, p. 420). That model was originally replaced with the four-stage process which included the following stages: "forming," "storming," "norming," and "performing" (Tuckman et al., 1977, p. 420). After further revision, the model was finally amended to include a fifth stage: "adjourning" (Tuckman at al., 1977, p. 426). According to the model, the *forming* stage is characterized by the efforts to get acquainted with other team members and the task itself. It is a testing time for all members of a group who try to figure out what the task is and decide on how to complete it. During the *storming* stage, team members may express distrust and hostility toward each other as well as the leader, polarize into subgroups, and resist the task. Once the storming stage is completed, team members overcome mutual hostility and become more open to new ideas by trusting each other and dealing with disagreements in a constructive way. That stage is referred to as *norming*. While the *performing* stage is characterized by team members' focus on reaching goals and task accomplishment in a harmonious way, the *adjourning* stage is marked by conclusion of team's work and coping with the issues pertinent to team members' separation.

Gray (1989) put forward another three-stage model of collaborative process, applicable, in his opinion, to any kind of collaboration, "While there is not a clearly prescribed pattern that characterizes every collaboration, there appear to be some common issues that crop up repeatedly" (p. 55). Gray's (1989) model includes three major phases: "problem setting," "direction setting," and "implementation":

The three-phase model of collaboration…is predicated on the assumption that although certain phases may be more significant for some collaborations than for others, there remains a fundamental set of issues that must be addressed in the course of any collaboration. (Gray, 1989, p. 56)

According to Gray (1989), the first phase referred to as a *problem setting*, "requires identification of the stakeholders, mutual acknowledgment of the issues that join them, and building commitment to address these issues through face-to-face negotiations" (p. 56). Within that phase, problems or "major issues of concern," need to be defined, and committed "stakeholders" with appropriate expertise identified (p. 58). In some collaborations, however, the issue of resources also need to be dealt with within the first phase, "One final aspect of problem setting may be securing enough resources to ensure that stakeholders may participate equally in the proceedings" (p. 73). The second phase, *direction setting*, in Gray's (1989) model, is associated with important procedural and substantive issues, "During direction setting, stakeholders identify the interests that brought them to the table. They sort out which of their interests are the same, which are opposed, and which are unique or different, and can form the basis for eventual trade-offs" (p. 74). During this phase, stakeholders need to reach an agreement on ground rules, establish outline for acceptable and unacceptable behaviors for all involved parties, set the agenda, organize subgroups, and undertake joint information search. This phase also includes completion of such tasks as management of data, exploration of options, reaching agreement among the stakeholders, and finally closing the deal. The importance of the third phase, *implementation*, was expressed by Gray (1989) in the following statement:

> Carefully forged agreements can fall apart after agreement is reached unless deliberate attention is given to several issues during the implementation phase of collaboration. These issues are dealing with constituencies, building external support, structuring, and monitoring the agreement, and ensuring compliance. (p. 86)

Although all of the above-referenced models can be used as lenses to examine and understand collaboration, Austin et al. (1991) regards Gray's (1989) model to be most useful, "This model, which can be used to analyze the development of any team, seems to be one of the most useful theoretical models for understanding the stages through which faculty collaborators pass" (p. 68). Austin et al. (1991) further noted that, "Although each collaborative arrangement is distinctive, collaboration generally follows a common pattern" (p. 6).

Although small-group models might label the steps in the collaborative process somewhat differently, each effective collaborative team must proceed through four basic stages: (1) choosing colleagues or team members, (2) dividing the labor, (3) establishing work guidelines, and (4) terminating collaboration. The way collaborators execute each step influences the evolution and outcomes of the team's effort. (Austin et al., 1991, p. 6)

"The term collaboration implies a conscious mutuality by which individuals of somewhat equal standing work in conjunction with one another toward a unified purpose"

(Sperling, 1994, p. 227). The "'collaborative' practices...carry implications from a root term, 'community.' This now privileged term suggests 'conversation,' 'dialectic,' 'sharing,' and 'respecting many voices,' in what are imagined to be face-to-face encounters" (Miller, 1994, p. 284). Freed et al. (1997) argued that "collaboration involves learning new behaviors and changing the way people perceive their work" (p. 112). Collaborative planning, an essential part of teachers' collaboration, "is about people making meaning together–about providing a supportive social context for students or other writers to develop their ideas" (Flower et al., 1994, p. XI). Donaldson et al. (1996), as others before him, perceive collaboration as not only a state but also a process, "Collaborative work, though complex, has two fundamental components: a respectful relationship among the collaborators and a productive process that assists the collaborators to do their work" (p. 9).

A team is frequently defined as "a group of people working toward [a] common goal,...a joint effort by individuals in which the individual subordinates personal interests and opinions for the unity of the team" (Lane, 1993, p. 40). The term team has come to be accepted "to describe a group of people who are goal centered, interdependent, honest, open, supportive, and empowered. Members of a team develop strong feelings of allegiance that go beyond the mere grouping of individuals (Lewis et al., 1994, p. 191).

The elements that distinguish collaboration from team structure are not clear, and in many instances overlapping. According to Hewit et al. (1997), "The elements that define a team and the relationship among team members are very similar to those of collaboration, because the element of collaboration is what distinguishes a team from a group or committee"

11

(p. 130). Freed et al' (1997) concludes that "a team is a process, not a product. The challenge for anyone who is responsible for building a team is to develop a group of people so that they are able to lead, act, and think together" (p. 113).

CHAPTER 2

COLLABORATIVE TEACHING

Collaborative teaching represents opportunity to improve quality of higher education. Even though, from a practical standpoint, the topic may sound novel, concept of "interdisciplinarity is quite old, rooted in the ideas of Plato, Aristotle, Rabelais, Kant, Hegel, and other historical figures who have been described as 'interdisciplinary thinkers'" (Klein, 1990, p. 19). Their beliefs grounded in the notion that philosophers have the ability to collect all forms of knowledge in a general almost encyclopedic sense had a profound effect on interdisciplinary study. Today, however, with tough economic circumstances resulting in many universities having their budgets significantly reduced, it is difficult to find proponents of innovation for long-term improvement. Nonetheless, Zangwill (1993) submitted that economic factors and a pessimistic vision of the future "should not constitute a self-fulfilling prophecy in shaping the future of higher education, but notwithstanding, leadership should battle the poison of pessimism, using the antidote of innovation….In fact, top university leaders often use difficulties as a launching pad for innovation" (p. 3). Since it is the responsibility of higher education to teach models of effective living, it could be partially accomplished through the demonstration of community building through collaboration among units in a college or university, he concluded.

Organizational theorists, following biological and social scientists, embraced systems concepts and gradually identified with the movement in the latter part of the twentieth century (Kast et al., 1996). Kast et al. (1996) argued that "General systems theory seems to provide a relief from the limitations of more mechanistic approaches and a rationale for rejecting 'principles' based on relatively 'closed-systems' thinking" (p. 47). The theory provides a paradigm for organizations to "crank into their systems model" diverse knowledge from relevant underlying disciplines (p. 48). However, in spite of a long history of organismic and holistic thinking, the utilization of systems approaches did not become the accepted model for organizations until relatively recently. One of the basic contributions of general systems theory was the rejection of traditional closed-system mechanistic view of social organizations by emphasizing that "systems are organized–they are composed of interdependent components in some relationship" (p. 53). Open system theory did not free us entirely from its constraints, and even though we teach a general systems approach, we continue to practice a subsystems thinking (Kast et al., 1996).

> Each of the academic disciplines and each of us personally have limited perspective of the system we are studying. While proclaiming a broad systems viewpoint, we often dismiss variables outside our interest or competence as being irrelevant, opening our systems only to those inputs which we can handle with our "disciplinary bag of tools." (Kast et al., 1996, p. 54)

It seems natural, therefore, to know more about the individual elements (or subsystems) of an organization than the interrelationships and interactions that keep its cohesion:

> General systems theory forces us to consider those relationships about which we know the least. Consequently, we continue to elaborate on those aspects of the organization which we know best–and that is a partial systems view. Although general systems theory does not provide a panacea for solving all problems in organizations, it certainly ...facilitate[s] more thorough understanding of complex situations and increase the likelihood of appropriate action." (Kast et al., 1996, p. 63)

Barr et al. (1995) maintained that "A paradigm shift is taking hold in American higher education" (p. 13). The paradigm that has governed our colleges is moving subtly but profoundly from a collegial system that exists "to provide instruction" to a collegial system that exists "to produce learning." Barr et al. (1995) refers to the traditional dominant paradigm as the "Instruction Paradigm." Colleges have created structures to provide for the activity of teaching conceived primarily as delivering lectures. Saying that the purpose of colleges is to provide instruction, is like saying that "General Motors' business is to operate assembly lines, or that the purpose of medical care is to fill hospital beds," they assert (p. 14). The mission of the college is not limited merely to instruction but producing "learning" with every student by "whatever" means work best (p. 14). The shift to a "Learning Paradigm" liberates institutions from a set of difficult constraints, because "The Learning Paradigm ends the lecture's privileged position, honoring in its place whatever approaches serve best to prompt learning of particular knowledge by particular students" (p. 14). It envisions the institution as a center to continuously learn how to produce more learning with each entering student as a full participant. In the new paradigm, college takes responsibility for learning, not merely teaching. Students, the co-producers of learning, can and must take responsibility for their own learning, "In the Learning Paradigm, a college's purpose is not to transfer knowledge but to create environments and experiences that bring students to discover and construct knowledge for themselves, to make students members of communities of learners that make discoveries and solve problems" (p. 15). Under the instruction paradigm, a primary institutional purpose is to optimize students' success by focusing on teaching. In contrast, the learning paradigm's primary drive is to produce learning outcomes more efficiently, "In a Learning Paradigm, college is concerned with learning productivity, not teaching productivity" (p. 16). In the Learning Paradigm, a college degree would represent not time spent and credit hours accumulated, but instead certify that the student had demonstrably attained specified knowledge and skills through the development of critical-thinking skills, "Thus colleges would move away from educational atomism and move toward holistically treating the knowledge and skills required for a degree" (p. 21). Learning paradigm frames learning holistically thus recognizing that the chief agent in the process is a learner. Students become active discoverers and constructors of their own knowledge. In the learning paradigm, knowledge consists of frameworks that are created or constructed by the learner. Knowledge is not defined as cumulative and linear, like a "wall of bricks," but interaction of "frameworks and matrices," they further edify. The ability to apprehend the whole of something gives meaning to its elements. Roles begin to blur under the umbrella of the learning paradigm. As the structures of colleges begin to loosen up and accountability for results of learning tightens up, organizational control and command processes will have to change, "Teamwork and shared governance over time replace the line governance and independent work of the Instruction Paradigm's hierarchical and competitive organization" (p. 24). In learning paradigm, "interdisciplinary (or non-disciplinary) task-groups and design-teams become a major operating mode" (p. 24). Such teams, they conclude, could have the freedom, that no faculty member has in today's atomized framework–to organize the learning environment in ways that maximize student learning.

Haber (1991) distinguished "collaborative learning" from "collaborative teaching," and asserted that "Collaborative learning is covered extensively in scholarly journals, but the subject of collaborative teaching in college has received scant attention" (p. 2). In educational terms, "Team teaching... refers, most often, to the teaching done in interdisciplinary courses by several faculty members who have joined together to produce that course" (Davis, 1995, p. 6). Wilson et al. (1998), in their research based on four-semester long experience with collaborative teaching at the college level, identified three basic areas of collaborative integration: "1) coordination of course content among the three disciplines, 2) team teaching of strategies common to all disciplines, and 3) coordination of integrated course assignments" (p. 3). In coordinating course content, faculty planned lessons addressing curriculum standards in mathematics, science, and social studies, "Such coordination allows the students to draw inferences about standards in general, as well as gain specific information about each set" (p. 3). "Instructional strategies common to all three disciplines are taught once with examples drawn from various fields. These strategies include cooperative learning, authentic assessment, and questioning techniques" (p. 4), with major collaborative assignment requiring integration of all taught disciplines, "Journal assignments and field experiences are designed to include all three 'inquiry' disciplines" (p. 4). The extant literature provides ample of compelling evidence to support the relationship between faculty approaches to teaching and meaningful student learning. If the ultimate goal of higher education is to promote meaningful student learning, faculty teaching approaches become a critical aspect in determining the quality of student learning.

Research focused on teaching approaches suggests that a student-centered, learner-focused approach promotes deeper and more meaningful student learning, and that there is a significant relationship between faculty approaches and student learning (Prince and Felder, 2006). Prince and Felder (2006) conducted an extensive overview of "inductive teaching methods" such as problem- or case-based learning and concluded that collective evidence favors the inductive approach over traditional deductive pedagogy. The evidence is conclusive...inductive methods promote adoption of a deep approach to learning...intellectual development...and helping students acquire the critical thinking and self-directed learning skills that characterize expert scientists and engineers" (Prince and Felder, 2006, p. 135). Similarly, Smith et al. (2005) provide an overview of "pedagogies of engagement," a term used to describe active learning. In their overview, Smith et al. explain that student-centered pedagogies of engagement, such as cooperative learning, promote student outcomes in three major categories: academic success, quality of relationships, and psychological adjustment to college life.

Austin et al.'s (1991) observations indicated that academic collaboration is already well established in the institutions of higher learning: "In many fields of study, the image of the solitary scholar working alone in a library carrel or laboratory is no more than a fond memory or historic artifact." (p. 19). Today collaboration is clearly a fact of academic life. More and more professors teach cooperatively (p. 20).

> Remarkably little research and writing analyze the process of academic collaboration, and scarcely a handful of universities and professional organizations have developed systematic policies for regulating and evaluating collaborative practices and products. (Austin et al., 1991, p. 21)

Austin et al. (1991) put forth the notion that:

> While the theoretical models suggest useful ways to understand the collaborative process, those interested in engaging in collaboration, or encouraging colleagues to do so, will want to consider the practical details of successful team work. (p. 68)

> Successful collaborations involve a complex set of attributes and activities, each requiring careful attention from the parties

involved. Faculty who wish to collaborate, should be familiar with all aspects of this process. (p. 98)

Maeroff (1993) viewed collaboration as a novel approach in academia, contrasting sharply with a traditional isolated mode of work in educational institutions. Since, by nature, faculty are most comfortable doing things the way they have been taught, the subsequent change becomes difficult to implement. He believed, however, that change could occur when faculty decide to immerse themselves in one another's subjects to make the connections that will allow to show their students the interrelatedness of knowledge, "The point here is not that teachers are perfect but that they are imperfect. And because of their shortcoming, they need help to improve education" (p.5). According to Griggs et al. (1996), "The interaction between individuals not only lends itself to mutual support but also provides greater vigor, energy, invention, and enthusiasm; [we] learn best and accomplish more when we work together" (p. 1).

Davis (1995) proposed that universities should reflect reality as it is, which means presenting its realities' various aspects as interrelated, not separated from one another. He argued that "Many colleges and universities today are developing and offering interdisciplinary courses taught by teams of faculty members" (p. 3). In his view, collaborative teaching indicates the most significant integration between disciplines. Davis (1995) used the term "interdisciplinary" to refer to collaborative work of academic instructors in two or more disciplines, by bringing together, and to some extent, synthesizing their perspectives (Davis, 1995). Collaborative teaching has been also conceptualized on a continuum, starting with a limited amount of collaboration circumscribed primarily to planning individual segments of the course to be later delivered separately by individual instructors, all the way through to most extensive exchanges with in-depth interdisciplinary interactions and multiple instructors present in each session. At one end of the spectrum courses are planned by a group of faculty and then carried out in a series of segments by the individual members of the team. For example, three faculty members might plan a course to be delivered over a period of one semester, with each faculty member taking responsibility for one of the cognate part of the course respectively. They plan the general content of the course together, to avoid overlapping the topics, but once the general planning has been completed, they teach their own sections sequentially, one after the other. They do not attend each other's classes, but devise their own teaching strategies and deploy their own evaluation procedures. At the other end of the spectrum, there are courses planned and delivered by instructors working closely together as a team throughout the process. Collaborating faculty develops a common syllabus, integrate various perspectives within the planning stage, and come to an agreement about the order of topics, activities to be deployed throughout the course. Even though instructors do take primary responsibility for individual class sessions, they are involved in both planning and delivering the instruction for each class together. They attend every session and provide feedback in support of each other's teaching. Instructors work together on grading and evaluation procedures. The enrichment that comes from the synthesis of the multiple perspectives is what gives the course its distinctive character. Since most of the collaboratively taught courses will fall somewhere between these extremes, it may be useful to include in collaborative teaching all arrangements that involve two or more faculty including both planning and delivery of a course (Davis, 1995, p. 7).

According to Austin et al. (1991):

> faculty collaboration is a cooperative endeavor that involves common goals, coordinated effort, and outcomes or products for which the collaborators share responsibility and credit.... Fundamentally faculty collaboration takes two forms—collaboration in research and collaboration in teaching. (p. 5)

Robinson et al. (1995) argued that "We use 'collaborative teaching' to describe any academic experience in which two teachers work together in designing and teaching a course that itself uses group learning techniques" (p. 57). "A team is a process, not a product. The challenge for anyone who is responsible for building a team is to develop a group of people so that they are able to lead, act, and think together" (Freed et al., 1997, p. 113). Wiedmeyer et al. (1991) defined collaborative teaching as "a cooperative and interactive process between two teachers that allows them to develop creative solutions to mutual problems" (p. 7). In educational terms, "Team teaching...refers, most often, to the teaching done in interdisciplinary courses by several faculty members who have joined together to produce that course" (Davis, 1995, p. 6). Griggs et al.'s (1996) enthusiasm for collaborative teaching was expressed in the following statement: "The interaction between individuals not only lends to mutual support but also provides greater vigor, energy, invention, and enthusiasm; [we] learn best and accomplish more when we work together" (p. 1). Davis (1995) believes that universities should reflect life as it is, presenting various aspects of life as related, rather than separate entities. That might be the reason, he continues, why "Many colleges and universities today are developing and offering interdisciplinary courses taught by teams of faculty members" (p. 3). Davis (1995) further argues that "collaborative teaching indicates most significant integration and collaboration between disciplines" (p. 3).

Mayo et al. (1979) purported that "Team teaching is a particularly effective mode of interdisciplinary instruction. In fact, for certain types of interdisciplinary study team teaching is likely the most effective method" (p. 63). Fourteen years later, Bergen (1993) agreed with their opinion, adding that teacher preparation programs today do advocate team taught interdisciplinary approaches. She argued that movement from individualized teaching to collaborative teaching is a major element of the school organizational and curricular reform that is now being strongly advocated in journal articles, in-service meetings, and the educational media. Teachers and administrators alike are being required to rethink the one teacher in his or her closed-door classroom model so pervasive in the past, she asserts. The alternative model calls for a "team of professionals planning, teaching, and evaluating within and across open-door classrooms" (Bergen, 1995, p. 1). Bergen (1995) strongly emphasized that "the action models we provide speak much more loudly than the words we utter…,students will need to develop abilities to work in cooperative, interactive teams as they will need to demonstrate these abilities in order to join the 21st century job market" (p. 2). Bergen (1995) concluded by cautioning that:

> Learning the art and science of teamwork is a worthwhile activity not only for teachers, but also for all individuals in our society. If teachers can provide good models of such teamwork, students may go on to demonstrate those skills in the larger community and the world. (p. 2)

Geltner (1994) advised that a learning environment should prepare students for their future work setting. In recent years, the mainstream of American workplace has been changing in a very significant and far-reaching way. It is now characterized by teamwork, cooperation, collaboration, and participation, "The individual specialist working in solitude can no longer solve the problems facing us....What is replacing the isolated worker is the team composed of members with a variety of perspectives, experiences, skills, and know-how (p. 7). Freed et al. (1997) estimated that at the turn of the twentieth first century, most of corporate America would have their workforces structured as teams. A few years earlier, echoing the same sentiments, Fey (1993) noted that "Broadening classrooms as nurturing communities is imperative to our survival in the 21st century" (p. 10). College faculty need to find ways to foster collaborations that will move students away from their isolated, solitary study (on "mountain tops") and sensitize students to the larger community in which they are a part (Fey, 1993). Bensimon et al. (1993) looked at teams from the executive perspective, drawing the portrait of an ideal leader as someone "who knows how to find and bring together diverse minds–minds that reflect variety in their points of view, in their thinking processes, and in their question-asking and problem-solving strategies" (p.1). Indeed, Bensimon et al. (1993) foresaw the day in which individual leadership would become archaic and obsolete:

> As the world grows more complex–that is, as we come to appreciate its growing complexity–it is likely that we will stop thinking of leadership as the property or quality of just one person. We will begin to think of it in its collective form: leadership as occurring among and through a group of people who think and act together. (p. 2)

Bensimon (1993) emphasized the distinct advantages of teams over "solo leadership" by pointing to enhanced ability of creative problem solving among diversely oriented minds, peer support, and increased accountability. On the other hand, dangers of teamwork may include isolation of the team from the rest of the department, "groupthink" (in case of overly homogeneous teams), and suppression of different opposing views, or even the fact that teamwork is time consuming. Davis (1995) postulated that "Whatever one might think about the relative value of the contributions of individuals and teams, it does appear, at least for the near future, that teams will be used to achieve a variety of types of outcomes in almost every kind of organization" (p. 77). He further adds that today the issue is not whether to use teams, but how to use them effectively. The use of teams for teaching in higher education is only a part of a broader context in which team collaboration is coming to be highly valued. Smith et al. (1990) argued that collaboration was rarely mentioned in the literature of the '80s, nor was it part of the vocabulary of national studies of American education. Collaboration appeared to be neither part of the problem nor part of the solution when considering reform of education. There is, however, good news, "Collaboration is being increasingly recognized as not only a desirable but an essential characteristic of an effective school" (p. V).

According to Austin et al. (1991), collaboration represents one of the modes of averting atrophy in academe by incessantly responding to the evolving needs of a dynamic society. Working closely with others gives faculty the opportunity to explore new terrains and scholarly modes such as discovery, integration, application, or teaching, "Ideally, collaboration enables professors to stay fresh and vital by adding new dimensions to their work lives" (p.83). Personal benefits, such as satisfaction with work and overall psychological well-being are correlated with collaborative activities as well. A sufficient amount of evidence supports the claim that benefits of collaborative relationships are large enough to recommend them as a useful vehicle for extending academic resources and enriching academic life (Austin et al., 1991). Mayo et al. (1979) argued that all parties involved in collaboration benefit from it:

(1) Students improve in their ability to integrate and synthesize because they are able to observe their instructors engaging in these processes. (2) Course format allows faculty to share not only their fields of knowledge, but also their teaching techniques as they approach a comprehensive subject. (3) Collaboration of faculty from several disciplines allows for a more adequate treatment of a complex subject. (4) An impetus toward innovation in teaching method and curricular reform is produced by the interaction of faculty in these courses. (5) Faculty members experience a stimulus for professional development because they must learn new content areas as well as methods of team teaching. (6) The current concerns of students are better met because the course format is better suited to the study of contemporary problems than the traditional one-teacher, one-discipline course. (7) More opportunities are presented for students to work at individualized projects in conjunction with faculty. (p. 67)

Gray (1980) regards teamwork as an "ingrained" part of academic life in general. He contended that "Education is saturated with teams. As soon as a new idea or project is conceived, a team is set up to develop it" (p. 85). This is especially true of academic courses when team members set to work with the willful intention of producing discussion papers about philosophy, objectives, and criteria of evaluation. As the complexity of the world grows, due principally to technological advancements and trends toward globalization, those ideas appear even more relevant today. An example of collaborative teaching was provided by Northwest Missouri State University, which in the fall of '87 inaugurated an Electronic Campus project to accelerate learning opportunities for students and created a course named CS 130 Using Computers (VanDyke, 1995). The dichotomous nature of the lecture and laboratory components of the course pushed the administration to create classrooms where lectures and laboratories could be integrated. Significantly more effort was required to coordinate the class. A small core of instructors slowly evolved into a team that worked together to develop materials. By removing a significant amount of redundancy and allowing each instructor more time to improve the materials being used, in the opinion of VanDyke (1995), "Team approach used by this small group of instructors was very successful" (p. 27). As instructors observed the benefits of collaboration, more of them joined the teams. In the fall of '92, a single team was established and all assigned instructors began to work together. Although some disadvantages of collaborative teaching do exist, such as "the increased amount of time required, limited flexibility of course schedule," the advantages of collaboration far outweigh its downsides (VanDyke, 1995, p. 34).

Zidon (1994), in a qualitative case study on collaborative teaching, examined undergraduate student perceptions of the learning experience within a pre-service teacher education course. Students reported a number of benefits related to collaborative teaching such as increased diversity of perspectives and teaching methodology–which helped students learn. Students observed that collaborative teaching provides psycho-social support for instructors. However, several disadvantages were also reported. They included: 1) sending mixed messages, 2) disparities in grading and instructors' expectations, and 3) personal uneasiness in situations when instructors fought as a result of disagreement. Students concluded that collaborative teaching can be difficult if instructors differ philosophically or have incompatible personalities. Students' observations indicated also that collaborative teaching can be successful if collaborating instructors are compatible, reach for a common goal, share responsibilities, are open, honest, and communicate frequently with each other. Administration must be cognizant that collaborative teaching puts additional demands on instructors' time and should plan their teaching load accordingly. Eighty percent of the studied students concluded that given an opportunity to teach in the future, they would like to teach collaboratively.

CHAPTER 3

PURPOSE OF THE STUDY & DEFINITION OF TERMS

The purpose of this multiple qualitative case study was to explore and gain an in-depth understanding of the process of collaborative teaching as an alternative method of instruction in higher education. The collaborations were conducted by three teams of faculty members teaching in a major Midwestern research university. The primary intention of this two-year long study was to depict the process of collaborative teaching and identify issues involved in it. Final focus provided pedagogical and curricular implications for students, faculty, administrators, and broader academic community. According to Austin et al. (1991):

> Faculty who are accustomed to working alone should consider developing collaborative relationships. Carefully managed collaborative partnership can enrich academic life. To be successful, collaborators must know the dynamics of the collaboration process and be prepared to cope with collaboration's challenges as well as reap its rewards. (p. 7)

For the purpose of this study the following terms have been identified and defined:

Universities and Colleges

Academic American Encyclopedia (1996) defines "Universities and colleges [as] institutions that offer education beyond the secondary (preparatory or high school) level" (p. 469).

Discipline

Oxford English Dictionary (1989) defines discipline as "a branch of instruction or education; a department of learning or knowledge; a science or art in its educational aspect" (Simpson et al., p. 735). Davis (1995) defines discipline as:

> a discrete subject and its characteristics regimen of investigation and analysis–geography, political science, psychology, and English are examples. In most American colleges and universities, such realms are structurally accommodated in departments, which administer the teaching and research in the individual discipline. (p. 3)

Interdisciplinarity

Webster's New World Dictionary (1994) defines interdisciplinarity as "involving, or joining, two or more disciplines, or branches of learning" (Neufeldt, p. 703). Davis (1995) defines interdisciplinary courses as:

> those involving the subject matter and faculty expertise of two or (usually) more disciplines or professional specializations….In the more narrow definition, a discipline usually refers to a subject specialization in the arts and sciences; a broader definition, one more widely used today, would include the specializations that also occur within professional fields. (p. 4)

Thus, one might think of specializations within business as disciplines such as: accounting, marketing, or management; or of specializations within law such as: constitutional law, civil law, or international law.

Collaboration

Sperling (1994) asseverates that "term collaboration implies a conscious mutuality by which individuals of somewhat equal standing work in conjunction with one another toward a unified purpose" (p. 227). The "'collaborative' practices...,carry implications from a root term, 'community.' This now privileged term suggests 'conversation,' 'dialectic,' 'sharing,' and 'respecting many voices,' in what are imagined to be face-to-face encounters" (Miller, 1994, p. 284). Freed et al. (1997) stated that "collaboration involves learning new behaviors and changing the way people perceive their work" (p. 112). Collaborative planning, according to Flower et al. (1994), is an essential part of teachers' collaboration; it is "about people making meaning together–about providing a supportive social context for students or other writers to develop their ideas" (p. XI). Donaldson et al., (1996) declared collaboration to be a state as well as process: "Collaborative work, though complex, has two fundamental components: a respectful relationship among the collaborators and a productive process that assists the collaborators to do their work" (p. 9).

Team

Most frequently, a team's definition would denote "a group of people working toward [a] common goal...a joint effort by individuals in which the individual subordinates personal interests and opinions for the unity of the team" (Lane, 1993, p. 40). Consequently, the term "team" has come to be accepted "to describe a group of people who are goal centered, interdependent, honest, open, supportive, and empowered. Members of a team develop strong feelings of allegiance that go beyond the mere grouping of individuals" (Lewis et al., 1994, p. 191).

Collaboration versus Team

The elements that distinguish collaboration from team structure are not always clear and in many instances overlap. According to Hewit et al., (1997), "The elements that define a team and the relationship among team members are very similar to those of collaboration because the element of collaboration is what distinguishes a team from a group or committee" (p. 130).

Teaching Team

"A team is a process, not a product. The challenge for anyone who is responsible for building a team is to develop a group of people so that they are able to lead, act, and think together" (Freed et al., 1997, p. 113). In educational terms, "Team teaching...refers, most often, to the teaching done in interdisciplinary courses by several faculty members who have joined together to produce that course" (Davis, 1995, p. 6).

Collaborative Teaching

According to Austin and Baldwin (1991):

> Faculty collaboration is a cooperative endeavor that involves common goals, coordinated effort, and outcomes or products for which the collaborators share responsibility and credit.... Fundamentally faculty collaboration takes two forms—collaboration in research and collaboration in teaching. (p. 5)

Wiedmeyer et al. (1991) defined collaborative teaching as "a cooperative and interactive process between two teachers that allows them to develop creative solutions to mutual problems" (p. 7). Robinson et al. (1995) believed academics "use 'collaborative teaching' to describe any academic experience in which two teachers work together in designing and teaching a course that itself uses group learning techniques" (p. 57).

CHAPTER 4

Extant Research

Reward System & Specialization

(3) The reward system in academia, both financial and symbolic, had developed around disciplines and department. This may hinder the development and support of team-taught interdisciplinary courses if there are no other structures within the institution to sponsor them. (4) Faculty cultures centered on fields' specialization may foster a parochialism which makes faculty unable or unwilling to undertake interdisciplinary team-taught courses. (Mayo & Gilliland, 1979, p. 67)

Hausman (1979) observed that within the past century, disciplines began to multiply and developed new branches such as social sciences, economics, or psychology. Each discipline became increasingly specialized, autonomous, and competitive. Having "the autonomy of disciplines… ,with their own integrity and administrative competition, cause much of the resistance to interdisciplinary study" (p. 2). Hausman (1979) further postulated there are two basic reasons for objecting interdisciplinarity in higher education. One is pragmatic, with administrative (departmental) competition for resources at the helm; the other theoretical, driven by ever deepening specialization and autonomy of each discipline. The similar notion was later propounded by Jurkovich et al., (1984), who stated:

University based disciplines, then, can be seen as particular ways of institutionalizing commitments and inculcating skills for conducting research in a well-defined area which also provides jobs and careers on the basis of original contributions to that area. (p. 16)

Communication

Practicing administrators often point to communication to be among the primary barriers to effective utilization of collaboration in academia. Banta (1993), vice chancellor for planning and institutional improvement at Indiana University-Purdue University Indianapolis, deprecated poor utilization of communication in most institutions of higher learning. She observed that faculty in many departments communicate almost exclusively with similar specialists in their discipline often on distant campuses more readily than with their own colleagues from other disciplines, even within their own department. She was convinced that cross-functional teams could be established to effect improvements in many areas of academic life. Wondering, however, how many universities would actually approach their critical processes in this manner, she concluded on a rather pessimistic note: "By virtue of their training and tradition, academics tend to work alone" (p. 147). Since collaboration on critical processes is important, cross-functional teams of faculty and staff must be trained to work together in an effort to improve all aspects of the services colleges provide–collaboration won't just happen (Bant, 1993).

Socialization

Like many before him, Baer et al. (1993) stressed that faculty are trained in discrete disciplines. Consequently, loyalty and specialization become focused on disciplines, rather than the broader values of the university. As a result, according to Baer et al. (1993), there has been a greater emphasis placed by faculty on promoting disciplinary sub-cultures in lieu of promoting a larger campus culture. Similar strain of thought was expressed by Strenski (1988), who asserted that faculty, predominantly in research universities, find any notion of collaboration difficult to accept, "They are preoccupied with having enough time for their research and their need to publish it for tenure or promotion and with a corresponding sense of obligation to their subjects" (p. 34).

Evaluation & Promotion

According to Lewis et al. (1994), even though organizations had traditionally been formed around tasks, the concept of teams and collaboration has become increasingly important in the last two decades. Human resource management professionals had historically emphasized the recruitment, placement, compensation, development, and evaluation of individuals–not groups. It has only recently become interpreted, though, as contributing to rivalries, competition, favoritism, and self-centeredness, which collectively counter the focus of the organization on its two most important functions: accomplishing the mission and servicing to the customers. Teams, with their needs for such skills as cooperation, interpersonal communication, and collective decision-making should present a shift in how work within colleges and universities is viewed. Yet, "Presently, cooperation among administrative divisions and academic departments is not encouraged. The predominant practice is individual advancement" (p. 191). This is encouraged by administration with such practices as management by objectives and individual performance evaluation and promotion. On the academic side, faculty members are expected to work alone, and even compete for limited resources, such as grant money, they conclude.

Cultural Individualism

The concept of working in teams in American colleges and universities is complicated by several factors, not the least of which has much to do with deeply rooted traditional values on which this country was founded: "Obstacles to teamwork include the tradition of academic freedom, the competitiveness of individual departments for funds and students, and a fundamental American individualism" (Freed et al., 1997, p. 112). Since academic decision-makers in colleges and universities act autonomously, faculty members are accustomed to working independently. The idea of working together to improve quality, suggests uniformity and conformity with which American faculty members are not comfortable, they added. Therefore, gaining acceptance for the idea of collaboration, particularly on the academic side, may be a challenge for any institution. For the quality principles to be successfully implemented in higher education, collaboration must become the cultural norm.

Carothers et al. (1993) further alluded to the notion of cultural individualism by recognizing that reward system in academe has traditionally reinforced individual achievement, both for students and faculty. Competition, not collaboration, is the norm. Quality can happen best at the team level through synergy, where the combined insights and skills of the group exceed the performance of any one individual, "The challenge is to devise reward structures which stimulate group-thinking and team efforts, and which reinforce the successful efforts of departments or centers toward the end of advancing the vision" (p. 190). Strenski (1988) argued that while faculty resistance to team teaching is common at all colleges, it is "especially acute at a research university where the problem of available time is compounded by an epistemology...that values the accumulation and broadcasting of 'facts'" (p. 35). Watson (1996), referring to the same issue, added: "I suspect this problem may be even more severe in the sciences, than in the humanities" (p. 3).

Commitment

According Austin et al. (1998):

> It is imperative that both instructors be committed to the process of team teaching. Both must be willing to spend additional time in planning future lessons, in reflecting on and improving completed one, and in jointly grading integrated projects....Both must be willing to solve problems as they arise rather than terminating the team teaching experience. (p. 9)

> We have also discovered that it is important that both teachers be committed to the process of continuous improvement. Only with this spirit, can we move beyond merely co-teaching to truly working as a team. (p. 9)

Trust

Wilson et al. (1998), on the basis of their experience with collaborative teaching, noted: "Finally, we have learned that it takes time to develop the trust that is so essential to the development of the team teaching experience. After two years, we are able to quite easily give–and take–constructive criticism" (p. 9). Robinson et al. (1995) noted that,

> Just as trust develops slowly between students and teachers, it must be actively cultivated in the relationship between co-teachers. Developing trust and airing disagreements in front of students involve risks, but the payoff is invaluable in terms of helping students, as well as yourselves, learn how to handle differences. (p. 58)

Philosophy of Teaching

A study guide for the National Teachers Examination (Educational Testing Service, 1992, p. 118) submitted the following question: If team teaching is to be successful, the teachers involved must possess which of the following characteristics?

(A) Equal popularity with the students they teach
(B) Equivalent amounts of experiences
(C) Similar backgrounds or training
(D) Similar philosophies in terms of learning objectives
(E) Similar approaches to the subject matter taught

The answer is (D). Team teaching cannot be successful if teachers differ significantly in terms of their approach to students' learning processes. According to Wilson et al. (1998), "If the philosophies are shared, differences in the other elements–experience, backgrounds, and approaches–only enrich the team-teaching experience for both teachers and students" (p. 8).

Robinson et al. (1995), on the basis of many years of experience with collaborative teaching, suggested that if you aspire to teach collaboratively, you should "early on, discuss your teaching philosophy and methods. Present your honest–not your ideal self" (p. 57). Robinson et al.'s (1995) extensive collaborative experience also taught them the following:

> Find out, for example, what kinds of collaborative learning exercises each is willing to undertake (e.g., large- and small-group discussions, group exams, peer review of papers, out-of-class

study groups). How much structure and closure does each of you need to feel satisfied with a class session? What kinds of testing and assessment does each think appropriate for the course? (p. 57)

Rank Differentiation

Watson (1996), an instructor whose assignment was to put into place a collaborative "writing across the curriculum" project at the University of Wisconsin at Milwaukee's engineering college, quickly found out that this would be a difficult task. In his opinion, this collaborative teaching venture failed for at least two reasons. First, there were too many differences in professional rank on the collaborating team—in this case, a full professor joined forces with an instructor. That, in turn, led to focusing on different aspects of presented material. McCarthy et al. (1988) noted that successful collaborations often occur between "two equal-status professionals agreeing to explore answers to questions they both cared a great deal about" (p. 81). The difference of past experiences and knowledge base among team members may cause misunderstandings and negatively impact the efficacy of the team.

These problems are only aggravated by what Davis (1995) had referred to as "normal problems" with faculty teams. According to Davis (1995), when faculty members, especially tenured faculty, join any kind of a team, they are entering a situation where they are sure to feel anxiety about knowing what they are doing and are put into a position where they may suddenly find that they are not necessarily the experts anymore, "They find themselves immersed in a collaborative process with other people from other disciplines, who also don't know exactly what they are doing" (Davis, 1995, p. 47). What they all bring to the process is their disciplinary perspective, which might become a problem in team-taught courses if everyone comes into the room with strong beliefs about what students need to know. Bowles (1994) further argued that "Professional status is always a factor in a collaboration of faculty members," especially when dealing with specialists from various disciplines (p. 18).

Austin et al. (1991) perceived teaching collaboration as a mutually beneficial Relationship, with two-way benefits. In this kind of symbiotic collaboration, senior academic can introduce the junior partner to "the practices and mores" of their discipline and academic profession in general. On the other hand, his or her junior counterpart, fresh from graduate school, can expose senior professors to recent developments in their fields, new methods of teaching or research, and fresh intellectual perspectives. Austin et al. (1991) encourage professors to consider the merits of collaborations, because working closely with a variety of people inevitably exposes individuals to a wider range of information. However, research on small group development demonstrates that individuals assembled to work as a team organize themselves along lines of status or prestige even when no formal group structure is provided (Fennell et. al, 1983, qtd. in Austin et al, 1991, p. 75).

Wilson and Martin (1998), in their research article encouraging involvement of faculty members in collaborative teaching, pointed to their own positive experience and its variegated advantages:

> For us, the benefits of team teaching have been substantial. First and foremost, the junior faculty member, in her first year at Muskingum College, had an ideal mentor in the senior faculty member. Administrative details, as well as scholastic expectations, were communicated; answers to questions about process and procedures were easily obtained. (p. 9)

Resistance to Change

Another challenge collaborating instructors may face is resistance to change itself. When Albert Ellis (1985), a psychologist, analyzed nature of people's resistance to change, he found that "resistance...is exceptionally common and is often an expected part of the normal human condition" (Ellis, 1985, p. 7). He noted that "Perhaps the most common, and often one of the strongest, kinds of resistance is that stemming from low frustration tolerance," or what *Rational-Emotive* therapists ET call "discomfort anxiety" (Ellis, 1985, p. 10). It seems, in general, human beings unwillingness to leave comfort zones of what's familiar and known to be principle defining many of their actions. Maeroff (1993) noted that "Teachers tend to teach the way that they were taught. This is the method that they have seen most, know best, and have the most confidence" (p. 6).

Vulnerability

According to Guarasci and Cornwell (1997), academic teams are the basic components of the learning communities, "Learning communities are conscious curricular structures that link two or more disciplines around the exploration of a common theme" (p. 109). Extant research on faculty collaboration suggests that many factors might seriously affect effectiveness of teaching. Those factors include: "(1) Faculty must teach under the scrutiny of their peers from other disciplines...,(2) Course format demands a greater commitment of faculty time" (Mayo & Gilliland, 1979, p. 67). Jurkovich and Paelinck (1984) noted that the need to expand the knowledge by leaving the boundaries of their own discipline, in a way, frees instructors, but also leaves them intellectually vulnerable, "Leaving their own field, they can no longer judge the soundness of the results they are confronted with," which, in many cases, engenders the feelings of uncertainty and discomfort (p. 48).

Personal Characteristics

Wilson and Martin (1998), when discussing prerequisite personal traits for effective collaborative teaching, identified a "strong personality" as one of the key elements of a successful collaborator:

Another prerequisite is a strong psyche. Team teachers share the stage in the classroom. One's teaching is constantly observed– and evaluated–by the other. The center of authority is constantly moving, with teachers being equal one moment and in a more or less dominant position the next. In addition, students are privy to the team-teaching relationship and as such are witnesses to apparent or implied differences of opinion. (p. 8)

Robinson and Schaible (1995), based on their six years of experience with collaborative teaching, advised: "Look for a co-teacher with a healthy psyche. Choose a person who doesn't appear to have a strong need for power or control, who is comfortable with him- or herself, and who is not easily offended or put on the defensive" (p. 57).

Griggs and Stuart (1996) identified a number of characteristics shaping faculty attitudes toward successful collaboration: 1) readiness to accept change, novel ideas and people–as opposed to shyness and reticence, 2) appropriately developed social and interpersonal skills–dealing with preference for working in a closely knit team vis-à-vis a solitary individual, 3) ability of prolonged cooperation with others–for preparation, organization of the material and its evaluation, and 4) ability to communicate properly. Essentially, team members who cannot reach out to each other, even when united by a common mission, cannot actualize team goals: "Frequently members of academe have difficulty sharing experiences with common problems" (p. 2).

Flexibility

According to Wilson and Martin (1998), it takes a great amount of discipline not to overstep and infringe upon the time of the collaborator. In the same token, material covered by one instructor should not be "rehashed" by the other collaborator: "A team teacher must be flexible. Both time and intended coverage of subject matter must be adjusted to accommodate the other team member" (p. 8).

Isolation

Robinson and Schaible (1995) claimed that "collaborative teaching can help us overcome the frequent sense of isolation felt by many faculty members" (p. 59). They further elaborate:

> Most of our exchanges with colleagues about teaching are restricted to grousing over poor student writing or the frustrations of lackluster discussions. Collaborative teachers offer each other a much-needed sounding board for sharing the excitements as well as the perplexities and disappointments of particular class sessions. They also develop, out of their common experience, the chance to engage in more philosophical explorations about teaching. (p. 59)

Maeroff (1993) echoed similar sentiment by noting that "Teaching is an activity that people almost always do alone....Teamwork for any purpose is foreign to most teachers. The measure of their success usually rests on how adept they are at working on their own" (p. 7). Guarasci and Cornwell

(1997) lamented that educational faculty chooses to isolate themselves by becoming victims of disciplinary "narcissism" immersed in fights over resources. That attitude does not teach students that learning liberates them from isolation and frees them to engage with the world rather than simply living in it, "If faculty fail to demonstrate how learning is about conversation and about the ability to enlarge that discourse continually, they will fail our students; they will be teaching them that learning is only about institutional politics and not about the expansion of human personality" (p. 14). They further continued: "Colleges are not privileged islands apart from society....Specialized knowledge and the explosion of scientific research are marbled in departmental and divisional separations that many times result in a disconnected and somewhat incoherent undergraduate experience as well as balkanized and byzantine academic politics" (p. 15).

Professional Development

Although team building has many obstacles to overcome, it represents underlying principles that could be made integral to professional development of academic faculty. Implicit in the team approach, in the opinion of Maeroff (1993), is professional development orienting faculty toward the continuous intellectual renewal, suggesting creation of teaching units through which students learn as much as teachers do, "A true learning community would be one in which all members, adults included, were constantly expanding themselves" (p. 12).

Robinson and Schaible (1995) looked at the benefits of developing a team-taught course: "Research on collaborative learning indicates that its benefits for students include higher achievement, greater retention, improved interpersonal skills, and an increase in regard for positive interdependence. We find that collaborative teaching benefits us as well" (p. 58). They further reported that collaborative teaching encourages instructors to keep in check their ingrained tendency to "slip back" into the style of teaching with the student as a "passive receptacle":

We have found that the collaborative arrangement spurs each partner to locate, share, and experiment with fresh ideas for structuring class sessions, creating more effective writing assignments, and improving our skills at critiquing student papers....There are many pressures in the academy to play out our role as experts—as conference presenters, published authors, commentators in the media....The objective of creating a student-centered classroom is not easy and demands we change our behavior....When teaching collaboratively, however, we can rely on each other to reinforce our new styles of teaching. To do so, of course, we must know how to give and receive constructive criticism. We must be willing to ask ourselves and each other if we are reverting to earlier ways. Are we talking too much in class? Are we getting caught up in performing our expertise? Are we missing important cues from our students? (p. 59)

Wilson and Martin (1998) developed great appreciation for innovative ideas that developed during their discussions and arguments while teaching collaboratively:

We both highly value the creative ideas that develop as we discuss each lesson. The 'give and take' of our discussions nearly always result[s] in plans that are more complex and more complete than we could have developed on our own....We push each other to higher standards of teaching. With a colleague in the classroom, we strive constantly to do our best. We know, too, that our efforts, our insights, and our occasional moments of brilliance will be recognized and affirmed. (p. 9)

Austin and Baldwin (1991) argued that "When faculty collaborate around their teaching, three kinds of benefits occur: development of their teaching ability, new intellectual stimulation, and a closer connection to the university or college as a community" (p. 57).

"Tag Teams" versus "True Teams"

Drexler and Forrester (1998) distinguished between "tag teams" and "true teams," "A true team is similar to a yoke of oxen, all pulling together toward a common goal. A tag team, on the other hand, comprises members who furnish expertise and then pass the project to another team member, much like 'tag team' wrestling" (p. 59). They used Albert Einstein as an example of a tag team member. Even though, Einstein did an excellent job as a tag team member, he would, in their judgment, be very unhappy and ineffective if included in a true team. Similarly, academic faculty represent an awfully awkward fit for true teams:

> Organizing university faculty into true teams also does not work very well. Faculty are highly educated individuals, with narrow fields of expertise; they resist and resent others deciding how they should perform their work. At most, they will accept some direction concerning the process, but will vehemently reject attempts to dictate content. Faculty refer to this as 'academic freedom'; we see it as part of the tag team process. (p. 62)

When Wilson and Martin (1998) began their experience with collaborative teaching at Muskingum College, Ohio, they were both relatively skillful in working with other people. In spite of that, however, "most of our early teaching was in fact merely co-teaching, a 'you do this, and I'll do that' strategy, which Bocchino and Bocchino (1997) call a 'tag team'" (p. 6). They further recalled:

> We have retained this strategy but have added to our repertoire: 1) 'Speak and Chart,' in which one of us writes while the other talks, 2) 'Perform and Comment,' in which one of us models a teaching strategy or technique while the other comments on the performance, and 3) 'Speak and Add,' in which one member presents information while the other adds 'color' with stories, examples, and humor. Occasionally, we hit the epitome of teaming, the 'Duet,' in which both present the lesson in a seamless whole. (p. 6)

Division of Roles

While sharing their experiences on collaborative teaching, Wilson and Martin (1998) noted: "As we become more experienced in team teaching, we find ourselves taking on and developing many different roles. Among the personae we have adopted are co-planner, muse, cheerleader, and critic (p. 4). Over time, however, as collaborators familiarized themselves with each other's styles, or even language, planning part became continuously less time consuming:

As we become more accustomed to working together, we find that we are spending less time in planning. We know each other's material, strategies, and even punch lines, so blending our material to support and reinforce common objectives has become relatively easy. We have also developed a common vocabulary: it is no longer necessary to explain each lesson to each other. We know what is meant by "the bread lesson," "the PRAXIS introduction," and "the Curriculum Fair." (p. 3)

The role of a "muse" frequently came to play an important function, often appearing out of nowhere through, for example, an interesting insight of the collaborating instructor during the class-session:

Our many and varied experiences in all kinds of educational settings mean a collective wealth of creative ideas. Lack of inspiration by one of us is nearly always countered by a useful–and sometimes brilliant–suggestion by the other. This role, too, has changed as we become more experienced with working together. In our early weeks of team teaching, we looked for help primarily during planning. Now we feel free to interject ideas as the lesson is progressing, often prompting stories of insights that we know the other one has in her repertoire. (p. 5)

When things do not go as smoothly as planned, when students do not respond to "a perfectly-worded fascinating question," when things fall apart and students get bored, it is important to have someone to rely on, "As cheerleaders for each other, we counter the often-deadening isolation of the classroom" (Wilson and Martin, 1998, p. 5).

It is comforting to have an understanding colleague to say, 'Some days are diamonds, some days are stone.' And as critics, we hold the mirror of serious reflection for each other, assuring that our failures are examined and improved, we are assured that our triumphs will be celebrated. (Wilson & Martin, 1998, p. 5)

We also occasionally serve as a "dive-master,'...the person who watches the students for signs of distress while the instructor teaches. As observers not immediately on the stage we are able to clear up students' misunderstandings in instruction" (Wilson & Martin, 1998, p. 5). The last, but not the least, Wilson and Martin (1998) identified the role of a "teacher's aide" to be of import during their collaboration. Whenever more attention was needed to individual students or groups, one of them was always free to help:

> When we're short a copy, or when the masking tape that is usually in the classroom has walked away, we are available to handle the logistics without unduly disrupting the flow of the class. One of us is always available to give extra attention to individual students or groups. (p. 5)

Risk Taking

According to Wilson and Martin (1998), the unexpected, though welcome benefit of collaborative teaching, was increased level of risk-taking by the collaborating professors, "An unexpected benefit is the support for risk-taking that team teaching affords (p. 10).

We each feel that with the other's encouragement and professional insight, we can try new strategies, knowing that the debriefing will be supportive and encouraging and will result in improved future lessons. (Wilson & Martin, 1998, p. 10)

Reflection & Feedback

Wilson and Martin (1998) identified mutual feedback and reflection as the benefit of collaborative teaching that solitary teaching does not afford,

> Good team teaching necessarily results in a more reflective approach to teaching. We spend a great amount of time—often over lunch—discussing the course activities and reflecting on those strategies that seem to work and on those that do not work as well. Insights from the observing (as opposed to the actively teaching) partner often result in better adaptations of strategies to meet student needs and preferences. Immediate feedback from a peer is gratifying, especially when the class is less than demonstrative! (p. 10)

Benefits for Students

Wilson and Martin (1998), while reflecting upon their own experience with collaborative teaching, observed the development of acute sensitivity of learning modalities among all involved in the process: "Because of the differences in our learning styles, we have become much more aware of the differences in those of our students" (p. 6). Consequently, at the outset of each term, they administer a learning styles inventory to each student, and then perform analysis of the results to construct a more accurate picture of students' learning style preferences. Accoutered with those tools, they plan lessons strategically, so that each day had at least some preferred activities: visual, auditory, kinesthetic, group, individual, etc–allowing students plenty of freedom and choices within those perimeters.

As a result of the constant barrage of ideas and concepts from various fields of knowledge, Wilson and Martin (1998) recognized that as a result of their collaboration, "We have become much more adept at recognizing areas of integration....We now integrate teaching of assessment, curriculum, multiple intelligences, national and state standards, classroom management techniques, and lesson planning" (p. 7).

> These topics cut across discipline lines and are taught much more efficiently once rather than in each of several methods courses. We find that we are able to reinforce important concepts, using example from many areas, rather than boring students with multiple cursory overviews of the elements common to all disciplines. (Wilson & Martin, 1998, p.7)

Their collaborative effort Martin and Wilson (1998) made them more adept at the art of integrating variety of disciplines in the classroom:

> We have also become more aware of opportunities for discipline integration....We are quite adept at incorporating into nearly any lesson the process skills usually taught in science, the graphs and charts, sometimes reserved for mathematics, and the reading strategies typically found in social and the language arts. (p. 7)

In conclusion, Wilson and Martin (1998) found that grading objectivity improved as a result of their collaboration: "We each serve as the other's sounding board, particularly in matters of student testing and grading. With two of us examining a situation, students are held to high academic standards while being guaranteed that their work is evaluated fairly" (p. 9).

During the fall semester 1991, the Communication Department at the University of Texas at Arlington, offered an innovative news editing course taught collaboratively by a journalism professor and an editor of the "Fort Worth Star-Telegram," a metropolitan daily newspaper. Students' reactions to the course were evaluated by means of an attitude test in the form of a five-point Likert scale. Two statements, provided by students, attracted special attention of the researchers: 1) "I compare this course favorably with other journalism courses," and 2) "This course provided a meaningful learning experience for me'" (Haber, 1991, p. 7). Further evaluating the level of success with collaborative teaching in this particular case, Haber acknowledged that "While recognizing some shortcomings, I still consider our innovative class to be a success. I would encourage other journalism teachers to design a collaboratively taught editing class and to use collaboration in other communication subjects" (p. 10).

Robinson and Schaible (1995), based on anonymous surveys of three separate courses led by three different pairs of instructors, found relatively positive evaluations of students' learning environment and experiences. They caution, however, against reaching foregone conclusions, "Still, problems do arise. Some students find it confusing to have two teachers; they feel uncertain about what is expected on assignments" (p. 58).

Modeling of Collaboration

Robinson and Schaible (1995) claimed that "Collaborative pedagogy holds much promise, but only if faculty members themselves can learn to become better collaborators" (p. 59).

They also added:

> Both our classroom research and literature on learning indicate that students learn from the behavior we model—whether we are mindful of it or not. If we preach collaboration but practice in isolation, or team-teach with inadequate preparation, students get a confused message. Through learning to 'walk the talk,' we can reap the double advantage of improving our teaching as well

as students' learning. At the same time, we will contribute to the rebuilding of a sense of community in higher education. (p. 59)

One of the biggest concerns for Wilson and Martin (1998) was the lack of real models of collaborating teachers that would translate into students working in teams during the class-time, "Another problem we struggle with is the lack of team teaching role models for our students. In few of the field experience classrooms do students get to see 'real' teachers working collaboratively with others" (p. 12). Students' evaluations of Wilson and Martin' (1998) collaborative teaching showed that students valued and enjoyed multiple teachers in the classroom, some wondering why anyone would ever want to teach alone. Teachers noted:

As team teachers, we provide our students with an effective model of collaborative teaching. They directly experience the increases in creativity, discussion, and social interaction that inevitably come with tasks shared by companionable peers. (p. 10)

Team's Composition

According to Austin and Baldwin (1991), "Several factors must be considered when attempting to assemble a workable collaborative team, including the values and goals of collaborating partners, their work habits and standards, the nature of the task to be completed, and the size of the group" (p. 71). They also add: "Although effective collaborators might differ on intellectual factors, they probably need to match rather than complement each other on their basic approach to work" (p. 72). The bottom line is clear: "Without shared goals and a strong commitment to the collaborative process, successful collaboration is not viable" (Parker, 1990, qtd. in Austin & Baldwin, 1991, p. 72).

Leadership

Austin and Baldwin (1991) asserted that "formats for team teaching vary with regard to the degree of hierarchy versus equality among the faculty members and the degree of interaction among the team members….In some models, one faculty member takes the lead while the other team members take less time-consuming and less involved roles" (p. 52).

Autonomy

Austin and Baldwin (1991) cautioned future collaborators that "Faculty also might be initially uncomfortable with the loss of autonomy inherent in successful collaboration" (p. 60), underlying cause for which, according to Austin and Baldwin (1991), lies in the fact that "teaching is typically a solitary activity, some adjustment is required to the presence of another faculty member in the classroom" (p. 60).

Providing Various Perspectives

Wilson and Martin (1998) agreed that by allowing students to witness their differences of opinion, they opened themselves to a more profound scrutiny. That vulnerability, however, allowed students to see them not only as professors, but people as well. The openness of interactions that followed, they believe, greatly improved student-teacher relationship, which was reflected in students' evaluations. Wilson and Martin (1998) reported that "Students overwhelmingly agreed that having two teachers–especially for a three-hour block of time!–is simply more interesting than having one. We agree" (p. 11). Additionally, Wilson and Martin (1998) noted:

> The students also benefit from experiencing two perspectives on complex issues. Often we agree: sometimes we disagree. It becomes apparent to students that there is often no one 'right' answer, only the opportunity to discuss the pros and cons of each alternative, to question reasons for a specific position, and to decide for oneself how the issue should be addressed or the problem solved. (p. 11)

Austin and Baldwin (1991), however, cautioned against Pollyannaish confidence that collaborative efforts inevitably lead to a broader presentation of the studied material. Collaborative teaching may achieve that objective, they assert, but it won't be accomplished by sheer numbers of instructors present in the classroom. Thorough planning, coordination of topics and activities are of paramount importance: "While team-taught courses offer students variety, diverse perspectives on a topic, and the opportunity to learn from a number of professors, they also have the potential to fall short of these advantages" (p. 61). Austin and Baldwin (1991) strongly advised potential collaborators to take ample time to plan and coordinate activities as a team. Without putting significant amount of time in preparing the course and individual sessions, classes could be "repetitive," "disjointed," cancelling out desired benefits of the collaborative effort: "Faculty collaborators must be aware of these potential problems to ensure the likelihood of a productive course and successful collaboration" (p. 61).

Time Commitment

According to Wilson and Martin (1998), "The primary problem with our team teaching experiment is the great amount of time it takes" (p. 11),

> One team teacher receives six hours of course credit for teaching the block: the other receives two. We each spend an additional two to three hours per week in class beyond what our course load assumes, as well as additional one to two hours of planning. Luckily, our offices are close, and our schedules allow us to do much of our planning over lunch. (p. 11)

Austin and Baldwin (1991) point to the same issue:

> A realistic assessment of the pros and cons of faculty collaboration around teaching points to several potential tensions. First, collaborative work, especially in teaching, takes time. Faculty collaborators must fit team meetings into their schedules to handle the necessary planning and coordination involved in team teaching and to nurture the trusting, open relationship essential to a productive relationship. (p. 60)

Size of the Collaborating Team

Robinson and Schaible (1995), based on their half-dozen years of experience with collaborative teaching, instructed: "Unless there are compelling reasons for doing otherwise, restrict the teaching team to two. Good collaborative teaching is too complex to do it well with more" (p.

57). Zander (1979), however, believed that nature of the task should dictate number of assigned instructors, and suggested less restrictive model:

> No optimum or even maximum size can easily be prescribed. Research on group dynamics indicates that on a given task, a group's performance seems to decline as the group increases in size. On the other hand, larger groups perform better on some kinds of tasks because they contain larger numbers of knowledgeable and able people. (Zander, 1979, qtd. in Austin and Baldwin, 1991, p. 72)

Austin and Baldwin (1991) asserted that, "Much of the literature on collaboration cautions against large teams, however" (p. 72). According to Seaman (1981), in general, as groups grow larger, the number of problems they experience also increases proportionately. Communication becomes more complex and indirect, as large groups find it difficult to interact directly on a regular basis (Seaman, 1981, qtd. in Austin & Baldwin, 1991, p. 72). The potential for disagreement on substantive and methodological issues grows as more people are involved in a research project. "Typically, more time is required for meetings and telephone conversations to negotiate plans and delegate responsibility" (Fox, & Faver, 1982, qtd. in Austin & Baldwin, 1991, p. 72). In sum, according to Austin and Baldwin (1991) "as groups increase in size, creative energies could be diverted from primary goals to logistical arrangements required to keep the team functioning smoothly" (p. 73).

The Team's Structure

According to Austin and Baldwin (1991), "The team's structure is also a factor that influences how collaborating groups operate….Indeed, no single type of structure is always superior" (p. 73). "Equality of power and authority is not unconditionally the best structure for collaborative arrangement" (Nobel, 1986, qtd. in Austin & Baldwin, 1991, p. 73).

> Although no consensus emerges from the literature on the best structural arrangements, agreement is widespread that some clear and consistent structure is preferable to no structure at all. The absence of structure, formal or informal, in a research team inhibits

the interaction and communication essential to collaboration. (Fennell & Sandefur, 1983, cited in Austin & Baldwin, 1991, p. 73)

According to Austin and Baldwin (1991), "Elaborate rules and rigid bureaucratic structures are not necessary to ensure successful collaboration, but smooth functioning requires a clear idea of authority and operational procedures" (p. 73).

Communication

"Communication is closely intertwined with the group's structure. Hence, it is another key feature associated with the success of collaborative activities" (Austin & Baldwin, 1991, p.73). They further noted:

A great deal of dialogue is required for collaboration to work in most cases. Communication enables team members to work out common goals, resolve differences, and strengthen each individual's commitment to a joint project....The structure of collaborative teams helps to shape the process of communicating. When the structure of a team is ambiguous, members might find it difficult to communicate efficiently. (p. 74)

Fairness in Collaboration

Austin and Baldwin (1991) claimed that, "Collaboration among faculty often raises issues of power, influence, professional identity, and integrity" (p. 7). As a result:

Evaluating individual contributions to collaborative endeavors and allocating credit fairly among partners are difficult challenges that frequently plague collaborators. Exploitation of lower-status parties in collaborative groups (women, minorities, junior colleagues, students, for example) is another problem that sometimes results when academics pool their talents. Most professional societies and higher education institutions have not implemented policies for resolving complex problems[;] more standard in the academic profession, clear policies are needed to ensure that faculty derive the maximum benefit from working together. (p. 7)

Collaboration is Fun

For Wilson and Martin (1998), "team teaching has been just plain fun. We both missed the company of other adults when we taught in the public schools and enjoy the camaraderie evident in our joint classroom" (p. 10).

Collaboration Represents Growth & Future

Teaching that encourages professors to learn from one another and to adopt interactive modes of instruction promotes greater intellectual community and hence vitality among faculty. Although collaborative teaching presents professors with some difficult challenges, it offers a flexible mechanism for enriching academic careers and for responding to the complex instructional tasks professors confront as the new century approaches. (Austin & Baldwin, 1991, p. 61)

CHAPTER 5

RESEARCH METHODOLOGY

The study conducted by the researcher is expected to build on the existing models and theories, which will serve as a point of reference for summaries and conclusions conducted in the latter part of the book. By vicariously living through the experiences presented in the description, the readers will be able to compare the conclusions of previous theorists and eventually make their own interpretations of the studied events.

Qualitative Paradigm

Qualitative research methods were utilized in this study to collect information from professors who were teaching collaboratively three separate courses in various departments, on both undergraduate and graduate level. The design of this study evolved on an ongoing basis throughout the duration of the collaborative teaching. Due to the nature of the investigated issues, the qualitative paradigm seemed most appropriate for this study. Qualitative research is most adequate when the researcher seeks in-depth understanding of a particular social interaction, group, or situation (Locke, Spirduso, & Silverman, 1987). Studied cases were teams of academic professors collaboratively teaching courses in higher education institutions. Collaborative teaching is a very complex process, multiple realities of which can only be constructed when the participants' voices and interpretations are revealed. According to Creswell (1994), a qualitative researcher assumes that studied reality is multiple and subjective and the researcher becomes the instrument of data collection through interaction with informants.

Within the past two decades, there has been increased interest in an interpretive, qualitative approach to research and theory, especially in social sciences: "Where only statistics, experimental designs, and survey research once stood, researchers have opened up to ethnography, unstructured interviewing, textual analysis" (Denzin & Lincoln, 1994, p. IX). Merriam (1988) noted that, "a case study is an examination of a specific phenomenon such as a program, an event, a person, a process, an institution, or a social group" (p. 9). Hamel, Dufour, and Fortin (1993) list Bronislaw Malinowski (a Polish-born Austrian) and Frederic Le Play, members of the Chicago School, as the first individuals associated with the case study. According to Hamel et al. (1993), "The case study has proven to be in complete harmony with the three key words that characterize any qualitative method: describing, understanding, and explaining" (p. 39). Guba and Lincoln (1989) substituted the "naturalistic" with "constructivist" form of expression, defining the role of the constructivist investigator as "teasing out" the constructions that actors might hold. Yin (1989a) introduced a distinction between "analytical generality" and "statistical generality." In his opinion, "case study, like the experiment, does not represent a 'sample,' and the investigator's goal is to expand and generalize theories (analytical generalization) and not to enumerate frequencies (statistical generalizations)" (Yin, 1989a, p. 21). Stake (1995) edified that the real interest of case study is "particularization," not "generalization." He claimed that first emphasis should be on in-depth understanding of the case itself: "We take a particular case and come to know it well, not primarily as to how it is different from others but what it is, what it does" (Stake, 1995, p. 8). According to Merriam (1988), a researcher might want to study several cases, "In doing so, one increases the potential for generalizing beyond the particular case. An interpretation based on evidence from several cases can be more compelling to a reader than results based on a single instance" (p. 154). In qualitative studies, an inductive model of thinking is used, in which a theory may emerge during the data collection and analysis phase of the research (Creswell, 1994). Hamel et al., (1993) explains that "Although the case study is an inductive approach, perhaps even the ideal inductive approach, that does not mean the definition of the object is a matter of chance or conjecture" (p. 41).

Research Design

A collective, multi-site, instrumental case study was utilized in this study. When more than one case is studied, it is referred to as a collective case study (Stake, 1995). Several programs (as contrasted with a single program) constitute a multi-site study (Creswell, 1998). When the focus of the study is on the issue or issues, with the case used instrumentally to illustrate the issue, we refer to this arrangement as an instrumental case study. On the other hand, in an intrinsic case study, the focus is on understanding a particular case whether it be persons, programs or events (Stake, 1995). Merriam (1988) noted that case studies use an inductive rather than deductive mode of thinking about the problem and data analysis, having as its primary goal discovery of theory, not its verification: "A qualitative, inductive, multi case study seeks to build abstractions across cases" (p. 154).

Three separate case studies were conducted at two colleges within the University of Nebraska, Lincoln. Data was collected by direct observations, interviews with collaborating instructors, and reviewing documents related to collaborative teaching. The interviewees were purposely selected. Interviews were taped and transcribed into a written narrative. Issues emerged by analyzing the information collected from the interviews, observations, and related documents. An attempt was made to describe the entire process as reported by the informants. Before the case study research began, a pilot study was completed, which became the first of three cases analyzed in this study. The focus of the pilot study was to gather information to be used in organizing the interview protocol. The interview protocol was used to further facilitate interviews with the research subjects in the individual cases.

Setting

Informants in this collective case study represented two colleges at the University of Nebraska, located in Lincoln Nebraska. Lincoln is a state capital city with a population of approximately 235,000. The university, located at its heart, at the time of the study had an enrollment of over 26,000 students. The first case (pilot study) took place at the College of Agriculture and Natural Resources. The second and third case took place at the Teachers' College.

Actors

Stake (1995) referred to research subjects as "actors" and explained that qualitative researchers ought to "enter the scene with a sincere interest in learning how they function in their ordinary pursuits and milieus and with a willingness to put aside many presumptions while we learn" (p. 1). Creswell (1994) indicated that the qualitative researcher should purposefully select informants who are best qualified to answer the research questions. He stressed that no attempt should be made to randomly select the informants. The first case consisted of a team of two professors representing Department of Agriculture and Natural Resources. Both instructors were involved in collaborative teaching of undergraduate class of approximately seventy students. The second case involved two professors: one representing the Department of Educational Administration; second representing the Department of Adult Education. Both professors taught collaboratively an undergraduate class of seventy seven students. The third case involved three professors representing the Department of Educational Administration. They were teaching collaboratively a graduate class of thirty students. Most (but not all) of the selected informants had previous experience with collaborative teaching. Only instructors who showed interest and commitment to work as a team, as well as ability to articulate their beliefs and experiences related to collaborative teaching, were sought for this study.

Ethical Considerations

Soltis (1990) believed that "Ethics is ubiquitous....Honesty is essential to research quality as well as to our everyday dealings with others...education is, at base, a moral enterprise. Education is ultimately about the formation of persons" (p. 247), "It is about developing and contributing to the good life of individuals and society" (p. 248). Smith (1990) proclaimed that "The two most important principles for the protection of human subjects are informed consent and anonymity" (p. 260).

Five basic steps were taken to secure the rights of the participants in this study:

1. Approval by the Institutional Review Board for the Protection of Human Subjects to conduct the study was secured prior to the initiation of the study.
2. Written agreement to conduct the study was obtained from the participants.
3. The participants were educated on all the activities and data collection methods they could expect during the study, including recording devices.

4. The decision regarding informant anonymity was left to participant discretion. All of the participants provided their permissions to use their real names in this study.
5. Reporting information that might be in any way harmful to research participants were seriously considered from the ethical perspective.

To ensure ethical approach toward informants, permission was secured from the participants to conduct the interviews. The informants were provided with informed consent forms. The research participants were informed of: (1) potential risks and discomforts, (2) guaranteed anonymity, if requested, (3) use of pseudonyms guaranteed, if requested, (4) time expected to spend on the study, (5) security of the collected data, and (6) detailed description of data collection procedure.

Methods of Data Collection

The researcher used a case study approach. This study represented "a bounded system" by being restricted to one event (single course), limited by time (one semester), and location (Midwestern university) (Stake, 1995, p. 2). The institution was a typical public university of average student body size. The researcher used purposeful sampling strategy and chose three teams of faculty members, who collaboratively taught both undergraduate and graduate courses at the University of Nebraska, Lincoln. Qualitative research methods were selected for this study because the researcher did not know *a priori* what he would find and wanted to generate data rich in detail embedded in the context. Merriam (1988) describes the end product of the case study as "a rich, 'thick' description," depicting case studies as being very particularistic and descriptive by nature (p. 11).

Creswell (1998) noted that a case study researcher should "look for contextual material about the setting of the 'case'" (p. 40). He listed five basic sources of information available to the case study researcher: "observations, interviews, audio-visual material, documents, and reports" (p. 61). Consistent with the features of qualitative case study design, data for this study was collected from the following multiple sources:

1. Unstructured open-ended interviews.
2. Taped and transcribed verbatim participants' responses.

3. Analyzed documents (class syllabus, course description, and students' evaluations).
4. Direct observations of classroom activities.
5. Direct observations of participants' out-of-classroom activities (meetings, planning sessions, and reflective sessions).
6. Informal meetings and discussions.

The researcher conducted six open-ended interviews with every informant in the conducted study with the exception of the first case (pilot study), which was limited to one interview with every participant. All interviews were audio-taped and transcribed verbatim. The interviews occurred throughout the course of collaboration as well as before and after the course termination, where appropriate. The interviews began with the following open-ended questions:

1. What is the process of collaborative teaching?
2. What are the issues related to collaborative teaching?

Subsequent questions were conversational in an attempt to get the interviewees to discuss further something he or she mentioned in a preceding answer. The researcher pursued issues raised by the research subjects and asked preconceived questions only if the informant did not spontaneously address an issue of interest to him or her. The researcher attended and observed every planning meeting of the collaborating team before the course began and during the course, including all regular class sessions throughout the semester. The researcher participated in informal meetings and discussions conducted by collaborating instructors, which further contributed to a better understanding of identified issues. After observations of regular class sessions and analysis of transcribed interviews, questions arose for which the researcher needed answers and clarifications in order to ascertain his conclusions. These questions were added to reflect an accurate understanding of the researched process. When early questions were not working and new issues became apparent, the design was changed, the procedure referred to by Parlett and Hamilton (1976) as "progressive focusing" (p. 148).

Methods of Data Analysis

Armed with an interest in a particular phenomenon and perhaps some assumptions about what one might find, case study investigators immerse themselves in the totality of the case. As the setting becomes familiar, and as data are being collected, the researcher looks for underlying patterns–conceptual categories that make sense out of the phenomenon. (Merriam, 1988, p. 60)

Creswell (1998) recognized that when multiple cases are chosen, a typical format would be to "first provide a detailed description of each case and themes within the case, called a within-case analysis, followed by a thematic analysis across the cases, called a cross-case analysis, as well as assertions or interpretations of the meaning of the case," the final interpretive phase "lessons learned" (p. 63). In the similar way, Bogdan and Biklen (1992) noted that "Analysis involves working with the data, organizing them, breaking them into manageable units, synthesizing them, searching for patterns, discovering what is important and what is to be learned, and deciding what you will tell others" (p. 153). Merriam (1988) noted: "Cross-case analysis differs little from analysis of data in a single qualitative case study. Analysis can be little more than a unified description across cases; it can build categories, themes, or typologies that conceptualize the data from all the cases" (p. 156). Stake (1995) taught that the pursuit of complex meanings cannot be designed or caught retrospectively, "It seems to require continuous attention, an attention seldom sustained when the dominant instruments of data gathering are objectively interpretable checklists or survey items. An ongoing interpretive role of the researcher is prominent in qualitative case study" (p. 43).

Analysis of collected data in this study was ongoing. Analysis of transcribed interviews began as soon as transcriptions were made available. Codes that emerged from the participants' descriptions of their collaborative experiences were generated inductively. All interviews and transcripts were re-read specifically for codes that emerged from later interviews. As patterns were identified, their segregation was carried out by re-coding for the developed dimensions or properties of a given theme. Further questions and possible routes of inquiry were devised to answer the queries that emerged in the research process. In the final phase of data analysis, the researcher, through inductive reasoning, produced generalizations and conclusions, which he referred to as "empirical assertions," (Erickson, 1986, p. 146). Another basic task of data analysis "is to establish an evidentiary warrant for the assertions one wishes to make" (Erickson, 1986, p. 146). This was achieved by reviewing collected data, seeking confirming, as well as disconfirming evidence. Each interview was re-read with the objective of writing individual short interview summary. These summaries allowed the researcher to see threads that ran through the interviews and thereby maintain the context for the quotes that were lifted out of the interviews and used as examples in writing up the research findings. Stake (1995) noticed: "There is no particular moment when data analysis begins. Analysis is a matter of giving meaning to first impressions as well as to final compilations….Analysis essentially means taking something apart" (p. 71). For a case study, "analysis consists of making a detailed description of the case and its setting" (Creswell, 1998, p. 153). For that reason, in the first part of the analysis, the researcher provided the reader with a rich description of all events involved in the process in a chronological order analyzing the multiple sources of data to "determine evidence for each step or phase in the evolution of the case" (Creswell, 1998, p. 153). The researcher emphasized the chronology of events because "To the qualitative scholar, the understanding of human experience is a matter of chronologies more than of causes and effects" (Stake, 1995, p. 39). In the second part of analysis, the researcher provided a detailed analysis of all issues that emerged during the research process. According to Stake (1995), there are two strategic ways a researcher can use to reach new meanings about cases. They include "direct interpretation of the individual instance and through aggregation of instances until something can be said about them as a class" (p. 74). Although sometimes we find a significant meaning in a single instance, usually the important meanings come from the re-appearance of the concept over and over again: "The search for meaning often is a search for patterns, for consistency within certain conditions, which we call 'correspondence'" (Stake, 1995, p. 78). After analysis and pulling the case apart and providing readers with a detailed description of the context and the emerging issues the researcher pulled the pieces together with the intention of providing readers with his interpretations of the process and assertions, especially those that reflected on the design literature about collaborative teaching–for future researchers to explore those issues even deeper: "The qualitative researcher concentrates on the instance, trying to pull it apart and put it back together again more meaningfully–analysis and synthesis in direct interpretation" (Stake, 1995, p. 75).

Methods of Verification

All research is concerned with producing valid and reliable knowledge in an ethical manner. A qualitative case study is no exception. In fact, because of the nature of this type of research, these concerns may loom larger than in experimental designs wherein validity and reliability are accounted for at the start. (Merriam, 1988, p. 163)

Eisner and Peshkin (1990) state that "Validity, in a basic sense, pertains to the congruence of the researcher's claims to the reality his or her claims seek to represent....Valid interpretations and conclusions function as surrogates through which readers of research reports can know a situation they have not experienced directly" (p. 97).

Denzin (1970) defined a triangulated perspective as the one in which "Participant observation was seen as combining survey interviewing, document analysis, direct observation, and observer participation" (p. 297).Validation of data in this study was achieved by triangulation of methods–by comparing instructors' perspectives with those of the participants, plus information gained from variety of documents made available to the researcher.

The researcher addressed the issues of validity and reliability using "qualitative terms." Guba and Lincoln (1985) defined "credibility," "transferability," and "dependability" as terms more applicable for establishing the trustworthiness of qualitative research. The researcher paid special attention to the internal and external validity of the study. Internal validity or "credibility" concerns the question of how precisely one's findings match reality (Merriam, 1988). The researcher conducted interviews, direct observations, participant observations, and document reviews to incorporate the elements of triangulation. Additionally, member checks were used by asking all involved in research study informants to verify the accuracy of findings and data interpretations.

The following member checking procedures were used in the study:

1) Informants had an opportunity to review and respond to observations the researcher made throughout the study.
2) Informants had an opportunity to review and respond to the issues identified by the researcher on the basis of interviews and informal meetings with research participants.

3) Informants had an opportunity to read and express their opinion on the conclusions about the process of collaborative teaching constructed by the researcher.

External validity, to which qualitative researchers refer as "transferability," refers to the extent to which one's findings can be applied to other similar situations, beyond the immediate study (Yin, 1989). Although Merriam (1988) noted that the purpose of qualitative research is not generalizability, but the interpretation of unique events, through careful selection, this study focused around the typical cases. The studied cases were located in various situational contexts like: graduate and undergraduate courses, professors representing various colleges and departments (cross-site analysis). The transferability of this study was also increased by providing a "rich, thick description" of the events in chronological order that enhanced the opportunity of creating "naturalistic generalizations" by the readers themselves. According to Stake (1995), "Naturalistic generalizations are conclusions arrived at through personal engagement in life's affairs or by vicarious experience so well constructed that the person feels as if it happened to themselves" (p. 85). As predicted by Stake (1994), the use of multiple sites and multiple informants increased the complexity of this study, enhancing, at the same time, the probability that results will be applicable to other similar educational settings.

Reliability commonly refers to the "dependability" of the measuring tool–in case of the qualitative study that is a researcher him- or herself. Merriam (1988) defined reliability as the extent to which one's findings can be replicated: "Reliability is problematic in the social sciences as a whole simply because human behavior is never static....Reliability in a research design is based on the assumption that there is a single reality which if studied repeatedly will give the same results" (p. 170).

Reliability, undoubtedly, presented challenges in this study, because informants did change their opinions along the process of collaboration, occasionally presenting contradictory statements and opinions to those they expressed earlier during the study. As a result, two different researchers conducting the same study at various stages of the collaborative process might reach different, even contradictory conclusions. This research project clearly asserted the view that human thoughts are dynamic by nature, and professors do change their opinions and thoughts on issues as the collaboration progresses. Triangulation of data increased reliability by using multiple interviews, direct observations, participant observations, and theoretical models identified in relevant literature. To ensure that informants were represented accurately in written accounts and that research findings were supported by the data, the researcher asked a few faculty members to serve as reviewers or "devil's advocates" in this research study. Dr. Fred Wendel, associate professor of education at the University of Nebraska, Lincoln, conducted the audit of case study #1. Due to extremely dynamic changes in informants' opinions during the course of case study #2, the researcher decided to utilize the help of two independent reviewers in order to further increase reliability of the presented data and conclusions. Dr. Stephen Stimpfle, associate professor of anthropology at the University of Nebraska, Lincoln, and Dr. Barbara LaCoste, associate professor of education at the University of Nebraska, Lincoln, reviewed the data collected for case study #2. Dr. Marilyn Grady, associate professor of education at the University of Nebraska, Lincoln, served as a reviewer of data collected for case study #3. Finally, the researcher conducted a personal audit, under the guidance of Dr. Sheldon Stick, associate professor of education at the University of Nebraska, Lincoln, for the purpose of documenting the results of this study. Particular attention was placed on the process and the product to ensure accuracy of the findings supported by the data. Dr. Larry Dlugosh, chairman of the Educational Administration department at the University of Nebraska–Lincoln, monitored the process to verify the authenticity of the audit.

Reporting the Findings

Stake (1995) noticed that complexity of the case needs to be observed and probed. That is why "questions, the context, the history, the case itself need more than to be described, they need to be developed" (p. 123). To organize the case study report, the researcher decided to use the model presented by Stake (1995, p. 123), and include five key sections:

Section 1: Entry Vignette

In this section, readers, through vicarious experience, are expected to develop the "feel" for the place and the time of the event under investigation.

Section 2: Purpose and Methods

In this section, the researcher introduces readers "to how the study came to be," and reviews the methods used in the study. The researcher introduces the most significant issues that in his estimation will best help the readers understand the case.

Section 3: Narrative Description

In this section, the researcher, like a "witness," presents all the available facts to the reader in a chronological order of events.

Section 4: Development of Issues

In this section, the researcher develops issues to better understand and highlight the complexity of the case.

Section 5: Descriptive Data

In this section, the researcher, through triangulation, attempts to "confirm" or "disconfirm" those issues that need further probing. Using documents and quotations, the researcher builds up on the issues identified in the previous section.

Researcher's Role

According to Smith (1990), "In general, qualitative or 'naturalistic' research is 'noninterventionist' in form.....That sets it in contrast to experimental inquiry, where studied variables are frequently manipulated. Events such as schooling, curricular approaches, or classroom interaction occur...normally, and the investigator observes and interprets them" (p. 258). It was the researcher's intention to conduct the research in the most unobtrusive way, in order to reflect reality as it was, not to change or modify it in the way he might see fit influenced by his perceptions, assumptions, presuppositions, or expectations. Qualitative research by nature requires opinions and interpretations produced by the researcher. Despite the best intentions of the researcher, readers have to assume the researcher's inevitable bias, which makes findings subject to multiple meanings and interpretations (Bogdan & Biklen, 1992). Research bias in this study was addressed by the clearly stated expectations of the researcher, which assured that "the reader is aware of and understands the researcher's position prior to being exposed to research findings. The pilot study, conducted prior to the initiation of the major part of the research project, served as a check for content validity. As a result, the pilot study allowed the researcher to modify and clarify questions that were later used during the interviews with research participants.

Functions of the Literature Review

All research should take into account previous work in the same area. An investigator who ignores prior research and theory chances pursuing a trivial problem, duplicating a study already done, or repeating others' mistakes. The goal of research–contributing to the knowledge base of the field–may then never be realized. (Merriam, 1988, p. 61)

Merriam (1988) further continues: "The thrust of an independent literature review is to present the state of the art with regard to a certain topic. Such reviews usually assess the work to date and may even offer suggestions for future inquiry" (p. 62). Cooper (1984) suggests several things a new reviewer can look for in past review:

First, past reviews can be employed to identify the positions of other scholars in the field. In particular, past reviews can be used to determine whether conflicting conclusions exist about the evidence and, if they do, what has caused the conflict. Second, a review of past reviews can assess the earlier efforts' completeness and validity….Past reviews can also be a significant help in identifying interacting variables that the new reviewer might wish to examine. Rather than restart the compilation of potential moderating variables, past reviewers will undoubtedly offer many suggestions based on previous efforts and their own intellect. If more than one review of an area has been conducted, the new review will be able to incorporate all of the suggestions. Finally, past review allow the researcher to begin the compilation of a relevant bibliography. (p. 29)

According to Glaser (1978), a review of relevant literature serves as a comparison with one's work and "provides a degree of support for it, as the analyst discovers how he fits into the literature and where his contributions lie" (p. 32). Glaser (1978) further added: "Reading for ideas, style, and support generate sensitivity which in turn generates stimulation for the drugless trip" (p. 32).

PART II

PROCESS OF COLLABORATIVE TEACHING IN HIGHER EDUCATION

CHAPTER 6

PROCESS OF COLLABORATIVE TEACHING <u>ANALYSIS</u>

CASE STUDY #1
(PILOT STUDY)
Entry Vignette

In this section, the researcher intends to answer the following questions that guide this journey into the complex world of collaboration: 1) What is the process of collaborative teaching? 2) What are the issues related to collaborative teaching? The researcher will also provide readers with an illuminating description of the context in which collaborative teaching took place and the profound benefits and consequences.

Collaborative teaching as an alternative method of instruction is slowly catching attention of academicians across universities and colleges. The University of Nebraska–Lincoln is part of that movement. The University puts emphasis on innovative approaches to teaching and learning. For the majority of faculty members, collaborative teaching is an abstraction far removed from their quotidian reality of ivory tower. Even though collaborative teaching is not a novel idea whatsoever, changing dynamics of everyday life makes it especially relevant today. That is why more and more departments within the university experiment with collaboration. The College of Agricultural and Natural Resources at the University of Nebraska–Lincoln realized the need for a change by proposing a new course taught collaboratively by two faculty members from different departments within the college. What is the process of collaborative teaching? What are the issues related to collaborative teaching? The observations presented here are designed to produce insights into these questions at one college of the University of Nebraska–Lincoln.

Course Objectives

Ethical issues permeate the agricultural and natural resource profession. Practitioners face multifaceted ethical dilemmas. Many decisions are of a broader scope calling for societal responses in the policy arena. College graduates therefore need to be able to reflect critically on ethical quandaries they will face upon graduation while applying proper conceptual tools to solve them. The purpose of this course was to integrate students' previously gained knowledge with ethical models by ensuring application of sound ethical reasoning.

Purpose & Methods

The course was taught in an interactive format with plenty of time devoted to discussion and experiential learning. Case studies and team assignments were used liberally throughout the course. The goal was to establish a learning community where spirited discussions and debates lead to in-depth understanding of discussed issues. The instructors acted as facilitators providing structure and stimulus to allow for optimal critical thinking and effective group dynamics to evolve. Class attendance and active student participation was mandatory. Each student was expected to complete the assigned readings and projects on time to facilitate class discussions. Midterm and final exams in essay format were given. Students were required to complete a set of assignments including an on-going analytic journal of events related to current agricultural and natural resources events. Additionally, a major final team project was also assigned. A number of educational experiences were designed to enhance students' oral and written communication skills. Written assignments were graded for presentation quality as well as content. Various class exercises involved peer evaluations.

Narrative Description
The Campus and the Classroom

On Thursday afternoon in the middle of fall 1998 semester at 2:30 p.m., the autumnal specter of the East Campus splendidly displayed its majesty with the nacreous embroidery of foliage. Leaves began their annual descent, making the ground look like an ornate Persian carpet. Barely a few students walked by while other college students sped through the campus in their motley assortment of cars (many with an urgent need of a muffler!). A sturdy building with a large epigraph above its entrance: "Dairy Industry," stood proudly right by the bus stop. The building was part of the larger Food Industry Complex and perhaps by design the three-story structure featured entrances on three sides. It was pleasant to see the building well-maintained with brightly lit halls and rooms. Shining floors, neat offices, and fresh flower arrangements filled the polished interior of the building. Smiling staff and faculty members were well-dressed in crisp office attire and ready to serve their students if requested. Everything seemed purposefully orchestrated to welcome students and make them want to stay. In the basement, a few students talked quietly creating a barely audible susurration that didn't seem to disturb anybody. Right across the room, however, a group of rowdy young men and women robustly cachinnated as if the entire room belonged just to them. Long, winding corridors led to the classroom no. forty-two, where the course took place. Large uncovered cables hang on the ceiling along the narrow and curvy corridors. pale walls and clean floors soften the otherwise industrial ambience of the basement. Regardless, the austerely pragmatic space gave the impression of walking through a well-preserved military base somewhere in Siberia, Russia. The classroom was located on the left side at the end of the corridor. A white door led to a squared room with yellow walls and a white ceiling, matching that of the corridor outside the classroom. The room was almost full with students, except for maybe several seats still not occupied a few minutes before scheduled time. Blue seats accompanied twenty rows of brown tables. Three black speakers hang from the ceiling right above the board, complemented by a full technical outfit of the room. At the upper left corner, a large black television set hang facing the audience. With the deep reflection of lights on the pitch black screen, it looked like the entrance to the hollow channel leading to some cyber space on the other side of the wall. Two substantial windows at the back wall led to control rooms. While Dr. Bruce Johnson was lecturing, Dr. Gerald Parsons–the collaborating instructor, was sitting close by his side facing the blackboard. It was not long before Dr. Parsons took over, leaving Dr. Johnson leaning against the wall observing the class and his colleague in action. Both instructors were tenured professors. One of the faculty members represented Department of Agricultural Economics, another Department of Agricultural Leadership. At the time, they were both involved in collaborative teaching of the described in this case undergraduate course named: "Ethics in Agriculture and Natural Resources."

Development of Issues
Selecting Partners

Although Dr. Gerald Parsons and Dr. Bruce Johnson had been teaching at the University of Nebraska–Lincoln for a number of decades, it was only recently when the idea of their collaborative venture gestated. The course originated in 1990 when Dr. Johnson became interested in creating a course in the area of agricultural ethics. Through a workshop offered by the college, he became aware of another colleague–Dr. Cassarie–who was also interested in creating a new course. Dr. Cassarie and Dr. Johnson visited further and decided to lay out the proposal for the new course called "Ethics in Agricultural and Natural Resources." After Dr. Cassarie retired, Dr. Parsons expressed an interest in teaching that course collaboratively with Dr. Johnson. That was the second semester of their working together. Dr. Parsons immediately jumped at this opportunity, claiming that "I have worked with Bruce collaboratively. My first experience was a good one, so there was no problem with doing it again."

Teaching/Learning Philosophy

Although any time two people teach together, one might expect differences in styles of teaching preferences to result in potentially dysfunctional conflict to emerge. That was not the case here. Both instructors showed a lot of flexibility by carefully treading in each other's comfort zones. Dr. Parsons offered his insight: "I think you can have a lot of flexibility. It's just simply a matter of making sure that you know we are talking about the same things in terms of goals and objectives that we are talking about the same things in terms of the number of assignments and expectations."

Joy of Working with Others

While sitting in the classroom together, a warm–almost friendly–camaraderie could be detected between those two collaborating instructors. "There is certainly high level of collegiality and a mutually satisfying environment," said Dr. Johnson, "I really do see that as synergistic–the whole is much greater than the sum of the parts that is achieved." He found working with Dr. Parsons rather unique, "It's one of high level of mutuality and very positive in terms of working." Dr. Parsons shared similar sentiments and found collaborative teaching to be a positive experience, "I find it an enjoyable collaboration. There is nothing onerous about it or wrong. It's not like I will be looking for the opportunity to end it or work with someone else. Well I feel very positive about it. This is the only class that I have taught collaboratively in a formal kind of way where two faculty members are actually in the same classroom." Dr. Parsons, on the other hand, had already taught collaboratively before. He taught a technical communication course and worked very closely with his colleagues. They put together the syllabus and made sure they were "all on the same page, making assignments that had consistency. So that is another notion of collaboration which comes in many forms," concluded Dr. Parsons.

Professional Development

Based on the experiences of collaborating professors in different disciplines, they found their experience growing and mutually enhancing in many ways. Dr. Parsons felt that "We complement each other in terms of our knowledge base very well. I am learning from him. I appreciate the illustrations of the examples, but he can pull from his more direct experiences in agriculture and economics." Dr. Johnson shared his colleague's observation, "The strength of one would complement the other and that would be sections that we would be more responsible for than the other members, depending what we were bringing to the table."

Variety of Perspectives

The collaborating professors found this experience beneficial for the students as well as their own development, "Even if we were overseeing students' projects and so forth, we each had different perspectives that we could, I think, provide for students to get a broader kind of input" stated Dr. Johnson. They both agreed that modern education calls for the interdisciplinary approach to learning, and collaborative teaching is in Dr. Parsons words, "an interdisciplinary approach at work. I think it's healthy for this department to be reaching out and finding opportunities of collaboration in other departments." Both instructors shared the view that two heads are better than one, and more they collaborate the better the process become. Indeed they noticed benefits early on while developing the concept of the course. Each of them had a network of people who had particular interest in collaboration and the topic of interest keenly shaped. They could easily call upon any of them when needs arose. The process wasn't always smooth, "We had some differences of opinions and so forth," acknowledged Dr. Johnson, "but we were civil and we recognized and respected one another, one another's opinions, and we worked out those differences. It was the course that was stronger because of the presence of two people, and not just one."

Knowledge Construction

The single most satisfying experience was learning the process. And that could only happen when two or more opinions confront one another. For Dr. Parsons, "Satisfaction has always been in terms of what I get back from collaborators, colleagues, and students. And for me it is the most satisfying experience when you are learning as much as you hopefully impart." Dr. Johnson assessed their collaboration from the perspective of students' learning dynamics that ensued, "Certainly from this position two heads are better than one, a broader perspective and a broader depth and more diversity of creative thinking as you collaborate."

Diversity

According to Dr. Parsons, diversity and its value for all parties involved was of paramount import, "We give emphasis in this university to the importance of diversity, cultural diversity. I think you could probably draw some connection between the importance in interrelatedness of knowledge. For instance, I don't think you could separate from the study of a subject matter its ethical component." Both instructors found the ethics component crucial for this particular course, "because ethics in agricultural and natural resources would bring together a mix of people of different value sets. That is providing classroom time which is really a microcosm of the real world," argued Dr. Johnson.

Active Learning

The main thrust of the researcher's inquiry in this study was to understand issues that emerge in the process of collaborative teaching. Informants' persistent insights into how this experience influenced student's learning kept coming back over and over again. It was evident students were extremely important to them personally and professionally. They both emphasized the significance of active learning that collaborative approach facilitates, "We each have different value sets. We even have conflicting value sets. And to provide for that active student learning environment and the dynamic of working through ethical issues requires more than one person," noted Dr. Johnsons. Dr. Parsons put special emphasis on the value and importance of working together closely with the colleague during the early stages of collaboration, especially when putting together the syllabus, "Being on the same page is crucial for students' benefit, from knowing there is a consistency on instruction for a common subject matter."

Real World

The opportunity to model real world for students was an essential byproduct of collaborative teaching. To the follow-up question: What does he mean by the "real world experience"? Dr. Johnson answered without hesitation, "Even though it was in the classroom, setting the value sets that were present were very much as diverse and as strong as you would see in the real world. So it is a great laboratory for student active learning that can take place within. I felt that we are more facilitators than lecturers or professors whose role is to proclaim truth for them to absorb. We were there to facilitate, to challenge, to confront, to encourage active learning environment, to deal with issues and from those issues understand better the process rather than rote memorization of facts and truth."

Collaboration beyond the Classroom

The aspect of collaboration within the classroom was easily verifiable by simple observation of classroom activities. Something that researcher could not see or observe, however, was the instructors' informal meetings and casual conversations that constitute a vital part of collaborators' daily interactions. To the question about their adventitious encounters outside the classroom walls, Dr. Parsons replied after a short pause that "In general, we talk to each other pretty frequently over the phone. I bring some materials to Bruce's office or he comes here, and we maintain a good open line of communications. We visit what we want to do or how we are going to assign the tasks to a given class prior to the class. Then after the class if I have given a presentation, I will request a feedback from him or we will talk about what we think. And you know if one of us has any suggestion, so we are in constant contact with each other." To the same question Dr. Johnson responded, "The flow of communication is open, collegial, and effective. This is different from the courses taught in a more traditional, individual way. Faculty collaboration can be and often is very sporadic, and communication may be nonexistent."

Consensus Building

When reflecting upon the initial planning stage of collaboration Dr. Johnson responded, "This stage of collaboration is probably the most important because whatever happens here will reflect upon the whole course and its effectiveness. It is the time to decide what will be taught how and in what sequence. This cannot be left for later, because later may be too late. I think first of all you need to have is a consensus over what you want to see happen in that particular course. If you can agree on the general philosophy and set of educational outcomes that you want to accomplish, and the general idea of process you can agree on, then you could move towards a contract in essence to work together to develop such a program. That contract is not the within idea of okay I will develop the first part of the course and you develop the last part. It is a much higher time commitment of saying: let's sit down and discuss how we see this course evolving over the semester regarding the critical components. And then step by step we would interact and develop a course flow and organizational format." Dr. Parsons had a similar take on the issue, "We sat and suggested what would be the topics that we'd like to do. For example, I suggested that we read at least one primary philosopher rather than reading second hand or third hand texts. So he was very open to that and we had students read by any account a reasonably difficult text on utilitarianism by John Stuart Mill. We had several meetings in summer what it is that we want to do by way of organizing the course. We were both in strong agreement that the course meet all of the criteria of integrated studies."

Mutual Facilitation

The fact of having different often divergent views on agricultural and environmental ethics did not hinder classroom performance. Dr. Parsons argued he "is in a constant process of discovering Bruce's thinking as well as my own thinking. I just think he is more utilitarian-minded than I am. He will reveal himself to be guided by another kind of theory or principle that's not so completely utilitarian. I mean there is a real tension in this class between the way an agriculturist is going to look at land use, water use, and so on, and the student in actual resources or environmental studies is going to look at. There is a potential for real conflict here." For Dr. Johnson, effective collaborative teaching demands the constant presence of both collaborators in the classroom, "First of all, I think it's critical that facilitators here are for the most part in the classroom simultaneously most of the time, and basically you can expect that there are times that only one needs to be there. If you are engaging in much more student active learning, it's not the case of heavy duty delivery of knowledge it's facilitating the interactive dynamic," noticed Dr. Johnson. There is however not always a real need for collaborators to be together in the classroom. There are times that it can be adequately done by just one person, but generally the students need to see the fact that there is a team of people involved here and each person has their own personality. There are times that students even gain from the fact that each facilitator has different opinion. To see Jerry and I approach an issue differently and sometimes even disagree on an outcome is healthy because again that's the real world. It even encourages students in their group dynamics to say I respectfully disagree. Conflict resolution skills, and group coordination, and that sort of thing certainly imply that you don't have to be totally passive." Dr. Johnson emphasized the importance of passion and engagement in the work, "There has to be some passion involved in the issues and I think the vibrant educational experience is going to require some passion in order for it to hook students and their interests and get them engaged. To a great extent that happens via facilitators as you bounce off one another you joke with each other you express feelings of intensity, and you get to be people rather than professors."

Division of Labor

To the question of how instructors evaluate students' performance, Dr. Parsons answered, "When it comes to determining final grades obviously he and I are going to have reconciliation, a meeting where we review the grades and assign a final grade. What we are doing now for the various reading journals that we make students do we basically randomly divide the stack into two and he reads one and I read the other and we do provide students with the criteria sheet or a set of clear objectives that they know what the criteria is for that particular assignment." Similarly, Dr. Johnson's responded, "As far as assignments, we randomly take half of them and we will grade them out with some preconceived general ideas as far as format for grading and what we intend to see is a kind of a particular level of expectations. Jerry grades half. I grade my half. We distribute them and the next assignment we take another random half. Over the course of semester, the probability of Jerry grading all of one student's assignments and me grading all of them is remote."

CHAPTER 7

PROCESS OF COLLABORATIVE TEACHING <u>ANALYSIS</u>

CASE STUDY #2

In this section, the researcher intends to answer the following questions that guide this journey into the complex world of collaboration: 1) What is the process of collaborative teaching? 2) What are the issues related to collaborative teaching? The researcher will also provide readers with an illuminating description of the context in which collaborative teaching took place and the profound benefits and consequences.

Entry Vignette

When it comes to providing quality education, University of Nebraska–Lincoln has been associated with the tradition of distinguished academic achievement since it opened in 1869. Excellence and quality are currently subjects of intense debate in education, business, and public institutions. Lack of agreement on what constitutes excellence and quality in higher education enhances the challenge of the discourse. Practitioners and policy makers have not always welcomed new innovative approaches to instruction delivery with utmost joy and enthusiasm. As leaders of changes and instigators of novel approaches in higher education, the Teachers' College bears a particularly heavy responsibility. The Teachers' College at the University of Nebraska–Lincoln constantly innovates trying to face the changing reality around them and equip their graduates with quality education and skills to allow them to successfully realize their personal and professional objectives. Among numerous efforts of the college, collaborative teaching caught the special attention of the researcher.

The City and the Campus

Lincoln, Nebraska's state capital and second largest city, is located in the eastern part of the state. Surrounded by fields, lakes and parks. This friendly "Star City" has received numerous national awards, including designations such as "All-American City" and "Most livable City." The city's quaint downtown, a short walk from the capacious main campus, features restaurants, museums, theaters, and the historic Hay-Market District. Nebraska's architectural wonder, its State Capitol Building, towers over downtown and is plainly visible from various points of the city. The university is proud of its cultural diversity. Through activities sponsored by students, faculty, and staff, cultural diversity is experienced through such events as the International Bazaar, the Food Fest, Asian Night, Black History Month, Hispanic Heritage Month, and the Native American Awareness Week. The arts also flourish on campus. Focal points of visual arts are represented by artistic sites such as the Sheldon Memorial Art Gallery and the Sculpture Garden, which has been nationally recognized for its permanent collection of twentieth century art. The number of international students and faculty has been increasing year after year. In 1999, the enrollment of international students exceeded twelve hundred. Fifteen hundred faculty members from around the world endeavor to carry on the high quality of education offered by the university as it ushers in the new millennium.

Collaborating Instructors

Coach, teacher, minister, administrator, and now academic teammate! Mr. Gene Armstrong was born in a small town of four thousand people located in North Central Nebraska. His childhood and adolescent's memories center on this small place somewhere in the fields of the very heart of the American continent. Growing up in a small town with even smaller elementary and high school allowed him to be involved in multiple activities. His upbringing has taught him many useful lessons. He explains, "I took advantage of about everything offered in high school. I participated in everything from athletics to art." After high school graduation, Mr. Armstrong left his home town for Kearney State College, Nebraska which was a growing experience for still just a teenage boy, "So, here I was, an eighteen year old high school graduate participating with twenty-five and twenty-six year old Korean vets." That experience, as he later recalled, made a big impression on him. It was then that Mr. Armstrong considered career of a Methodist pastor. That idea, however, was never realized. Right after graduation, at the age of twenty-four, Mr. Armstrong got married and began his life-long career in education. He started as a biology and physical education teacher. He was a football and basketball coach. Finally, time came for school administration. Mr. Armstrong is proud to stay loyal to the state of Nebraska, never leaving it for any professional position. He was, however, most proud of his legacy of four kids–all married–eight grandchildren, and five dogs. During the time of this research study, Mr. Armstrong was a graduate assistant pursuing doctoral degree in the Department of Educational Administration at the University of Nebraska–Lincoln, teaching undergraduate as well as graduate courses. During the spring of 1999, Mr. Armstrong was assigned to teach collaboratively with Dr. Steven Eggland: ED 131 Foundation of Modern Education.

Globetrotter, teacher, administrator, consultant, and now academic teammate! At the age of fifty-seven, Dr. Steven Eggland had visited more places in the world than most mortals can ever dream about. He conquered most of Europe: Austria, Switzerland, France, Norway, Italy, Greece, and other places: Hawaii, Canada, India, Africa, Pakistan, China, Hong Kong, Peru, Mexico, Honduras, Nicaragua, Guatemala, Costa Rica, and the list goes on. True educator that he is, Dr. Eggland has visited over thirty countries. He knows the world and the world knows him. He stands well over six-feet tall, sporting fashionably gray hair. His straight posture and broad shoulders would make him an excellent subject for a statue. With Norwegian blood streaming through his veins, he is definitely a man of action, "I love skiing, fishing. I do some woodworking. I have a huge collection of antique woodworking tools. I like to garden and collect antique furniture. I like to go to auctions," he reminisced. He was born in 1942, in a small town of predominantly Norwegian community in central Iowa. Although he was single at the time of this research study, he did not feel alone. He has a thirty-one year old son named Erik and a twenty-eight daughter Erin. Although both of his children are married, he is still patiently awaiting his first grandchild. His elementary and secondary education takes him back to his family town of Roland, Nebraska. At the tender age of eighteen in 1960, young Steve moved out of his family town and started college education at the University of Iowa. At the college, "I kind of floundered around. I wasn't particularly serious about college. Somewhere after the second year of college I decided to become a teacher, "I don't know why I chose teaching, maybe I saw the writing on the wall or something" he joked. About two years later, he received Bachelor's degree in business education with marketing emphasis. Following graduation, he moved to Wisconsin got a job as a high school marketing teacher in a community outside Milwaukee and taught there for two years. Soon after, he moved to Madison to complete his doctoral study. It took him two and a half years to graduate from the University of Wisconsin majoring in Curriculum and Instruction, with a minor in Adult Education. In the fall of 1971, Dr. Eggland came to the University of Nebraska–Lincoln, Department of Business Education, teaching courses in vocational education, marketing education, and cooperative education. During this research project, Dr. Eggland was a professor and chair of the department of Vocational and Adult Education. the fall of 1998, he and Mr. Gene Armstrong were assigned to teach collaboratively an introductory course for education majors: ED 131 Foundation of Modern Education. The course was offered in the spring semester of 1999. It was a required class that all beginning students majoring in education were required to take. "Many years earlier, the same course was taught by graduate assistants from the Department of Educational Psychology and students complained about the quality of instruction," confessed Dr. Eggland. As a result, administration decided to reshape the course and assured undergraduate students that the course would be taught by senior professors in a way that would encourage critical thinking, career exploration, and a thoughtful look at the teaching profession, while simultaneously giving students a realistic view of the social, economic, governmental, political, and historical milieus of education. Dr. Eggland has taught the course twelve times so far, with only a short break during the last five years. At all times he was individually responsible for the classroom leadership and the number of students did not exceed thirty. More recently, the dean of the Teachers' College experienced difficult time getting senior professors to teach the course and one of the solutions was to create the course with a larger number of students taught by two collaborating professors. Dr. Eggland had never taught collaboratively before. He taught prior with some help of graduate assistants, but never did he experience collaboration that would involve full-blown partnership with a colleague.

Course Objectives

Course ED 131 Foundation of Modern Education is a first course in the sequence of professional preparation for elementary and secondary school teachers. It was designed as a critical thinking module developed around relevant educational issues emphasizing writing as a primary mode of expression and demonstration of clear reasoning and judgment. Prospective young teachers become acquainted with the role of schools and educators in the larger society. It was expected that the course would provide a foundation for subsequent courses in the sequence of professional development. The course was organized around five topics: 1) Who should go to school? 2) What is the purpose of schools in the United States? 3) How should equity be promoted in schools? 4) What subjects should be taught? 5) Who should decide? 6) The future of the educational reform. Upon completion of the course, students were expected to: 1) Have a clear understanding of schooling in America, 2) Have a clear understanding of the process by which data are collected and decisions made about schooling, 3) Have the ability to express their ideas clearly and concisely in both written and spoken forms, 4) Demonstrate the ability to work collaboratively, 5) Develop data-gathering skills, 6) Enhance technology skills. Participation in discussions during the course was critical. Any unexcused absences beyond two resulted in a reduced course grade. Professionalism included regular and punctual attendance, turning in assignments on time, contributions to class discussions, and completion of all required class activities. The intentions of Mr. Armstrong and Dr. Eggland were to create a learning environment, which would recognize and support student diversity in terms of gender, race, pluralism, physical ability, age, and economic status.

Narrative Description
First Meeting

It was a clear winter day on Thursday afternoon, December 17, 1998, when the two collaborating instructors met for the first time. The weather was surprisingly warm for the usually frigid Nebraska winter. The shining sun added extra cheerfulness to the already happy ambience directly preceding Christmas break. The fall semester was over and the noise of the usually busy corridor leading to the departmental library, where the meeting took place, was almost nonexistent. The library was located on the first floor of the Seaton Hall where offices of the Educational Administration Department were located. The building was part of the "Selleck Quadrangle," which constituted one of the assets belonging to the University of Nebraska–Lincoln. The room in which the meeting took place, though called a library, did not quite fit the common definition of the word. The relatively small space of about five square meters in diameter was filled with doctoral dissertations, Master's theses, and variety of academic journals. Books, with black and red covers, were stocked interchangeably on four grey bookshelves to the right of the entrance. Deeper into the room, right by the window, a number of donated books, educational magazines, and newspapers were neatly arranged on the adjacent table. Right across the room, a neat brown glass bookcase stood proudly displaying motley colored books, which contrasted starkly with the white walls of the room. The bookcase was filled with the historical documents for the department. On the right side of the bookcase, a picture of the White House commemorating President Ronald Reagan was dedicated to Dr. Anne Campbell in appreciation of her commitments in promoting excellence in education. The overall display of neatly arranged furniture gave the room a distinguished look and ambience of history and sophistication. Both instructors seated against the picture of President Reagan in the background gave the impression of watching a political debate on television. Slightly subdued sun rays found their way through the shaded windows. In addition to straw-colored shades, all windows were accoutered with opaque curtains that precisely matched the carpet. The room was cozy yet distinguished, which reflected the ambience of the entire department as the meeting that was about to begin. The meeting started at 3:50 p.m. Both professors appeared cheerful and enthusiastic about the prospect of working together. Although they never met before, after a few minutes of a chit-chat, it was evident that those two individuals genuinely liked and respected each other. They started by introducing a brief biography of their educational experiences. Both were similar in many ways. They shared an excellent sense of humor, seasoned attitude to life, and easygoing personalities that reflected the Midwestern culture surrounding and nurturing the entire university. After a short introduction, which took about ten minutes, they shifted gears and went straight to the business at hand. They spoke about the professional aspects of their expected collaboration. Scheduling, teaching methodology, students' evaluation, and even clarification of the concept of collaboration itself constituted the essence of the meeting. Although they were only able to discuss those issues in a general sense, it was apparent that all those issues would have to be resolved on an ongoing basis via regular meetings throughout the semester. Mr. Armstrong made it clear that their work would be characterized by full collaboration, which meant that both instructors would be involved in all course-related activities in and out of the classroom in the most interactive way possible. In that context, Mr. Armstrong made a fine distinction between "collaborative teaching" and "turn-teaching." They agreed the latter method would mean instructors taking turns in lecturing depending on the topic, and that would not be their method of choice in this class. Both instructors agreed also to be present in the classroom on an ongoing basis throughout the semester. They agreed to regular meetings, which would allow them a better understanding of their own expectations for each other and for their students. That would also give them opportunity of mutual feedback and reflection. They suggested meeting once a week, but where and when exactly meeting would take place was to be determined later. Instructors compromised on the topics to be covered in the course and defined tentative distributive leadership arrangement in which each of them would take the leadership stance depending on the topic covered. Another important issue discussed at the meeting touched upon the assessment of students work and ultimately grades. Instructors then established their priorities, objectives for the course, reading materials, sequence of presentations, use of visual aids, and active engagement of students. Mr. Armstrong emphasized the need to break the ice in the class, the importance of which was underlined by the fact that this class consisted predominantly of freshmen–"intellectual virgins"–using words of Dr. Eggland. Mr. Armstrong suggested taking a picture of every student accompanied by a short vignette to allow for better familiarity with students. In the meantime, Mr. Armstrong proposed the idea of "intentionally structured groups" that would promote more structure during the beginning stages of the course, which would then be gradually loosened up as the semester progressed. After establishing and agreeing on all course-relevant issues in the final five minutes of the meeting, the instructors switched back to more personal issues, which gave them yet another opportunity to get to know each other a little bit more. They shared their interests, found mutual grounds, and talked about their careers. Before departing, they established ways of communication, exchanged e-mail addresses, phone numbers, and office locations.

First Class

One can never know what kind of weather to expect in Nebraska. It was January 11, 1999, when snow with glacial temperatures was forecasted and expected. Despite the gloomy predictions, the first day of spring semester was surprisingly warm and sunny. It was around noon and the students seemed rather relaxed, some almost feigned a lackadaisical attitude. No doubt the beautiful weather, with the radiant sun juxtaposed against the austerity of winter, contributed to that jovial mood in the middle of Nebraska's severest season. Although the number of students attending university was approximated twenty-six thousand that year, the campus did not appear overly crowded. Although the temperature was in the low 20s, some students wore simple T-shirts while others sported heavy coats carefully wrapped up to their noses in some solemn expectation of a snowstorm. The ground was partially covered with a thin layer of snow. Exiguous patches of grass resolutely sprang from under the melting snow. "Henzlik Hall," where the class took place, was a relatively large, two-story building located at the southern part of the campus. It was surrounded by "Mabel Lee Hall" from the north and "Bancroft Hall" from the east. On the western side of the building, a huge field spread out where athletes spent majority of their time off practicing football. On the southern side of the building, solidly square fraternity houses lined up like chess pieces with a street and a parking lot behind them. Henzlik Hall, a sizable construction belonging to Teachers' College, seemed uncomfortably squeezed on a relatively small patch of ground. Upon entering the building, three options emerged: first, going straight to the design center with a small dining area; second, turning left to the long corridor with classrooms and offices on both sides; third, choosing stairs leading down to the basement where collaborating instructors were scheduled to teach their class. A long, curvy corridor led to the destination classroom no. 53. The solid blue door opened to the capacious classroom. Six long rows of chairs with small tables affixed to them amounted to a total of eighty seats. The classroom with its rather grand architecture and slightly slanted floor reminded one of a large amphitheater rather than the traditional classroom. The mild slope enabled every student to see clearly the board, peers, and instructors. By 12:30 in the afternoon, almost all seats were filled with students. During the first few minutes of the class, students sat silent deeply engrossed in their own thoughts patiently awaiting the professor to start the class. Mr. Armstrong stood right by the entrance and distributed yellow cards to newly arrived students. Each card had a number and blank space for students to fill in with their personal data such as major and age. The numbers on the cards were used to assign students into groups. At about 12:40 p.m., all who wanted to be in the class on that day finally arrived. The class was comprised of mostly Caucasian students with only three students of African-American origin. Mr. Armstrong briskly distributed hard copies of syllabi explaining that class would be taught in a collaborative fashion with one more instructor, Dr. Steven Eggland, who due to other departmental obligations could not attend the first two sessions. Mr. Armstrong introduced himself sharing with students his brief biography. The entire session was introductory in nature which allowed students to get to know the instructors and better understand expectations and assignments scheduled for the course. Somewhere in the middle of the session, to get the ball rolling, Mr. Armstrong divided students into groups and allowed fifteen minutes for an informal chat. Then a student from each group stood up and presented their newly acquired friends to the rest of the class. The students' introductions confirmed the rather obvious racial and ethnic homogeneity of students. The introductions, however, also revealed that the geographical origins of the students was richly varied, with students hailing from various states including New York and California and anything in-between. Most of the students were eighteen-years-old freshmen majoring in education with two relatively older nontraditional seniors, who at the end of their undergraduate work decided to explore educational profession. Most of the students planned to teach at the elementary level with approximately twenty-five percent of students aspiring to teach at the secondary level. Overall, the session was very lively and productive and ended at the scheduled time.

Second Class

Hardly two days passed since the previous session and temperature dropped well below zero. A mild wind blew falling snow askance which made breathing in the open air almost impossible without some face buffer. Even Henzlik Hall looked slightly different on that day with the ominous clouds gathering in the sky as if announcing to all that winter was back with a vengeance. Ten minutes before 12:30 p.m., some students waited for the locked classroom to open. Soon after, Mr. Armstrong sprang to the door unlocked it and with a welcoming smile announced, "Come in." Students poured into the classroom, rushing through the narrow entrance. The temperature in the room was temperately comfortable. A few energetic male students wore typically Nebraskan baseball hats. Mr. Armstrong was the only instructor in the classroom again. As planned, Dr. Eggland was still out of town. When most of the students were comfortably seated, Mr. Armstrong asked students to form earlier pre-assigned groups. The silence was broken almost instantaneously with a burst of commotion and buzz of interacting happy students. At the same time, the two guest speakers appeared in the classroom almost unnoticeable. They entered rather unobtrusively, indeed remained unnoticed by most students until Mr. Armstrong asked for their attention. Mr. Mike Dempsey, one of the visiting speakers, approached the center of the classroom and took charge of the class for about ten minutes. Soon after, his colleague, Ms. Peggy Quinn took over for another fifteen minutes. They were both technology experts responsible for lab activities, which were part of the course requirements. They spoke about assignments, timing, and scheduling of activities. Meanwhile, Mr. Armstrong stood on the side and encouraged students to ask questions. Despite his best intentions, no one volunteered except for Mr. Armstrong who inquired about the textbook. For the remainder of the class, Mr. Armstrong asked students to discuss in groups characteristics and qualities of "an educated person." Most students were actively involved in the discussion, but occasionally individual slumping bodies could be spotted leaning lazily against the chair, taking the role of passive observers.

Third Class

A week has passed since the last class took place due to the university's scheduled break for Martin Luther Day on the preceding Monday. Students were gradually pouring into the classroom, slowly filling in their designated by now seats. The dampened level of enthusiasm and energy reflected the oppressive winter weather. In the front row, a female student was reading a newspaper, others conversing casually, all awaiting instructor's arrival. Since Dr. Eggland could not appear in the class again, it devolved upon Mr. Armstrong to take individual leadership for the third time in row. The class was dominated by group activities, this time focused around the topic of "seven intelligences" by Gardner and their applications for students as future teachers. Somewhere towards the middle of the session, Mr. Armstrong introduced the topic of illegal immigration in American schools. The article dealt with a hypothetical problem faced by an elementary school in Nebraska and took a critical view of the issue of providing education to the small daughter of illegal immigrants from a Central American Country. Two slightly different vignettes were provided to stimulate critical thinking. As usual, the class was instantly filled with buzz and commotion. Students read, discussed, some even argued using lively facial expressions and animated body language. The discussion that followed proved that most students felt passionate about the topic. Opinions were as divergent as the places from which the students originated. Mr. Armstrong, although pleased with the students' involvement, had to eventually stop the discussion since the time to wrap the session up had arrived. The class ended and students left the classroom with thoughtful expressions on their faces as if still thinking about the moot case discussed during the past hour.

Fourth Class

On Monday, 12:15 p.m., on January 25, 1999, the two collaborating professors finally met in the classroom. Immediately upon entering the class, both instructors looked hastily through their lecture notes, occasionally conversing with each other. From a distance both instructors looked very much alike. Both were rather tall, wearing glasses which added proper dignity to their professorial demeanor and scholarly image so scrupulously forged from years of earnest lucubration. Even the classroom looked a little different that day. Some of the lights were off, with a few dim fixtures left on to allow for safe movement around. The attendance was, as usual, almost perfect, with only a handful of empty seats. Students formed their respective groups. Mr. Armstrong opened the class with a question, "What is your understanding of the differences between 'expulsion' from the school and 'suspension' from the school?" While Mr. Armstrong confronted students with a task, Dr. Eggland stood silently nearby observing students. Upon task completion, instructors promptly collected the cards with students' answers. Next, Mr. Armstrong referred to the topic addressed last week and initiated conversation about applications of Gardner's "Intelligences." At the same time, Dr. Eggland's confident posture remained unchanged with right side of his body leaning against the wall observing Mr. Armstrong and students interacting with one another. Soon after, Mr. Armstrong revisited the case of Gabriela, a daughter of illegal immigrants. This time a controversy shifted from ethical and moral considerations to the purely legal and completely unemotional aspects of the case. During the discussion, Mr. Armstrong, while experiencing some sort of memory lapse, referred to Dr. Eggland who helped him recover temporarily forgotten facts. At the time of the discussion, the class was filled with the hushed but intense susurration of the students. While Mr. Armstrong kept wandering around the classroom mingling with the students, Dr. Eggland searched through his stack of notes. At some point, Mr. Armstrong approached Dr. Eggland, who so far did not have an opportunity to address students directly. That was about to change. After a short introduction by Mr. Armstrong, Dr. Eggland described the journey of his professional life with references related to the course. Dr. Eggland distributed an article with the last reading assignment for the day. The leading theme of the article was "weapons in schools." While students were reading and discussing the article, both instructors walked among the groups, listening to students, occasionally participating in their discussions. After approximately ten minutes, Dr. Eggland posed two questions: "Which groups think Chris should be expelled and why?" Mr. Armstrong restlessly jumped in and added: "What would you do in this case?" After a brief pause, students began to express their ideas freely. Dr. Eggland responded to students' responses by elaborating on the topic with stories from his own experience with guns in schools. When the students were almost ready to leave the classroom, Dr. Eggland swiftly distributed articles about guns in schools. While Dr. Eggland was still passing around the articles, Mr. Armstrong presented the assignment for the next class. Although the work was over for students that day, it was not for the collaborating instructors. They had already scheduled another meeting to take place immediately after the class in that very classroom.

Second Meeting

Students were slowly exiting the classroom, when both instructors began to plan and organize their future work in more detail. It was 1:50 p.m., but one group of students was still in the classroom discussing their group project. Mr. Armstrong sat behind the brown desk placed in front of the board facing Dr. Eggland who took one of the students' chairs in the front row. The ambience of the meeting was very relaxed but both instructors were conscious of the time spent on collaboration that would not have been necessary if either had taught the class independently. The instructors seemed overwhelmed with busy schedules and other out-of-class responsibilities. They started by mutually assuring each other that everything went right during the last class. They agreed the class went mostly as planned and the time was ripe to think about the next Wednesday. Mr. Armstrong suggested a few topics for the next session. In the meantime, the rest of the lingering students rushed out of the classroom, leaving behind much desired quietude. After a brief cross-check of ideas, they agreed to truncate certain materials deemed redundant. Dr. Eggland offered to take the lead of the next class saying, "I will carry the next day." Mr. Armstrong concurred and offered to take care of "housekeeping" tasks in the meantime. Towards the end of the meeting, they focused on sequencing of activities and agreed to wind up the issue of "weapons in schools" during the next week session. The productive meeting ended after about fifteen minutes.

Fifth Class

Two days passed and students showed up on time slowly streaming into the classroom. They have already acquired a hebdomadal routine of forming groups from the very outset. An almost buoyant atmosphere was palpable when students struck conversations with their peers and instructors. It was comparable to sitting in a theater shortly before opening act of a highly anticipated spectacle. The audience patiently awaited actors to begin. Their forbearance was finally rewarded when Mr. Armstrong stepped into the center and initiated another group discussion, which by now became a routine part of each session. This time students were asked to define the concept of "societal induction," the topic introduced during the preceding session by Dr. Eggland. After a few minutes of reflection,

Dr. Eggland briskly stepped onto "the stage," and embarked on introducing the topic. He posed the question: "What does 'societal induction' mean to you?" At the same time, Mr. Armstrong finished collecting cards with students' answers and discreetly removed himself to the side of the class, away from the limelight. Since the lights above the board were dimmed, students could not see the instructions clearly. Mr. Armstrong almost instinctively jumped to the switchboard and turned the lights on. That allowed Dr. Eggland to finish his trail of thoughts uninterruptedly. He continued his lecture, occasionally referring to Mr. Armstrong to retrieve some facts that temporarily escaped his memory. In each case, Mr. Armstrong eagerly infused his insights, occasionally elaborating on the discussed issues even further. Initially students appeared to be listening rather passively (or perhaps not listening at all). However, over time, clearly stimulated by the exchanges between collaborating instructors, students became increasingly more engaged reacting vigorously to examples and suggestions posed by both instructors. After sufficiently exhausting the topic, Mr. Armstrong took over the lead by switching students' attention to the papers that groups were expected to share with each other before today's session. Almost instantaneously, a sonorous scream surfaced from across the room, "Oh, no! I forgot the paper." After the discussion, instructors informed students of the next project. While Mr. Armstrong was explaining the assignment, Dr. Eggland adjusted the lighting in the classroom to make the reading easier. Soon after, while Mr. Armstrong was still speaking, Dr. Eggland assiduously looked through the students' responses on what the "societal induction" meant to them. He singled out the best definitions, dividing them to various categories such as: funny, creative, concise etc. During the last fifteen minutes of the session, Dr. Eggland referred back to the earlier discussed issue of weapons in the classroom. Again even though discussion started rather slowly it ended up with fireworks. To the delight of the instructors, students provided quite profound insights. Evidently students found the topic emotionally charged and some thoughtful answers surprised even instructors.

Sixth Class

On February 1, 1999, students and instructors alike seemed comfortably ensconced in their new routines. Their hearts began to beat in the same rhythm. Students acquainted with the teachers' styles and expectations appeared relaxed in forming their assigned groups almost instinctively without any prompts. Mr. Armstrong appeared in the classroom twenty minutes before scheduled time to ensure everything worked properly and class was ready to launch at the moment's notice. Dr. Eggland appeared ten minutes later and both instructors began browsing through their lecture notes. When students were still entering the class, Dr. Eggland took off his jacket and mingled with students for some informal chats. Right on time, Dr. Eggland brought entire class to attention by randomly choosing students to summarize articles assigned for that session. Out of five presented articles, the one dealing with senior citizens' volunteer involvement in helping educators do their jobs spurred most interest and response from the students. While Dr. Eggland led the discussion, Mr. Armstrong, stood nearby leaning against the wall occasionally interpolating his comments into the discussion. Having exhausted the subject, Dr. Eggland asked students to hand in their articles. For a short while, the classroom transformed into a wild horse race of sort with students struggling to move around closely cramped rows of seats. After the commotion subsided sufficiently enough and students were successfully reined in back into their seats again, Dr. Eggland read a scenario that set the stage for the next topic of the day—"religion in schools" and the role of religious schools in American society. Dr. Eggland introduced the subject matter by reviewing current legislature that constitutes the basis for administrative decisions in public and private education. When deliberation ended, Mr. Armstrong took over the leadership by introducing a short film. The lights went off and large screen rolled down from the ceiling. Instructors removed themselves from the students' sight and began the film projection. A murmuration passed through the audience and then died away. Soon after classroom was instantly filled with a silent anticipation, characteristic of an audience curiously anticipating the opening act of a theatrical spectacle. While Mr. Armstrong quietly walked toward the right side of the classroom, Dr. Eggland sat on the stairs right by the classroom entrance. As announced the film addressed future of private religious schools with the specific focus on allowing parents the freedom to choose the kind of education they wanted for their children. The thirty-minute film and Dr. Eggland adjusted the classroom lighting. Mr. Armstrong inquired into students' reactions. After eliciting quite a number of responses, the class came to an end. Mr. Armstrong requested that students pick up their graded papers from the front desk. The noise in the classroom increased instantaneously when students looked through their graded papers—most of them excited—some looking a bit dejected—perhaps mourning lower than expected grades. Right before students' departure, Dr. Eggland announced a homework assignment in which students were asked to argue for and against the test scores as an alternative way to certify teachers. Students left the classroom, but the work of the instructors was not finished. They stayed longer to assess the past week and plan for the next one.

Third Meeting

Dr. Eggland and Mr. Armstrong began their meeting at 1:45 p.m. Students had already left the classroom, leaving behind a messy disarray of chairs twisted in all possible directions. Instructors were seated in the same positions as they were during the previous meeting facing each other. They hastily browsed through a tall stack of students' papers. Dr. Eggland, while marking something in his notes, agreed to lead a group activity that starts each session. They agreed that stretching the discussion on the selected film would be desirable. After a short pause, Dr. Eggland proposed the dichotomous approach to instruction delivery by differentiating between "what we teach" and "how we teach." That triggered in Mr. Armstrong a question that perhaps would not have occurred to him, had it not been for Dr. Eggland's suggestion. He inquisitively inquired, "When do students really get to the issue of 'how to teach' in their program?" Dr. Eggland paused for a few seconds and concluded that "Students take methodology classes, but basically all other courses somehow relate to that aspect of student development." That was quite surprising to Mr. Armstrong, who took only one or two methodology classes during his entire education. He strongly concurred that "This class should contribute somehow to the students' methodological development." With this in mind, the instructors adjourned in quite vivacious spirits.

Seventh Class

It was surprising to see students wearing T-shirts on the unseasonably warm day on February 3, 1999. The lights in the classroom were already on. Instructors conversed in a somewhat subdued manner. It was obvious they were planning the class and sequencing of events in this long seventy-five minute session. Generally speaking, the atmosphere was exuberant on that day. Dr. Eggland took leadership of the class with Mr. Armstrong helping to sort through class activities and stimulate group discussions. The room was quiet with the exception of occasional giggles coming from a couple of female students seated at the very back of the class. After approximately ten minutes, Dr. Eggland started discussion on students' written responses. At the same time, Mr. Armstrong and one of the students left the classroom rather quietly. Mr. Armstrong asked the student to be his partner during the activity that followed. The student, young African-American woman, had spent plenty of time in various parts of the world and could serve as a tremendous resource for both students and instructors. The instructors did not waste that opportunity and after a short while, and they both returned to the class and the selected student delivered an inspiring presentation related to her wide spectrum of experiences around the world. During the discussion, one of the students asked Dr. Eggland about the requirements for teacher certification in private schools. Instantaneously, Dr. Eggland urged Mr. Armstrong, "Gene, you can answer this?!" Mr. Armstrong heartily responded with a short but comprehensive list of the requirements. Minutes later, instructors provided students with sheets of paper outlining state regulations for nonpublic schools. The students' task was to select "true/false" answers. At that moment, a group of conversing students burst in the room. While students were searching for correct answers, both instructors stood by the front desk browsing through the papers. After a fervent discussion, the class was ended with a number of students approaching both instructors with individual questions. Both instructors gladly obliged and provided ample opportunities for students' Q & A session.

Eighth Class

On February 8, 1999, at 12:30 a.m., the instructors began the class by distributing graded assignments. Dr. Eggland called students' names and Mr. Armstrong approached students individually personally delivering each paper. For the most part the class was filled with the sanguine buzz of celebration. A group of students sitting at the back of the classroom clapped loudly averring, "We did good!" While the students were still celebrating, the instructors met at the front desk shuffling quickly through their notes. No more than five minutes elapsed, when Mr. Armstrong interrupted the classroom clamor with a prolonged "Okay!" After a short congratulatory note for the job well done, Mr. Armstrong referred to the earlier prepared list of rules, helpful guide to writing a scholarly paper. At the same time, Dr. Eggland browsed through the papers at the front desk. When students were not able to answer the question put forward by Mr. Armstrong, he requested Dr. Eggland to leap in with helpful hints, which prompted a series of arguments. On another occasion, due mainly to lack of students' responses, Dr. Eggland interjected again somewhat unexpectedly pointing to the student who was raising his hand but went unnoticed by Mr. Armstrong. In the following activity, Mr. Armstrong posed a question, "Is mere exposure to education enough for students to learn?" Students after completing assigned activity went on to discuss the topic with one representative student summarizing the responses in the front of the classroom. At that time both instructors were standing together on the side, carefully observing the interacting students. After approximately fifteen minutes, Mr. Armstrong asked the students to "Write down some thoughts about a teacher who had a strong impact on your personal development listing as many adjectives as possible." Immediately, the class was filled with tangible sensation of highly focused students. In the meantime, Dr. Eggland exited the classroom leaving Mr. Armstrong wandering among the silently reflecting students. Just when Dr. Eggland appeared in the classroom anew, Mr. Armstrong resumed the discussion. That was the last activity of the day. When students began to leave the classroom, the collaborating instructors prepared for their weekly meeting.

Fourth Meeting

Upon completion of the course, Dr. John Sheer entered the classroom. He was a tall, slim man in his early fifties. Light khaki pants, a blue shirt, and a brown tight vest made him an excellent match for his crisply attired teammates. At about 2:00 p.m., the classroom was practically empty when Mr. Armstrong and Dr. Eggland sat by the computer trying to implement what they had just learned. While still digesting newly acquired knowledge, Mr. Armstrong began the review of the material for the next class. He turned to Dr. Eggland with the statement, "This is where you pick up next time." In the meantime, Dr. Sheer continued his disquisition on his experience with the course and the most effective way to apply technology with utmost efficacy. It took collaborators another hour of practice to gain relative familiarity and comfort with the freshly introduced program. Upon finishing the meeting, all three left the classroom. Mr. Armstrong switched off the lights and locked up the door.

Ninth Class

Something unusual happened on February 10, 1999. Black suits, ties, crisp white shirts constituted the sartorial standard of the day. It appeared as if something unusual was about to happen. Indeed, a guest speaker, Dr. Jody Isernhagen from the department of Educational Administration, visited the class to edify students and hopefully instructors on biases and treatment of women and minorities in educational institutions. Her highly professional dress code composed of a perfectly fitted skirt, jacket, and dark blouse underneath put pressure on the collaborating instructors to dress up for the occasion. Dr. Eggland took a seat next to Dr. Isernhagen behind the front desk, leaving Mr. Armstrong casually conversing with the students. A short while later, Mr. Armstrong pulled down the screen to present students with another group activity related to the topic of the day. After approximately ten minutes, the instructors collected cards with students' responses. Dr. Eggland picked the most interesting responses and read them aloud, contributing occasional editorials along the way. Meanwhile, Mr. Armstrong standing on the side contributed a few examples of his own in support of his colleague's arguments. Soon after, Mr. Armstrong took control of the class, switched off the projector, and clearly enunciated, "One third of our course is behind us." He turned to the visiting professor, Dr. Isernhagen, who briskly approached the center of the classroom and gave a short introduction of her educational experiences. For the remainder of the session, the collaborating instructors removed themselves from the students' view, leaning against the wall and listening to guest's presentation. The class finished at 1:45 p.m. sharp.

Tenth Class

On February 16, 1999, Dr. Eggland faced the students alone in the classroom for the first time. "Gene left town to make money," he started jokingly. With his sleeves pulled up Dr. Eggland was ready. He announced with a booming voice, "Let's get started!" Gradually the noise subsided and students began brief summaries of their articles. Of all the presented issues, respect for teaching profession–or the lack of it–generated the most discussion. That very issue became the catalyst that transformed this rather subdued discussion into an aggressive exchange of opinions of highly opinionated individuals. After a while, the focal topic of the day began to crystalize into the role schools and teachers should play in the society at large. The session ended with a documentary comparing and contrasting American and Japanese education system. Dr. Eggland ended the class with closing comments and a quick reminder of the readings assigned for the next session.

Fifth Meeting

On February 17, 1999, the collaborating instructors met to critically review their work performed thus far and prepare for the upcoming week. The meeting took place in the classroom at exactly 12:00 p.m., half an hour before the scheduled class start. Mr. Armstrong had already prepared the room, pulled down the screen and turned on the computer. The room was a bit stuffy and warm at the time of the meeting. Dr. Eggland, wearing a long coat with a black satchel hanging over his shoulder, entered the classroom. He swiftly took off his coat and approached Mr. Armstrong, who was arranging the class materials all over the desk. A moment later, both stood behind the familiar brown desk hurriedly shuffling through the material. "This is usually the time when the wheels start to waffle away," reflected Mr. Armstrong. Dr. Eggland showed him the students' completed assignments and briefly explained his intentions for today's class. Just then the first student showed up and took the seat in the front row. Seeing more students coming in, Dr. Eggland stood up declaring loudly, "That's it for today. How about next Monday?" "Fine," retorted Mr. Armstrong. Just then, the second student arrived saying "Hello." The meeting was over at 12:20 p.m.

Eleventh Class

Just when the instructors finished the meeting, a third student arrived greeting everybody with a cheerful "Hi." From that moment on, students were streaming into the classroom in droves. Even though the temperature dropped significantly that day, most of the students wore light jackets, perhaps subconsciously defying the reality it was still winter. Leaving Dr.

Eggland in charge at the front of the classroom, Mr. Armstrong took a seat at the very back of the class to update students' attendance. Dr. Eggland looked over Mr. Armstrong's shoulder saying, "There are some people here that don't show up too much for the class!" Mr. Armstrong peeked on the list and marked those who were absent most frequently. When most of the seats filled up, Mr. Armstrong approached the front of the classroom and greeted students with a boisterous "Good morning! It's time to get started." He read the list of students who miss classes most frequently and proceeded to an opening group activity of the day. Soon after, Dr. Eggland listed their responses on the board initiating the discussion. He was then joined by Mr. Armstrong who just finished updating students' attendance. He approached the class and commented on the controversial issue of "pay inequities" between men and women. While raising the issue of federal money for schools, Dr. Eggland referred to Mr. Armstrong with a request to clarify the issue for students. Mr. Armstrong gladly obliged and proceeded to collaborate on the issue from the perspective of his own administrative experience as elementary school administrator. After a brief summary of the most salient points, Dr. Eggland released the students who proceeded to sauntered out of the classroom.

Twelfth Class

On February 22, 1999, the capricious winter finally settled on a more characteristic temperature way below zero. Bitter cold and harsh wind accompanied heavy snowfall. That alone made the uneventful diurnal activities like commuting to work or school onerous, in some cases impossible. It was not surprising then that twenty percent of students did not show up for the class. At 12:10 p.m., Mr. Armstrong busily readied the classroom. Ten minutes later, Dr. Eggland entered the room wearing his easily recognizable light brown coat and a large book bag hanging over his right shoulder. Immediately instructors approached the desk, looked through the prepared material and hastily exchanged thoughts on presumably some class-related issues. Mr. Armstrong approached the front rows to talk to students with a predictable request. He asked them to start their group activities that opened each session. In the meantime, Dr. Eggland left the classroom, leaving Mr. Armstrong stranded among the rows of interacting students. The noise of the conversing students gradually filled the entire room. Just when Mr. Armstrong began the discussion, Dr.

Eggland returned to the classroom and both gathered cards with students' responses. While Mr. Armstrong led the discussion, Dr. Eggland took the seat behind the desk facing the students and began looking through the students' responses, taking attendance at the same time. The next task, which was also completed in small groups, filled the rest of the session. Dr. Eggland occasionally interrupted the discussion with questions and comments of his own. The activity ended with instructors distributing the sheets with homework assignment for the next class. Students spent a little bit more time than usual zipping their coats up to their very chins trying to create an impenetrable buffer against the wall of snow and wind awaiting them outside the building. Winter, "Nebraska style," had become a chilly reality.

Thirteenth Class

On February 24, 1999, the classroom was unusually hot and stuffy, which contrasted with the cold and murky day outside the building. "So hot in here!" exclaimed a female student upon entering the class. Instructors were talking behind the front desk looking through the papers. Both looked ready for an action. Right then, a stocky young man entered the classroom with a loud burp, as if saying "Here I am. We can start." Mr. Armstrong, familiar with the students' vernacular, turned to the class and said, "Okay! Three by six cards," referring to the session's opening group activities. While students were studiously writing their answers in absolute silence, Mr. Armstrong meandered toward the back of the room. At the same time, Dr. Eggland sat on the side observing the class. While Dr. Eggland continued to gather students' responses, Mr. Armstrong distributed white sheets of paper with past due assignments to the students who were absent on Monday. Mr. Armstrong started with a short debrief of what was covered so far. Dr. Eggland glanced through the students' responses taking their attendance at the same time. After this short introductory activity, Mr. Armstrong asked students to form their groups and initiated the exercise that covered the remainder of the session. When students were busily working on their assignment, instructors wandered among the students, who occasionally whispered to each other and looking through their lecture notes. In the final phase of the activity, instructors confronted students with the dilemma of a hypothetically cut school budget, "On the basis of your priorities, what areas of the curriculum would you cut and why?"

Students discussed the topic in groups with a representative team member sharing their final decisions. Instructors frequently commented on the discussion with probing questions, elaborating further on more insightful responses. The robust deliberation came to an end with everybody looking satisfied.

Sixth Meeting

On February 25, 1999, the collaborating instructors showed up at the departmental library at Seaton Hall at exactly 8:30 a.m. It was the same place where they met for the first time over two months ago to plan the course and get to know each other. Lights in the room were already on. Windows had their shades rolled half way down allowing in the limited daylight of the grey winter day. Instructors faced each other by taking seats on the opposite sides of the table, right by the entrance door. Dr. Eggland was professionally dressed as always in a black suit and a white crisp shirt. That contrasted sharply with Mr. Armstrong who sported jeans and sneakers for the occasion. The purpose of the meeting was to take a critical look at their real achievements thus far. They were determined to learn from previous mistakes and develop new constructive strategies for the remaining two months. Dr. Eggland started with a deep sigh and an opening statement, "So what is the overall objective for the near future?" After a brief pause of what seemed to be a deep reflective ponder, Dr. Eggland started a list, "Gender, age, sexual orientation, sport, age, and equity issue." "Ethics!" added Mr. Armstrong. "Of course," retorted Dr. Eggland, who picked up the list to review it again. "Attractiveness, handicapped, religion, feminist perspective," continued Mr. Armstrong. Both jotted down the ideas carefully and the more ideas appeared the more enthusiastic they became. After fifteen minutes of brainstorming, Dr. Eggland suggested to create a "matrix" to provide students with a chance to respond to it. Soon after, Dr. Eggland, who took the lead in the discussion, asked "Is there anybody we can bring from outside to help out?" Mr. Armstrong responded without hesitation, "How about 'University Diversity Players'?" "Yes, let's do it!" exclaimed ever more excited Dr. Eggland. Again, it seemed the more they bounced the concepts against each other, the more novel ideas they generated. Their excitement finally crescendoed when Dr. Eggland followed up with another suggestion, "How about legal issues? Do we have someone, a lawyer who could help us?" "I've got a lawyer in my office, he's in our department!" responded Mr. Armstrong, "In fact, he's probably here right now. Let me check" "Perfect!" exclaimed Dr. Eggland. The excitement grew by the minute. It wasn't more than three minutes when Mr. Armstrong came back accompanied by Mr. John McMillen, the above-referenced lawyer. After a few minutes of consultation his role in the upcoming session was outlined and agreed upon. Dr. Eggland excitedly added, "How about Kathy Shada to talk about diversity and ethics? I'll call her." During the last minutes of the meeting, instructors set deadlines for each task. The meeting ended after an hour with both instructors looking exuberant with the results. Mr. Armstrong concluded enthused, "I like it. I think we are getting into the meat!"

Fourteenth Class

On March 1, 1999, the students appeared quite exuberant. Loud laughs and chats echoed throughout the room in festive expectation of the upcoming spring break. A female student seated in the front row abruptly exclaimed, "I'm going to California!" as if announcing for everybody to hear. Dr. Eggland stepped into the center of the class to capture students' attention, but to no avail. He turned the lights on and off to signal the "picnic" was over and time arrived to start the class. He immediately asked for volunteers to share their assigned articles. Mr. Armstrong, seated behind the front desk, directly faced students. He submerged himself in the deluge of papers tossed right in front of him. Dr. Eggland, who led the discussion, occasionally referred to him asking questions about school funds and legal issues. Mr. Armstrong, always willing to share his experiences, readily elaborated on the discussed topics. After approximately twenty minutes, students handed in their articles and both instructors distributed assignments that preoccupied the remainder of the session. The students' task was to come up with novel approaches to current issues in education. While students struggled to find creative answers in their respective groups, Dr. Eggland approached Mr. Armstrong for clarification on one of his earlier comments. When noise in the classroom reached its crescendo, Dr. Eggland started a stimulating discussion. Every student had an opinion and wanted to talk. So much so that instructors had to hush the class down and started calling on students individually. Every student seemed to have a different idea on how to revive schools' budget, what to cut, and who to hire. The instructors were quite pleased with the results. Everybody could hear Dr. Eggland exclame to Mr. Armstrong, "This is great!" The animated wrangling filled the majority of the session with Dr. Eggland assuming the role of a leader. Mr. Armstrong, standing on the side, supported him with occasional comments and assisted with the overall control of the class. Mr. Armstrong ended the class with the closing comments about teachers and their roles in shaping the future of American education as he saw it fit.

Fifteenth Class

On March 3, 1999, minutes before the class started, students crowded around the instructors' desk to pick up their graded papers. Mr. Armstrong stood by the computer browsing through the materials prepared for the class. Right then, Dr. Eggland appeared at the doorstep. He immediately joined Mr. Armstrong who started by pointing to a number of organizational issues to be addressed. He turned to Dr. Eggland and asked, "Do you have anything else?" "Not really," he briefly retorted. Loud chatter gradually subsided to a soft susurrus and ultimately a complete silence. While students wrote down their individual responses, instructors whispered to each other, presumably preparing the next task or activity. Approximately ten minutes passed the students handed in their responses and Dr. Eggland started a debate. Instructors stood next to each other when first volunteers began to express their opinions. Dr. Eggland raised the issue of advertising in education. To which Mr. Armstrong added jokingly, "How about Budweiser!" That example obviously resounded quite well with most of the students. At times Dr. Eggland, referred to Mr. Armstrong to retrieve names and dates. Communication between instructors was, as usual, quite relaxed and easygoing. Mr. Armstrong moved to the left side of the classroom so that instructors practically faced each other with students strategically placed between them. In the middle of the discourse, Dr. Eggland introduced students to the notion of "equity" in schools. That topic would be carried on through the next five sessions. The discussion that followed filled the rest of the session.

Sixteenth Class

March 8, 1999 was marred by cold and wet snowstorm. Due to the inclement weather forecast, university administration considered canceling classes for the day but eventually decided against it. Nevertheless, many students did not attend the class, leaving classroom spotted with numerous patches of empty seats. Fifteen minutes before the class started, Mr. Armstrong stood rather animated at the front of the classroom talking to the guest speaker, Mr. John McMillen. As scheduled, Dr. Eggland was absent on that day. Mr. McMillen, a former Husker quarterback and a lawyer, was working on his doctoral degree in the Department of Educational Administration at the time of this research project. Mr. Armstrong briefly recapitulated concepts from the previous classes and smoothly segued to the subject of equity in schools. After a brief introduction, Mr. McMillen swiftly asserted leadership role. He started with a quick overview of "diversity laws" and began his disquisition that filled the remainder of the class. The arguments reached a real momentum when Mr. McMillen raised the issues of AIDS, gay and lesbian students, and the role of teachers in that context. A majority of the students wanted to express themselves and many appeared to have strong well-defined stance on the topic. Mr. Armstrong assumed the role of the facilitator occasionally inserting his own questions, short commentaries and elaborations on Mr. McMillan presentation. Frequently, he simply pointed to a student who had a question but inadvertently was not acknowledged by the guest speaker. Class ended at the scheduled time with unanimous applause for the speaker who contributed greatly to stimulating exchanges among students and the instructor.

Seventeenth Class

On March 10, 1999, two visiting female students were standing at the back of the class preparing their presentation, or rather demonstration. The invited guest speakers represented the "University Players"–a student organization promoting diversity among students. The idea of inviting the peer sophomore students to the class came up as a result of brainstorming during one of the instructors' meetings two weeks prior. While students completed their responses to the opening group activity, collaborating instructors stood on the left side of the classroom communicating in a customarily subdued fashion not to distract working students. Ten minutes passed when Mr. Armstrong asked the visiting students for a short introduction. The team immediately asked for a volunteer from the audience to join them, and three of them role-played the undesirable behaviors that might be offensive for people representing different races, sexual orientations, ethnic, national origins, or religious beliefs. For the most part, the classroom was filled with the murmur and chitchat of interacting students who commented on the displayed behaviors. The instructors, located at the very back of the classroom, took the roles of passive observers examining the quality of students' interactions with each other and the presenting team. In the final part of the session, the instructors summed up major learning points of the demonstration and, along with the rest of the class, gave a big hand to the performing team. Everybody left the class fifteen minutes before two o'clock in the afternoon.

Eighteenth Class

March 22, 1999 marked first class after spring break. Vernal frolicking was over and time quickly sped towards the finals. Dr. Kathy Shada, who taught parts of this course a few years prior, was invited as a guest speaker on that day. Her tiny stature starkly contrasted with the towering figure of Mr. Armstrong. Dr. Eggland was absent on that day. On a daily basis, Dr. Shada worked with disadvantaged minorities and her main objective was to promote "diversity awareness" among university students, especially those aspiring for teaching careers. Mr. Armstrong started with a warm, "Welcome back after the break!" An opening group activity soon ensued. While students busily filled out the assigned cards, Mr. Armstrong and Dr. Shada quietly conversed on the right side of the classroom. Completing the task did not take more than ten minutes, upon which Mr. Armstrong asked students to form new larger groups of seven students each. Once the students were comfortably ensconced in their new groups, Mr. Armstrong briefly introduced the guest speaker. Dr. Shada, using group activity and a short film, focused students' attention on the issue of diversity and sensitivity towards minorities, something students would need to be keenly aware in their future work as teachers. Mr. Armstrong strolled among rows of students listening attentively to their arguments occasionally responding to questions posed by the students. Class ended a few minutes after the scheduled time with loud applause for the quest speaker.

Seventh Meeting

On March 24, 1999, collaborators met again to revise the progress and plan for the final quarter of the course. Customarily in case of comprehensive meetings, they met in the departmental library located on the first floor of Seaton Hall. They arrived together at exactly 10:30 a.m., two hours before the class on the sunny but chilly morning. Both entered smiling and joking with each other. They took seats behind the tables as usual facing each other. Since Dr. Eggland was not present during the last class, Mr. Armstrong debriefed him on the material covered. "Is there something we can follow up on?" inquired Dr. Eggland. "That's what I'm thinking about," retorted Mr. Armstrong. Dr. Eggland kept jotting down the ideas offered by his collaborator. He concluded, "Since I will be gone next week, I would be happy to play a major role today." "It would be fine," responded Mr. Armstrong. "Censorship in schools"–the collaborators must have found the topic extremely important since it dominated over twenty minutes of their time. Since both had different understanding of the concept, Mr. Armstrong suggested "standing on different positions in front of the students?" "Yes, let's try to do this," Dr. Eggland responded without any hesitation. Poor involvement of majority of students in the class activities represented, in the view of Dr. Eggland, "underutilization of the great potential of every student." The instructors agreed on dividing students into smaller groups, hoping that would activate those students who never speak up. In the final part of this forty-minute meeting, the two collaborators scheduled the topics and assigned material for the rest of the semester. Soon before adjourning the meeting, Dr. Eggland asked, "How about the attendance?" "Out of seventy-seven students only three dropped out," responded Mr. Armstrong. "We need to be tougher then," jokingly concluded Dr. Eggland.

Nineteenth Class

One hour upon completion of the meeting, collaborating instructors met again to lead nineteenth session of the course. Mr. Armstrong started with a small group activity in which students were asked to provide examples of censorship in schools. Ten minutes later, while Mr. Armstrong was still collecting students' answers, Dr. Eggland stepped into the center and began the discussion. During the introduction, Mr.

Armstrong, standing on the side of the classroom, contributed once or twice by asking students to clarify their viewpoints. After approximately thirty minutes, Mr. Armstrong took over the leadership by asking students to create new groups. At first, students rather slowly began trekking around the classroom, eventually creating commotion that filled entire auditorium. It took only a few minutes for groups to form. While Mr. Armstrong explained the nature of the activity, Dr. Eggland distributed blank sheets of paper to the individual groups. Students were instructed to role- play various scenarios of depicted real-life situations. This small group activity concluded the class, evidently dividing students and causing unnecessary but unavoidable resentment among some of them.

Twentieth Class

On March 29, 1999, students arrived in the classroom dressed for spring, wearing primarily T-shirts and sweat pants. Mr. Armstrong stood in front of the classroom chatting with students lounging in the front row. Dr. Eggland was not present in the classroom again. Mr. Armstrong started class by asking two students, sitting in the first row, to read two excerpts from the articles covering previously broached topic of censorship in schools–this time from historical perspective. Following that activity, Mr. Armstrong pointed to the steps projected on the screen students must follow to complete their final group project. For the remainder of the class, students worked on the procedure and sequence of their presentations. They distributed workloads among individual group members and worked out timeframes for each part. Once compromises had been reached and final decisions made, students left the classroom.

Twenty-First Class

On March 31, 1999, Mr. Armstrong led the class all by himself. Dr. Eggland could not attend the class again. There were only four weeks left of the spring semester. One could already sense tangible tension accompanying speedily approaching finals. The focus of the session was organizational in nature with Mr. Armstrong assigning groups for the upcoming presentation sessions. The task took only fifteen minutes to complete. Nevertheless, the groups found it difficult to decide on the day most appropriate for their presentations. Eventually, after brief but intense negotiations, group assignments were finally completed and the classroom filled with relative ease again. That interval allowed Mr. Armstrong to elaborate on the nature of presentations and the technical aspects to be taken under consideration.

Eighth Meeting

On April 1, 1999, half an hour before scheduled class, Dr. Eggland and Mr. Armstrong met to prepare for the upcoming week of classes. Other than the instructors seated next to each by the front desk, the entire auditorium was empty. The brief meeting lasting only ten minutes focused on students' final presentations. Instructors selected groups each would supervise and the classrooms they would occupy. Dr. Eggland decided to stay in the original classroom no. 53 while Mr. Armstrong would move upstairs with his groups to classroom no. 116. Despite time constraints, they were able to quickly agree on the assessment standards. In the final three minutes of the meeting, Mr. Armstrong shared with his collaborator attendance numbers he recently calculated. Just when the first two students showed up for the class, the meeting ended at 12:20 p.m.

Twenty-Second Class

Five minutes after the meeting ended, the classroom began to fill up with students prepared to make their presentations. Since the weather was cold and rainy, students arrived with heavy drenched coats. As agreed during the meeting, Mr. Armstrong left and headed for classroom no. 116 one floor above to meet the groups assigned under his tutelage. Only students with projects due on that day were present. When fourteen students took their seats in the first row, Dr. Eggland asked the first group to begin their presentation. The mood in the classroom was rather quiet. Perhaps somewhat subconsciously, students projected the oppressive clime outside the class onto their own dejected spirits in addition to the pressure of formal presentations. Paralyzed by stage fright they remained still staring silently forward awaiting their turn. The first presentation took about twenty minutes and focused on "social interaction in the classroom" followed by a fifteen-minute discussion initiated by Dr. Eggland. The second group followed the suit. Dr. Eggland sat right behind the students in the second row filling out assessment rubrics, practically breathing at their necks. Mr. Armstrong's classroom was comparably much better lit and that very factor might have added somewhat to a comparably more cheerful ambience that accompanied students as groups progressed with their presentations. Five big windows filled the room with much needed sunlight. Mr. Armstrong, seated at the far back of the classroom, availed himself of a panoramic view of the entire room. Topics presented that day included "teenage pregnancy" and "gender discrimination." Some students role-played parts of their presentations making the experience very interactive and animated at times even comical. Each presentation took approximately fifteen minutes and was followed by a brief commentary courtesy of Mr. Armstrong, who related the presented topics to his years of experience as a principal. The entire session was quite vigorous with students frequently using their body language as a tool to relay their messages. Upon completion, Mr. Armstrong distributed evaluation forms to the participating students applauding everybody for their excellence.

Twenty-Third Class

April 7, 1999 welcomed students with a clear sky and beautiful sunny weather. The elusive spring imbued students with optimistic disposition and buoyant outlook. The instructors led their groups to the respective classrooms. Since more students presented on that day, both classes were filled with a large number of students. Dr. Eggland led his groups to room no. 53. All of the students congregated today at the very center of the auditorium. The session followed the patterns established two days prior with each group taking approximately fifteen minutes to present their topic followed by a fifteen-minute discussion led by Dr. Eggland. Topics included: "homosexuality," "homophobia," and "sex education." Mr. Armstrong occupying a room upstairs supervised three groups with total of nineteen students. This time most students got seated around the tables on the right side of the classroom. Mr. Armstrong kept the previously established procedure with each presentation followed by a short commentary of his own. All activities ended twenty minutes before the scheduled time. Prior to departure, students in both classrooms filled out course evaluations collected by the instructors.

Twenty-Fourth Class

On April 12, 1999 at 12:25 p.m., the auditorium was almost full. The desk, which customarily occupied space at the front of the classroom separating instructors from the students, was removed. That provided extra space to facilitate Mr. Armstrong's peripatetic style of teaching. Dr. Eggland could not attend the session leaving Mr. Armstrong all by himself again. The entire session had a reflective nature. Since there were only five sessions left, Mr. Armstrong looked retrospectively at the material covered so far outlining a brief draft of things to come. "Today, I want to focus on reflection of what we've learnt so far your teacher's interviews and your papers," he stated. While the initial part of the session focused on the excerpts Mr. Armstrong selected from the students' papers, the latter portion of the class was devoted almost entirely to reinforcing most salient points elicited from students' recently completed presentations.

Twenty-Fifth Class

On April 14, 1999, the entire session was unusually interactive. It was partially due to activities which required heavy physical involvement on the part of the students. Right at the outset, Mr. Armstrong divided students into eight groups arranged in circles. Every group received a ball with the instruction to pass it around in the shortest possible time. Every time the activity was repeated students were expected to cut the time in half. The exercise continued for a long time and was not completed until students realized that the only way to optimize the speed involved changing the paradigm–leaving the proverbial "box," or in this case the "circle." Students quickly reorganized by rearranging their positions. The entire activity was performed with gusto and enthusiasm. The primary objective of the task was to convey the message that future of teaching profession will require novel ways and innovative pedagogy, "What works today may not work tomorrow," Mr. Armstrong concluded the session.

Ninth Meeting

On April 19, 1999, collaborating instructors met in the departmental library at Seaton Hall to plan for the remaining two weeks of the semester. At 11:30 a.m., the bright sun was breaking through the windows when

Mr. Armstrong started the meeting by saying, "One of the best things of our meetings is that we can establish where we are going." After a short pause, Dr. Eggland responded, "There is going to be a shortage of teachers. So we need to talk more about the job market, compensation, salaries, and other job opportunities. If they decide not to teach, they'll know their options. Students don't know that." A few minutes later, while Mr. Armstrong outlined a list of requirements he prepared for students' final papers, Dr. Eggland sat straight and listened attentively jotting down occasional notes in his notebook. The assessment list included a grading system rubrics and areas students should emphasize in their papers. After a short review, Dr. Eggland agreed and proposed, "I'm going to grade two-thirds of the papers to compensate for your bigger load in the past." "No problem," retorted Mr. Armstrong. In the concluding part of this efficient meeting, the instructors brainstormed ideas for topics and activities to be included in the final four classes. The meeting finished at noon leaving just enough time to reach Henzlik Hall, and start the class.

Twenty-Sixth Class

On April 19, 1999, at 12:30 pm., Mr. Armstrong began class with a group activity. Instructors stood close by on the left side of the classroom watching students at work. Total silence saturated the room as students focused on writing down their responses. After about ten minutes, Mr. Armstrong stepped into the center of the class to summarize issues raised during the last session. At the same time, Dr. Eggland took a seat on the left side of the classroom which allowed him a clear view of Mr. Armstrong and the students. A few minutes passed and instructors distributed sheets of paper with designed during the prior meeting rubrics for students' final paper. While Mr. Armstrong elaborated on the rubrics point by point, Dr. Eggland returned to his seat browsing through some of his past due paperwork. When one of the students asked about the grades for the papers, Dr. Eggland quickly informed students that he would take responsibility for mailing the papers with his comments and the grades back to students. Approximately thirty minutes into the class, Mr. Armstrong gestured to Dr. Eggland to take over. While some students were still mulling over the assessment rubrics, Dr. Eggland introduced the topic of the day. The lecture that gradually segued into a lively discussion, recapitulated main issues of the course. Throughout the entire time, Mr.

Armstrong was seated at the back of the room occasionally contributing with comments of his own or delivering facts and figures whenever Dr. Eggland hesitated, looking anxiously for a bailout. The class ended with Mr. Armstrong's announcement of class cancellation on the following Wednesday. In lieu of a meeting, students were advised to work on their final papers. As predicted, the news was accepted with a cheerful "Great!"

Twenty-Seventh Class

The final two sessions of the course coincided with Mr. Armstrong's preparations for his final comprehensive doctoral exams. To alleviate his colleague's tight schedule, Dr. Eggland volunteered to cover the remaining two sessions alone. Mr. Armstrong, who merely stopped by to bid farewell, began with restating the outlined rubrics for the final project and finished by expressing his utmost gratitude for students' efforts to create stimulating learning environment clearly exhibited throughout the semester. After approximately ten minutes, Mr. Armstrong left the room. Dr. Eggland briskly stood up looked over the audience and stated, "Today I'd like to talk about the milieu of education." Dr. Eggland briefly recapitulated the basic steps of becoming a certified teacher. For the benefit of students who may have a change of heart and no longer desire to be teachers in the future, Dr. Eggland presented a number of viable alternatives to pursue in lieu of education. Despite a very animated discussion and a larger number of questions, Dr. Eggland handled the class with calm and composure ending the class right on time.

Twenty-Eighth Class

On April 29, 1999, one could detect a twinge of irony. Although it was Mr. Armstrong who was forced to start the course alone four months prior, the responsibility fell upon Dr. Eggland to officially end it. Since it was the last session, it did not come as a surprise that all enrolled in the class students were in attendance. In fact, there were so many students that couple of them had to sit on the stairs. The class started with Dr. Eggland distributing final course evaluations to the students to be filled out at the end of the session. For the final topic of the course, Dr. Eggland chose "violence" in schools. Due to the recent incident of high school shooting in Littleton, Colorado resulting in twelve students and one teacher dead, the subject seemed relevant. By allowing students to express their feelings about this tragic event, Dr. Eggland perhaps unintentionally created a platform for students' catharsis of suppressed emotions. Not surprisingly, students were deeply touched by this event. At 1:20 p.m., Dr. Eggland dismissed the class thanking everybody for their participation during the entire semester. He concluded, "It's been fun."

Development of Issues

In this section, the researcher intends to answer the second of the sub-questions: What are the issues related to collaborative teaching?

Course Design

A relatively limited involvement in the design of the course by the collaborating instructors has been found an important factor contributing negatively to the successful operations of the course. In lieu of allowing instructors to actively structure the course, a ready-to-go blueprint was presented to them, "It seems to me that in some ways the notion of collaborative teaching would be more free to follow its own course. If we were, meaning my collaborator and me, teaching a course that we developed on our own from scratch" reflected Dr. Eggland, "There are probably some constraints or restraints with the ED 131 course because to some degree it's kind of a cookie-cutter course. It's taught according to format or protocol a curriculum guide that already been created." Although Dr. Eggland had been deeply involved in creating and then developing the course in the past, collaborating instructors were not granted the opportunity to work on its design together. That "could enhance the spirit of ownership and a better understanding of the course direction. Gene and I have behaved more like diners at a buffet than as cooks," Dr. Eggland noted facetiously, "So, we kind of look at what's available when we plan and we say well this looks interesting that looks like fun I think they could learn something if we did this I'll do this. So we didn't exactly collaborate on all of the stages. A couple of the stages were already finished. The course was already created for the most part. We didn't work on the creation stage. We didn't work on the developmental stage. We didn't work on creating objectives a mission or evaluation strategy. We are simply collaborating on the delivery of the course and on the process associated with its delivery," noted Dr. Eggland visibly frustrated and somewhat resentful. Dr. Eggland was clearly unhappy about having no say in the design part of their work and strongly believed that a collaborative effort on the recreation of the course would be worth it, "There is an educational administrative philosophy followed from old times which is that 'people tend to support what they help to create.' I think if we would have been involved in the creation of the course more intimately and more recently, probably we would be more committed to it, more enthusiastic about it. Some days I feel a little bit like an automaton following the dots rather than a person actually building from the plan. To some degree, the cookie-cutter prescribed nature of the course precludes the value of or makes it unnecessary or reduces the need for collaboration. It seems to me that one of the collaborative outcomes should be creating interesting ways of doing things, deciding to go down a given path. Because of the prescribed nature of the course, it kinds of militates against that. We've done a few slightly unusual things but mostly that's all done for us–it's prescribed. There is always a concern about what it is that we ought to be teaching, what's the stuff the essential learning that they must have before they leave. There are probably the first few days that we could have locked the doors, so now we can say what the essential learning is that we want them to have. We didn't do that." Mr. Armstrong added, "Ideally what I would like to see is the collaborative teachers sit down for a day and lay out all the information that we expected to deliver pick out those things that really meet the needs of the students figure out how we are going to do that. How we are going to operate might be 'a pie in the sky' that would allow us to do the job right. If you are really going to do this right, you spend at least a day before you ever start."

Tag Team

The arrangement that professors created in their collaboration was teamwork to which Dr. Eggland referred to as a "relay race" or a "tag team," "I try, when I am a lead person in a course, to ask him what he thinks suggest or provide experiences describe experiences that he has had that are relevant but we don't plan that. For the most part, it's more like professional wrestling. There is something in professional wrestling called a tag team match when one person wrestles for a while and then another person takes over and then another person wrestles for a while. In track and field, it's called a relay race where one person runs for a while then another person runs for a while. It seems like we do more of that than we actually perform as a team." Mr. Armstrong agreed with Dr. Eggland's depiction of their collaboration in that regard, "Collaboration may be a word out there that really describes the fact that the Teacher's College says that if you have a certain number of students, there needs to be more than one of you teaching. I guess if there are going to be more than one of us in the course then we need to teach collaboratively. There is no reason to take turns. We should build on each other's strengths so we can work collaboratively." Due to Dr. Eggland's frequent absences throughout the semester, Mr. Armstrong was forced to lead the class on his own most of the time and admittedly felt somewhat disappointed about it, "I think I have handled the class by myself four or five times in his absence and–if it was true collaboration–we would be there together and we would be planning together."

In/Out of the Classroom Collaboration

Mr. Armstrong estimated the amount of collaboration out of the classroom was sufficient, "Our intention is to be fully collaborative. To the extent that we do meet after Monday sessions we talk about who we are delivering it to who would take the lead and when who would support what. And I think that's worked out pretty well as the key element of the successful collaborative teaching." When asked the same question a little later in the process, Mr. Armstrong appeared less optimistic, "I think we set out early we are going to meet after every Monday class and work out how we are going to present the material next week. That has been less than perfect I guess." When finally asked the same at the very end of the process, Mr. Armstrong's overall evaluation was positive, "I think outside of the classroom, as far as the planning part, I think it's going well. I think we've both seen opportunities where we can contribute to the development of the curriculum." Dr. Eggland frequently felt like a "guest speaker" in this course. Collaboration outside of the classroom presented a similar problem for Dr. Eggland, "It's not perfect either. I need to disclose that I am having a modest amount of guilt about my role in this. I really didn't agree to teach this class until toward the end of last semester and most of my plans and schedule for this semester was already made. I missed several sessions and wasn't able to put in the actual time or the appropriate amount of professional and psychic energy." Having said that, Dr. Eggland concluded, "I wish that, number one, the class was smaller and, number two, I had more time to devote to it." When interviewed at the end of the semester and having the perspective of the entire process, Dr. Eggland noted emphatically, "Today in particular, I feel a little negative about the class generally. Part of it is my own circumstances and part of it is just the arrangement of the university. I'm not against team teaching or collaboration, but I think that it hasn't helped either. I'm not sure why."

Getting Acquainted

The biggest stumbling block collaborating instructors confronted early on in the process had to do with a limited knowledge of each other's backgrounds experiences and teaching preferences, "Probably the first issue we had to deal with is to get acquainted with my partner," noted Mr. Armstrong, "I didn't know Steve before we started teaching together," Although instructors had a meeting arranged one month before the course started, their focus was on the technical aspects of the collaboration alone, "We talked more about management things, what we are going to do. We haven't spent a lot of time yet on what are the best techniques that we have experienced up to this point that have been preferable for our students." Understanding of each other's backgrounds appeared of paramount importance to Mr. Armstrong as the safeguards against surprises later on, "Just as anybody moving into the new environment, one of the hardest things to do is to socialize to get into the culture. I think we have a responsibility to each other to find out the culture of each other and develop a new culture based on collaboration. The better acquainted we are, the better the chance to optimally utilize and work off each other strengths and weaknesses. I think it is important because as we engage in various instructional strategies, it is important for us to know where the other one might have some measure of expertise that would embellish the topic in some way. I think that probably the level on which we know each other could be improved and should be improved. We really don't spend very much time together." In a separate interview, as if echoing that assessment, Dr. Eggland noticed, "We still really don't know one another. It might have been best if we would have been colleagues for the last ten years and we knew our experiences more intimately."

Teaching Styles

Early in the semester, Mr. Armstrong noted, "We are still kind of experimenting with each others' teaching style to see how they blend together." To make sure students are actively involved in learning, instead of passively regurgitating information, he was convinced that the clash of two different styles of teaching demonstrated by collaborating instructors would result in students actively participating in the development of their own learning and thus more learning would take place. However, he thought of potential downsides as well. Mr. Armstrong stated, "I may go too far to the extreme one way, he may go to the extreme to the other, but somewhere in the middle there is a nice mesh, which is teacher-centered versus student-centered. I would guess that if one would to veer to one side or the other, he would veer into instructional side [teacher-center] and I would veer into constructional side [student-center]. Not that either side is right or wrong, but I see that as differences in styles of teaching." Dr. Eggland did see their styles of teaching as different. However, it did not represented a problem for him, "I think it resulted in a fairly good mix of activities of instructional strategies for the students and so I think it's okay that we have different, slightly different styles." Dr. Eggland, who desired his postmortem epitaph to read, "He asked hard questions," described his style as the one with a preference "to engage in quite a bit of prodding probing poking and asking hard questions. Gene's style is more of a laissez-faire style in which he is not the content. I am certainly not against that, but I think given a choice I would use less of that than he does."

Roles Division

The roles collaborating instructors took upon each other emerged almost naturally throughout the entire process of working together, especially at the beginning, "I think, during the first stage of our relationship I basically delegated or deferred to him to be the logistics detail guy," reflected Dr. Eggland, "He is kind of an administrator manager, and I sometimes feel almost like I'm a guest lecturer, which is fine." At some other point in time, Dr. Eggland referred to his role as "planning consultant—a person to add ideas to the existing paradigm existing structure delivery package. However, the roles began to blend later in the course. I have been pulling more of my load in the form of an administration such as checking the attendance, which on occasion was done by my teaching assistants." His additional engagement was noted and appreciated by Mr. Armstrong, who described Dr. Eggland as "very supportive and willing to help. He's been very receptive to doing some of the management duties and I really appreciate it. From role taking, correcting half of the papers, development of the study, working together to developing diversity, he has never hesitated to do whatever he can. So it's a totally cooperative effort. He is willing to do anything he can and to make it as smooth as possible." Dr. Eggland reciprocated by stating that the division of roles that developed during their collaboration resulted from intuitive understanding of dynamics existing in their relationship, "The roles developed partly because he is a graduate assistant and I'm a professor, partly because he was tuned into the culture into the administrative portion of the course last semester, and partly because he seems to be willing to do that." From the very outset, Mr. Armstrong seemed to understand his role, "I was assigned as the lead teacher in this collaborative effort." That galvanized him to bear the main load of the organizational part of the work, as he himself admitted, "I was given responsibility from day one to be the lead teacher, so I took that to mean I'd better have things organized."

Divergent Experiences

"Our experiences are quite divergent," admitted Dr. Eggland, "I think it might be useful for us and I'll probably suggest it to him to figure out ways that we might leverage and put those experiences together in ways that they are synergistic. That synergism would result in students' having greater understanding of various issues." Different professional experiences of collaborating instructors indeed appeared to have practical implications in the classroom, "Gene is an administrator. One of the things that school administrators learn to do, especially school administrators who are directly responsible to a board of education, they learn to become political. They learn to mask their points of views. I haven't done that." Spending most of his professional career in academia, Dr. Eggland never felt compelled to hide his opinions, but he found the "politically correct" approach of Mr. Armstrong a useful ingredient stimulating enormously class discussions. Dr. Eggland stated, "School administrators are supposed to be political. They are not supposed to be participants in the political process. They are supposed to be hired hands carrying out the policy of the board. And

I find it quite an interesting mix." At the end of the semester, his views changed somewhat. Looking at their entire collaboration in retrospect, Dr. Eggland found his collaborator's experiences and approach to teaching resembling that of his own much more than he originally assumed, "In some ways, I've had some of the same experiences he had or at least have been close. I've been an administrator here and I've been a school-board president and I worked intimately with school administrators. As a result, I think the collaboration from the professional growth perspective might have been more valuable had I been working with let's say a fourth year elementary school woman teacher maybe or a school psychologist or somebody who was farther away from me professionally." For Mr. Armstrong, all of the collaborators' divergent experiences enriched the students' experience immensely and constituted the real strength of this collaboration, "My perception is that he looks at it from the perception of higher education looking back to the freshmen, and I am looking at the secondary level looking forward to the freshmen. So we've got them pinned in. I can look back at the experiences that they have had in the high school and relate to those aspects. He can stretch them beyond where they are now because he knows where they ought to be when they graduate from the university. His role broadens my knowledge base of what we are trying to accomplish with these college freshmen."

Convergent Perspectives

The collaborators' diverse but convergent experiences greatly strengthened the opportunity to achieve main objective of the course. Primary goal of the course, according to Dr. Eggland was "Students' learning to think about the entire enterprise of education in a critical way. However students tend to think about education in a rather mechanical way." That is why convergent perspectives inject into the classroom a very desirable element, "Positive because probably to some degree students can see the world, especially the world of education, through two different lenses and they are largely experiential," claimed Dr. Eggland, who while comparing himself to Mr. Armstrong, emphasized that "His experiences were running schools and my experience has been teaching in schools and thinking about schools. It's not to suggest that he hasn't thought about schools, but we thought about them from different perspectives. He's thought about the mechanical aspects: Where are we going to get money to do this? How are we going to answer this parent? I've been concerned with the psychology of teaching and learning, development of curriculum, that sort of things. I think one thing that's been good is that his teaching style differs from mine and students can get a taste of at least two different styles of teaching. They can see different models of thinking and approaches to schooling. I want to present a positive but realistic description of education to them, and I think together Gene and I can do that. I think another interesting addition to a team like that might be a current high school teacher. I think we ought to do that. First of all, it gives students exposure to different teaching styles because everybody has a different teaching style. When the news member of our staff talked to the class a few weeks ago, she brought another perspective but she also brought a style that certain students could tie into and say 'I can do that.' So, from the students' perspective, I think more ways we can deliver instruction collaboratively, the better they will be."

Learning

The diversity of knowledge bases and experiences presented by the collaborating instructors appeared beneficial not only for students but professors as well. When asked about that issue during the first weeks of the collaboration, Dr. Eggland confidently stated, "It's certainly good for me because it helps me see another perspective." Mr. Armstrong shared similar sentiments. When speaking of collaborative teaching, he clearly separated "mechanical" from "contextual" part of teaching arrangement, "It's not something that we are putting together because we have seventy-five or seventy-seven students. That's not the reason why you teach collaboratively. You teach collaboratively to enhance what each other's performance, to support each other, and get to know students much better." For Mr. Armstrong, the single most important aspect of collaboration was the ability to generate of novel ideas. That would be impossible if it wasn't for them working and thinking together. Mr. Armstrong explained, "He came up with some excellent ideas that I would have never thought of. I had some people that I could contact to help us deliver that part or this part. So I see that might have been the most collaborative thing we have done up to this point. His focus has been higher education so he lends that segment of the whole process that I don't have. So when he is up there talking, I am listening just as intently as the other students because I am learning while he is talking. I would hope that maybe he is learning when I'm talking." When making his final assessment at the end of the semester, Mr. Armstrong was absolutely convinced about the value of collaboration and the positive effect it had on his professional development, "I learned content, concepts that I didn't know that actually helped me on my 'comps' [final comprehensive doctoral examination applied after completing the program directly preceding dissertation stage]. The second rewarding aspect of collaboration was the receptivity of students. There are things we tried that worked very well. There were some things that I won't do again. However, content and techniques that would be the two major things." Although Dr. Eggland concurred that the technical mutual support seemed to be working well in their collaboration, when referring to intellectual aspect of his development he did not share Mr. Armstrong's optimism, "So I have not felt that there has been much in the form of mutual academic or intellectual support. It didn't bubble up yet. It hasn't congealed yet. And I am thinking it probably won't." On second thought, Dr. Eggland wasn't even sure they differed very much, "We are not so diverse. We are both Midwesterners, we are both white males, we were both socialized in the same way–educationally and otherwise I think. But to the extent that we do have divergent experiences, that's good for the students. But I don't see that either one of us has, or the synergy of us working together has had geometrically added synergy." To the question: What circumstances could contribute to their professional development? After a thoughtful pause, Dr. Eggland elucidated, "I think time together." He then recalled his times as a doctoral student, "When I and my professor were getting to an automobile and drove half way through the state of Wisconsin to teach a course and then drove all the way back, we were literally forced to share experiences, points of view, ideas, philosophies and information. Nothing like that happened in my work with Gene. Gene and I just don't spend so much time together. He does his things, and then we do this type team thing and now it's my turn to do something." To the question: Did you become a better professional as a result of this collaboration? Dr. Eggland answered, "No, no. I thought more about collaboration but I couldn't honestly say that I've become a better professional as a result. If I did it again and we had more time and I think circumstances were different, I might think differently about that. We don't spend a lot of time in any sort of critical analysis of what went on in the classroom. What did you think of this? What did you think of that? I wonder how we can make this better. We haven't spent that kind of time together. To some degree, I would take responsibility. I suppose I would be characterized as the senior member of the team, so the obligation is mine. I could probably force that to happen. Instruction took a back seat to some administrative junk that I had to deal with," Dr. Eggland regretfully concluded.

Complementation

When talking about the division of roles, especially while in classroom, Mr. Armstrong made it clear that the most important aspect of their collaboration is that of complementing each other's roles, "My role is to help him keep an eye on seventy-seven people and see if they are with him. Conversely, if I am out there with twelve groups interacting, he needs to be in there helping me to determine whether it's time to move on, whether they are focused on the topic or not. If they are not, then he needs to let me know." From observations and interviews conducted with the collaborating instructors, it was clear that Dr. Eggland felt more comfortable as a leader of classroom discussions, whereas Mr. Armstrong couldn't be happier as "a guide on the side." Although Dr. Eggland expected to be subject to some censure by being too directive, he seemed quite adamant in his conviction about the effectiveness of his approach, "I want to elicit clear cut demonstration about critical thinking and I want to know that this is going on. Gene seems more content trusting that students will do that critical thinking on their own in small groups. He might be right. I might be right. And I think this synergistic advantage is the best of both worlds, I hope." For Mr. Armstrong, "Complementary can occur in two ways. It can be total agreement which is complementary. Or we can disagree with one another and yet complement a viewpoint by giving a different viewpoint. Both can be useful in classroom discussions. So that maybe contradictory of each other, but can be complementary if there is such a thing. We can strengthen each other's case by giving opposite perceptions of the issue. To the extent that he will offer his experiences and I will offer mine." Dr. Eggland agreed that they did complement to some degree, "I think we would complement even more if I was a black woman having experiences of educational system of England, and he was a Pacific Islander educated in Japan or something. I'm coming from a teacher-professor perspective and he is an administrator. Although now I am too an administrator of sort and he is moving towards being a professor, so we are more homogeneous than we are heterogeneous." Nevertheless, Dr. Eggland became more and more convinced over time that "We are awfully alike. The only differences I was able to figure out were those of the political differences and modest educational differences."

Mutual Feedback

Perhaps the most precious aspect of the collaborative setting, as attested to by the observed instructors, is the potential of receiving and giving feedback to each other on an ongoing basis, "He and I almost daily evaluate one another," noted Mr. Armstrong. Dr. Eggland decided to teach collaboratively in part because of the opportunity to receive feedback from a colleague, "It's been good for me and I've done this in other settings too. This is one of the reasons I wanted to do it–to open myself up to some scrutiny frankly. It's useful to me just on the personal level, to open myself up to scrutiny of another professional." Dr. Eggland observed other positive effects of collaborative settings, "It keeps me honest. It keeps me working hard. It keeps me innovative. It gets me feedback–sometimes it's not spoken but I can tell when something I do, say, or develop is approved of by Gene." Although Dr. Eggland and Mr. Armstrong perceived a lot of potential value in mutual feedback as a result of collaborative setting, they did not believe this potential was truly utilized in their collaboration, "We have avoided that, or at least avoided being honestly critical about that." When asked about the reason, Dr. Eggland smiled and responded, "Partly because of our own socializations. That's difficult for Midwesterners, polite Midwesterners, to be critical, even in the supportive positive sense because it is considered dangerous to relationships, especially for relationships that probably won't sustain for a long time. I see Gene as a temporary one-semester colleague, probably. Plus, it takes a lot of energy. We do provide a modest amount of positive reinforcement to each other. I think it would be an ideal situation that two of us could move to a point of providing criticism of one another. I doubt that trust level will build up to that extent during this semester." To the same question regarding feedback, Mr. Armstrong put it bluntly, "It's non-existent. I haven't critiqued his teaching, he hasn't critiqued mine. We have done very little. We haven't reflected back on our teaching. We just haven't had enough time to just sit down and reflect on teaching styles and results. So it's nonexistent. However, I do think that a key strength of collaboration is observation of one teacher by another and critiquing each other."

Supervisors' Feedback

"The dean of the college doesn't come in to observe us. There is nobody to observe us for the purpose of watching. The only feedback we will get will be after the class is over and the students evaluate us and that is too late," claimed Mr. Armstrong, "They talk about continuous improvement but that not only goes for students. It should go for teachers as well. We could be continually improving if we had snippets or suggestions of how we can do better. But it doesn't happen. And this is the very thing we are trying to get away from in education. We are out there forging without the map. You go out there, you give it a shot. If it works great or if it doesn't, you can tune in and make it better as you go." Mr. Armstrong believed it would be very useful to have some sort of instruction before involvement in collaborative teaching, "Teacher Learning Center–I think that would be good. I would say that part of your commitment to doing something like we are doing is to commit to meeting with so many of these sections that deal strictly with how to teach collaboratively." Dr. Eggland expressed exact same concern, "The two of us haven't got any feedback, either from the dean or from the coordinator of the program. That's true in the university and that's probably true in other places too that people are expected to do things with no instruction on how to do it. There is a big emphasis on collaboration among your colleagues, but we don't have much of the experience with this. On the contrary, our culture at the University of Nebraska has been focused on the individualized growth and development, individualized achievement. We've also been asked to serve on committees and chair committees, but nobody has really ever taught us how to serve on the committee. Nobody taught me how to do it, what it means to be a chair of a department. So you as a group going to collaborate…Like it's going to happen like magic. What Gene and I have done is basically figure it out ourselves to the extent that we have collaborated. But in my opinion, we certainly don't have it right, not yet at least. Everybody makes an assumption that we can teach. People do that in all kinds of settings. And also people think that everybody who was in school for twelve years can be a teacher. Our religious system is the best example of that–we have a collection of Sunday school teachers. You don't have to know anything about teaching to be a Sunday school teacher. They don't think about curriculum development, the psychology of teaching and learning, program planning. They don't think about any of that kind of stuff. They just think about teaching as you just walk into room and say: 'Okay students, today we're going to do fractions!' So we behave the same way in the case of collaboration. We didn't talk about anything. What we are going to do with the results. We also didn't look at what the outcomes would be. We did a pretty poor job with that as well."

Reflection

The opportunity to debrief and reflect on what has been done and said in the classroom was, in the estimation of Mr. Armstrong, probably the biggest advantage of collaborative teaching. Mr. Armstrong reflected, "I think one of the important things is that, as much as possible, we need not only to teach together but we need to debrief together. One of the strengths of what we're doing is the fact that we meet every day after we present to kind of decode what we've been doing every session. Every Monday is followed by a session to plan and to debrief, reflect on what we've done to see what has gone well, what things we could have done differently." Mr. Armstrong would like however to see reflection emphasized more during their formal weekly meetings, "We need to do more of that. I can see two things happening in our Monday meetings and we probably need to pull them out so we make sure that we do that. One is let's reflect back and see what we did that was good, what we did that need to be improved. Then move on to okay what we are going to do next." On the basis of reviewed literature and his own experiences, Mr. Armstrong theorized that the lack of reflection may be the weakest aspect of the teaching profession, "We forget what has been done and we go on and we shouldn't do that. We need to look back and identify those things that are good and are not so good. So I would suggest that the next time we meet, I will advise that we reflect in the next debriefing meeting with Dr. Eggland. Reflection is an essential thing. One, we can do a better job as a result. We've done some, but we haven't formalized this to the extent that okay we are reflecting now, what went well, what didn't go well. We just kind of say, 'Well what do you think?' and we just chat a little bit about it." Dr. Eggland, although quite appreciative of the potential value of reflection on the improvement of his teaching, sadly acknowledged that

123

"I haven't done any of this hardly with Gene, and to be totally honest, I had not much time to reflect. I had many alligators in the swamp here, and when I get out of this class by the time I'm half way back over here in my office, I'm thinking about something else. I admit, and I think it's bad, but I had just not been able to commit the kind of time for reflection that this course would demand."

Conflict

"There is no interpersonal conflict between us," noticed Mr. Armstrong, "The only conflict I saw, the primary one, was that of the lack of time together. We are not located in the same building so that might create some problems. His willingness to come this way, we always meet in my office, tells me there is a commitment to get together. He's always been very willing to cooperate that way, but I just think that maybe it's a geography, maybe partially responsibilities that he has that takes him away from the classroom environment." Mr. Armstrong felt uncomfortable with the very notion of conflict and struggled to find a right word to express his feelings precisely. Trying to be politically correct, he finally uttered, "Maybe disequilibrium or maybe there is a better term—friction or disagreement on points of view." Mr. Armstrong persisted on referring to the "contextual" rather than "interpersonal" conflict when speaking of his collaboration with Dr. Eggland, "He is coming from the higher education perspective and I'm coming from the K-12 perspective. That can be very wholesome, because he can bring some things to this class that I don't know and I think I can bring some things that he doesn't know." Dr. Eggland agreed with the potential value of "contextual conflict," but in case of this collaboration neither was existent, "People will always have personal conflicts, but I have a feeling that Gene and I would never have very much of that because we are both people who would be inclined to avoid that conflict, try to compromise the ways so that to get rid of the conflict." When mulling over the value of conflict for their collaborative effort, after a short pause, Dr. Eggland responded, "I think some conflict would be good. Lack of conflict is a real Midwestern thing. People who live in the Midwest are inclined to avoid conflict at any cost. There is plenty of conflict but we tend to deny it and avoid it. Several times Gene said things in class that conflict with what I think, but I just basically blew it off and I expect I have done the same thing, said things that conflict with his value system.

124

He may agree with everything I say, or he may just figure that's easier than having a big argument and developing the big case for his point of view. With my closest friends, professional or otherwise, I believe I'm capable to explore conflicting points of views, conflicting ideas, agree or disagree, making a case with data. But Gene and I did not progress to that."

Freedom from Isolation

"There is a great potential for helping each other," noticed Mr. Armstrong, "You know my experience is that teachers cry for some help. Teaching in high school is nothing but a big box with a bunch of little boxes inside and each teacher is in a box alone with thirty students isolated. Collaborative teaching removes this isolation. But in collaborative teaching, especially at the higher education level, we are there together throughout the whole thing. It's just a built-in mechanism that allows that sort of things that sort of things to happen every time you teach." Dr. Eggland looked at this issue from his decades of experience in higher education, "The culture of teaching for years and years has been that the teacher works in a vacuum to a large degree. Vacuum may not be quite the right word, but professors work in isolation. Even though there are all kinds of teachers and all kinds of students in school, the culture of teaching has been that I as a teacher go into my classroom, shut the door and am not be particularly accountable to anybody for what goes on inside those doors. It is healthy not to be isolated. Some philosopher said that the 'unexamined life is not worth living.' I think an unexamined teacher is not worth very much either. And the collaboration affords examination in a positive sense—you can't hide." Although Mr. Armstrong was in a total agreement with Dr. Eggland about the reality of isolation of academic professors, he believed it had more to do with a choice on a part of professors, "You go up and down these halls, and I think I bet there are some collaborations going on but it's not formalized very much. And I think from what I've learnt so far university professors are hired as kind of private contractors, they are not hired to work as a team. It's becoming difficult for them to work as a team just by nature of the university setting."

Status Differentiation

In the conducted interviews, both instructors mentioned that differences in academic status, as defined by earned degrees and held positions, seriously affected dynamics of their relationship and eventually entire collaboration. Dr. Eggland received his PhD many years ago, whereas Mr. Armstrong at the time of the study was still a graduate assistant completing his doctoral program. "The whole thing started when I was approached by Dr. Stick and I was told that it was my responsibility to take the lead and that he would find somebody to be a support instructor," recalled Mr. Armstrong. He was surprised that Dr. Eggland was assigned as his support instructor, "Dr. Eggland was an experienced faculty member and then when I discovered that he was a department chair, I thought 'holy smoke, what am I doing taking a lead when we've got a department chair who's taught that course many times?'. But when I talked to him about it, he was comfortable with that. So here I am a lowly grad student, and here he is head of the department. Yet I am a lead teacher, and it's not anything to do with him personally as it has to do with positional power. I really shouldn't feel that way because I have nothing to lose by critiquing one way or another. I suspect that even if I became a tenured professor and he was a department chair with some twenty-eight years of experience at the university level, I would still feel that way." Mr. Armstrong felt strongly that this kind of dynamic inhibited more effective collaboration between them. Mr. Armstrong believed that, "If I had my PhD in hand, he would see me as one who's been through this. I've been through the world. I've jumped through the hoops. I have a PhD. So now I am at least at the PhD level that is consistent with his. I've got the benefit of lots of years of experience, but I don't have a degree." Not being entirely certain whether the academic status differences helped or inhibited the process, Dr. Eggland noticed similar dynamics, "Gene is a graduate student here working on a degree. The culture of the graduate students is that graduate students would probably not want to take the risk of being highly critical or would probably be very careful with that. It shouldn't be that way, but it is. So that's probably another barrier to frankness. It is a critical thing." Dr. Eggland could not see any positive outcomes that could come out of the existing dynamic, but he didn't see much of a negative side either, "I don't think I can see anything that is positive about it. I also don't see too much that's negative. The only thing that would be negative about it would be that he might be unwilling to risk honesty because of the obvious juxtaposition of our various roles in the college." Considering a hypothetical situation in which both instructors had the same academic standing and the extent to which that would affect their collaboration. Dr. Eggland argued, "Probably yes. The risk of two tenured faculty members talking to one another honestly is not as great as the graduate assistant criticizing full professor." To the same question, Mr. Armstrong responded less assuredly, "Maybe. I can't say for sure because I think it has to do with personalities of two people involved. But at this point there is a positional thing and this is my problem."

Trust

The development of trust was for Mr. Armstrong another key factor contributing to effective collaboration, "Development of trust to the point where you almost know what the other is going to do before he ever does it. You almost learn how to orchestrate the class so that you can support each other in the way that does more than twice support to people can do individually." Mr. Armstrong perceived collaborative teaching as an excellent tool to build the sense of unity and the spirit of teamwork in the entire department or even broader academic community—the context in which collaborative teaching takes place, "If you and I were teaching collaboratively and the trust level builds up to the level that we understand each other then we can individually go on and talk to other instructors and it not only helps the teaching but it helps the camaraderie among your own staff. I think the fact that we are in the university setting creates a certain understood trust because we are here and we are here for the same purpose. The trust is always there. Trust is more of a personal thing than it is a professional thing. There are certain things that we know about each other because we are in a certain environment. The culture of the university lends itself to a certain level of trust that is already there. If I can't trust you, how can I be sure that you are not going to undercut some of the things that I am trying to accomplish and vice versa. We are not in competition. We are in total collaboration, so trust has to be there." Although Dr. Eggland rated trust as "the mid-level importance," he concurred that, "a higher level of mutual trust would be helpful in our collaborative efforts." He also noticed that development of trust takes time, and neither of them truly committed themselves to work on that aspect of their work together, "The way things work in the Midwest, and I think they work around the world, is that it takes time to develop trust and we have not committed that time. We haven't been forced to do that. We haven't elected to do it. We are both busy guys. He is working on the doctoral program. I am trying to dismantle a department here. So we haven't taken the time."

Confidence

When trying to identify other stages, levels, or dimensions in the process of collaborative teaching, Mr. Armstrong paused slightly only to laser-focus on the notion of "confidence," "Maybe the word trust is little strong, maybe confidence. So you get the acquainted stage, and then you get the confidence stage when you understand what each of us is going to do. Then from the confidence would probably come a true understanding of the whole process. There is going to be a point that we understand what collaborative teaching really is because we experienced it frequently enough that we just think that's going be the way it's going be done. The word 'confidence' doesn't mean anything unless you are talking about self-confidence or confidence in each other. Again as the trust develops, as the knowledge of each other's teaching style develops, the confidence of each other develops. I think there are some innate confidences that are there because he's been there and I am getting there. So there is some sure confidence that comes with it. I can trust that if he gets in front of the students, things are going to go well. He needs to have a confidence that when I'm up there, we are all going towards the same goal. I think that's what I mean by confidence." Dr. Eggland had a slightly different take on this matter, "I'm not totally confident in Gene and what he can do and does, but I know what I can be confident about. I think and I'm confident that he will and can keep the course running that he will keep the heads over the water keep us in control of what's going on. I'm confident that he is really good at the administrative part of the course, keeping us appropriately scheduled and that sort of thing."

Collaboration is the Future

Mr. Armstrong had recently listened to a speech during which a question was posed: "Is your school Y2K ready?" One of the more important statements he recalled had to do with the concept of collaboration, "If you are producing students who cannot work together or give them opportunities to learn how to work together, they are not going to be Y2K ready. It is our obligation to model collaborative learning, collaborative teaching, collaborative problem solving, and critical thinking is a must. That's the way our society is going to grow toward. I am confident that two people working on the same thing will do more than twice what each of them would do working separately." Although he didn't outright reject individual work, he thought that "There are times that you need to work independently, but there has to be a comparison of notes so to speak. The product is going to be better than twice as good as two separate ones." Similarly Dr. Eggland noted, "We are more and more and more and more incapable of possessing, containing and using the information that we have to do the things that need to be done in business, education, and any other place. We are going to be forced to do the collaboration. If I wanted to teach a new course ten years ago, develop a new approach, I could do it almost all by myself. Twenty years ago when I was doing the research project, I could analyze the data by myself and write the project. I could do it all. Now, because of technology, I need help. So I think it was a great experience for me and perhaps for him too. It will have positive benefits coming out of that. I'm confident of that."

Modeling Collaboration

"Students read more than what you say, and if they can see collaboration as well as hear it, they will tend to model what they see," reflected Mr. Armstrong, who quoted Confucius, "'I can't hear what you are saying because what you are keeps ringing in my ears.' If through modeling our own behavior we cannot instill in students the ability to work in community with each other and do it effectively, we as teachers won't be successful. They won't believe what we say, if we are not modeling what we are trying to teach. For obvious reasons, the modeling of collaborative teaching was especially important in the context of this course which designed to train future teachers. How we deliver the instruction is at least as important as what we deliver. The process is at least as important as the product. So what we have to do is to show them how collaboration works. So in their teaching they can work collaboratively."

Learning Community

Mr. Armstrong deeply believed in the quality of education in which the teacher becomes the co-learner and along with students participates in the process of knowledge creation. When describing his role as a professor, he put it bluntly, "I'm not an instructor. I'm a constructor–not me–we are. There is a difference between being an instructor because it sounds like I am instructing you I am giving you instructions, but in collaborative teaching we are constructing knowledge and that means that students and collaborating teachers are working together to construct the knowledge. Maybe that's the end we are searching for. It is away from 'instruction' toward 'construction.'" As an example of how ideas gestated during this collaboration, Mr. Armstrong pointed to the opening group activities that started every class, "Several activities are a spin-off of something that he [Dr. Eggland] said on a side. One day we talked about research cause and effect and that triggered in my mind a question with the telephone pad exercise used in one of the classes. So again his expertise lends to the extension of my knowledge of how I can do some things for students. I wouldn't have done it if he wasn't there. Dr. Eggland's responsibility was to make sure that those students understand that it's not us imparting our knowledge to them. It's us constructing the knowledge together. Steven and I are both learners as well as the seventy-five that are in the class." Mr. Armstrong recalled another moment from one of the sessions, "When Dr. Eggland built the grid on the board and it was the students who filled in little squares inside and by doing so got more and more knowledge base they got more insights into what this whole thing is all about. So it's not him telling them, it's them developing the grid together and that's what we are doing–we are developing knowledge together." Dr. Eggland agreed with Mr. Armstrong's concept of a learning community, "I'm sure there are examples of things I have learned from him. He has very good concrete examples of things more stories that have occurred to him. They are reinforcing some of the philosophical notions that I bring to the table, so I think that we are constructing. I'm hoping that students are figuring it out."

Assessment

The assessment of students' papers initially appeared to be a straightforward though unexpectedly multifaceted project. The problems appeared in their first evaluation attempt when collaborating instructors divided the load equally, each taking half of the papers to grade. "I checked half the papers and I made comments all the way through. When I looked at Steve's papers that he graded–that he didn't grade by the way–he had an assistant to grade–no comments just a letter grade," noted visibly flustered Mr. Armstrong. Although that may be the area of disagreement with Dr. Eggland, Mr. Armstrong strongly believes that feedback provided to students on their papers was important. According to Mr. Armstrong, students approached him holding graded papers with various questions such as "What does it mean?" Another equally important issue in Mr. Armstrong's judgment was assessing not only what students know but more importantly what students do with what they know, "For me the day is gone when we strictly evaluate what they know. What we need to evaluate is not only what they know, but if they can use what they know to solve complex problems and not just simple problems. We are talking about a second order change. We are not talking just about tinkering. We are talking about significant change and the only way to do that is to give them opportunities to demonstrate they can use the knowledge to solve complex problems. Knowing is not enough."

Commitment to Collaboration

"I think the main thing is that we make the commitment to collaborative teaching. It's not something that we are putting together because we have seventy-five or seven-students. That's not the reason why you teach collaboratively," argued Mr. Armstrong, "At least my experience from the past was that people say they teach collaboratively but they don't–they 'turn teach'–they say you take today and I'll take it some other time. That's not collaboration. If you are going to be committed to collaborative teaching then that means that you plan together, you deliver instruction together, all those things together. These are all the terms that if you put them all in the basket, everything comes out saying: 'We are going to do that together!'" Although Mr. Armstrong did value Dr. Eggland as his collaborator, what was missing was time, "As far as collaboration is concerned, he is very valuable to the collaboration process. However I am discovering that true collaboration really requires total commitment of all the teachers involved and I realized again his commitment is there but his time isn't. If I were to analyze true collaborative teaching, I would say it has to have the commitment of all the people involved." Mr. Armstrong strongly believed that the roots of poor commitment were sown at the very inception of the collaboration, "We went to the department and said: 'you know it's your turn, find somebody in your department to teach.' So you go down and hunt for somebody who is willing to do it. It's not like I'm really committed to make this thing go. You get approached by somebody saying: Will you do this? Okay I'll do that for the semester. Well, there is not much commitment there."

Time Commitment

While trying to compare the amount of time needed to teach collaboratively, as contrasted with the traditional individual model, Mr. Armstrong did not think collaborative teaching overall takes more time. However he found scheduling to be a challenge, "Collaborative teaching takes more planning. When you teach alone you are the one to plan whenever you find time to do it, but in collaborative teaching you have to find time for both of you available to plan. The real term in this case would be 'synchronization.' If anything, it can probably speed it up because with two sets of ideas–if you are really working collaboratively you can control amount of planning." Dr. Eggland, to the contrary, claimed that collaborative teaching took slightly more time than traditional individual approach but "Not a lot more...somewhat more." He was questioning however if the increased amount of time put into collaborative teaching was worth it, "I'm kind of right in the middle on that. I think that there are some values, but I have also taught it by myself and with smaller groups of students: twenty, twenty-five, twenty-eight, and I would claim that the outcomes were as good when I was doing it myself than when I was collaborating."

Collaboration as Evolution

When referring to the entire collaboration process, Mr. Armstrong noted, "It's an evolutionary thing that will grow. It's started here and it will grow to full bloom–I hope by the end of the semester. We can look back then and say we saw collaboration growing, trust growing, we saw the understanding of each other's strengths in teaching styles and growth. But everything is going to be evolutionary. We can't identify stage one, two, three, four, five." As a follow up to the idea of evolution, Mr. Armstrong trying to conceptualize his understanding of the collaborative process that developed in their team named it "mitosis." He explained, "They taught it to us in stages but it doesn't appear that way when you see it under microscope. It just blends right into the next. I think that's what we are going to see here–the blending from the getting acquainted to kind of feeling each other and to see how we operate to a point that things go naturally. If there were two people that know each other very well that wouldn't be so evolutionary." Somewhat later in the collaborative process Mr. Armstrong reflected back on his previous comments, "Yeah, there are stages. I'm not sure it is a linear thing. I think it's more of a cyclical thing. But I see it as evolving into a team that kind of knows each other and we can support each other. If you can evolve to the point where you have complete trust, confidence, and all this stuff, then I think you have a true collaboration. The process is evolutionary not revolutionary. You don't just jump into it and boom you are doing everything right. You evolve in that situation." Although in his judgment, it was impossible to achieve perfect collaboration, progress was possible and important, "If we were to do it another semester together, after having evolved to this point, we are always in the process of becoming. I don't think we are ever going to come to the point when we are totally confident totally trusting and all this, but we are better than we were and that's why I said evolutionary." Dr. Eggland similarly admitted to perceiving collaboration as an evolutionary process, "I would think that if we did this four times, that would be better the fourth time than it was the first time. And we would have some of the confidence, trust, those kind of words. And right now we are still doing kind of a little dance on our own. The model I would use would be cyclical in which you constantly keep going around the circle. It's not the timeline but it would be a circle or a spiral or something where you keep going around you do more planning and then you plan some more and then you evaluate and then you plan some more and you evaluate some more and then you teach and then you plan. So yes there is a sequence, but the sequence is repetitive, I would say."

Course Design

"What I would like to have done which I didn't do because I didn't have time to do I would like to spend more time on planning, thinking, creating, idea generation, those kind of things," noted Dr. Eggland. He saw only three basic phases in this collaboration and neither course design nor its inception was one of them, "The very beginning was kind of a shakedown period in which we rather gingerly determined who was going to do what and who is going to be in charge of what. Another phase was when we kind of assumed some roles. He was kind of an administrator of the course. He was the PR guy for the course. And I was kind of senior citizen idea person. And then finally we both took kind of a caretaker role." Participation in designing the course is crucial because as Dr. Eggland put it, "There is an old saying that says: 'People tend to support what they create.' That's especially true in the realm of curriculum and I've seen that before and I think that's an important element. If we can create the time for success in collaborative experience, it would be to work in the creative mode in the first phase. Reality, however, in case of this collaboration was different. We basically skipped that step. We didn't spend any time 'philosophizing,' what the course should be, what kind of students there will be, what our roles will be, we didn't spend any time doing that. It was just like we were administrators like we administered the course." And that's one of the reasons for which, according to Dr. Eggland, "The combination of Gene and I didn't work as well as it might have. What he believes would contribute greatly to the success. To sit down before let's say two hours a day or an hour a day for two weeks and create this course, find resources, maybe have graduate students helping us, and then going to collaborative delivery mode. But instead, it was a cookie cutter boiler plate course with simple command—'Teach it!' So we only became conduits rather than creators. Not that we need to create everything. In fact, we probably couldn't create everything. We would assemble the things, create the sequence and the design, but use other people's materials. So I think we basically skipped the first step. We just launched right into doing it without any instruction, particularly how to do any thought discussion how to do. We just did it. I think it was a mistake." Dr. Eggland went even further suggesting that collaboration should start long before two instructors meet together. Formal training should be made available for instructors on how to teach collaboratively, "We should have read a couple of articles, talked to people who have done this before, gone to some seminar on what collaboration is, what it should be and so forth." Mr. Armstrong also tried to identify the beginning stages of their collaboration he regretfully stated, "Well, the very first step was identifying who it was.

Following that was getting the materials to him. The third step was to sit down together and kind of plan out. The last part of the course would be administrative. A few minutes later while Mr. Armstrong reflected again on the design part of the course itself, he stated, "That would be an excellent place to start. That even goes further back from that, that goes back to the dean of college. Because the dean has elaborated on the way he wants it taught." Although how professors presented the material was left to their own discretion, the design of the course was a given. This lack of impact on the design of the course had serious implications and resulted in decreased commitment from both instructors, "I think we feel now like we are delivering something that somebody else designed," concluded Mr. Armstrong.

Personal versus Professional

"There has to be a commitment to each other before you can ever have a commitment to the students," noted Mr. Armstrong, for whom developing personal relationship with Dr. Eggland would symbolize the beginning of fruitful and effective collaboration. Mr. Armstrong elaborated, "Sure you can do it by yourself, but the key issue is to develop all those attributes in such a way that when you step into that classroom with the students you know each other well enough that all these things come about: evaluation, confidence, trust, support of one another." At the same time, he was far from trying to disqualify professional aspects of collaboration as unimportant or insignificant. On the contrary when asked about the importance of the content knowledge itself, Mr. Armstrong responded, "Sure it's important, but knowledge of each other and the trust and all these things are at least as important. And if I had to balance one against the other, I would say maybe even more important." After a pause, Mr. Armstrong continued, "Well maybe not. I'd say they are equally important. You've got to know what you are teaching, but the how is at least as important because students can go to sleep on you if how isn't there." Dr. Eggland shared the opinion of Mr. Armstrong in this matter. When asked whether the development of personal aspects of the relationship with Mr. Armstrong has or could have effect on the effectiveness of their work, Dr. Eggland unambiguously declared, "Yes I would say that's possible, that's probable. I would say there is potential for that to develop." Somewhere in the middle of the semester, while trying to

135

evaluate the present state of his personal relationship with Mr. Armstrong, Dr. Eggland noted, "At the moment, I wouldn't say that Gene is my friend. We probably will be moving at that direction but at the moment we are colleagues doing a job doing it politely and in a friendly way, but we are not friends. We are friendly, but we are not friends. We don't go out to have a beer together. I don't go to his house or that sort of thing." He went even further by saying, "I have a feeling we are on different planes socially, culturally, and probably in several ways. It's not bad particularly. Not much has developed socially. Professionally it's been interesting, nice, sometimes reinforcing to work with him, but I'm not sure that I particularly learned a lot." However, Dr. Eggland was convinced that the development of the social bond would have a significant effect on their professional life in the classroom, "The bond that would get us to go out and have a beer would be a professional bond or at least that would be a common ground. We probably wouldn't talk about his grandchildren a lot. We probably wouldn't talk about his hobbies or mine. But the common ground that we have is the University of Nebraska, the Department of Educational Administration, this course, the professors who are my friends or acquaintances. We would talk about professional staff in a social setting. No matter how hard I try when I go to parties and so forth with people from the University of Nebraska community, we end up talking about University of Nebraska staff." When thinking about social aspects of their relationship in the context of their work within the classroom, Dr. Eggland paused for a while and noted, "I would imagine that our rhythm could be a little better than it is. I sometimes feel like we are not connected that he is working in a different sphere than I am. It's not good or bad, it's just different." Dr. Eggland believed that "If we had a social relationship, we would have little cues, little subtleties, little inside jokes, we would have more shared experiences, the connection between two of us would be more obvious to students I would imagine. It happens that I am reasonably friendly with Sheldon Stick and I can imagine team teaching with him. There would be a lot of banter, although I don't have a social relationship with him. I've known him for a long time and we think alike on a lot of things. Gene and I didn't come to this level or at least not quite and that's one of the things that I'd like to do in the classroom. It's kind of a disarming strategy, it gets me off of the pedestal with students and I'd like to shock them from time to time with various things. Gene and I haven't reached that level and I don't know if that happens spontaneously or if you have to work on it–I don't know." Dr. Eggland believed having a closer personal relationship between collaborators "would make students more alert. They would listen more carefully. They would watch for the subtleties. They would watch for the nuances and innuendoes."

Class Size

For Dr. Eggland, who taught this class for many years, the exorbitant number of seventy-seven students was astonishing, "Seventy-seven students in the classroom was too big, absolutely too big. I have taught this class ten times previously and in those cases students their numbers were in the twenty-five, twenty-seven, thirty range, never more than thirty students." Although Dr. Eggland admired herculean effort made by Mr. Armstrong to memorize students' names and a little bit about them, he was clearly uncomfortable with the fact that size of the class would preclude the opportunity to examine everybody's point of view, "Out of those seventy-seven people, there are probably only about fifteen you really ever hear from." Dr. Eggland's poor familiarity with students' names made his communication with the class profoundly limited, "Because I don't have all the names, I can't say: Joane! What do you think? Geofrey! What do you think? If I had a smaller class, I can deal with that better than we are able to in this setting. The bad news is that I don't think that students in this class are prodded or forced to think about that or seeing that. They just kind of come there and plop down and they can hide out in the anonymity of seventy-seven students and they don't have to explore all those issues. All they have to do is to read a couple things and write a little report." The inability to reach out to each and every student in the class to force students to formulate their opinions, to disagree with instructors or each other, to think critically was the most disappointing thing most seriously obstructing learning. There you can hide in that class hide intellectually you are not forced to engage in critical thinking and discussion. Kids raise their hands and have opinions and I've noticed a handful of them are really smart they are really thoughtful." Probably the biggest problem for Dr. Eggland was the challenge of developing a bond with students, "That class is too darn big to allow for what I consider to be a really good bonding. I don't know them intimately, intellectually, hardly any of them actually." Mr. Armstrong, on the other hand, when asked about the size of the class vis-à-vis learning processes taking place, presented slightly different perspective, "I have to withhold my thoughts totally on that because I think we've done some things. I've learned some things about large groups that would lead me to think that it can be done. I think there has to be some strategy developed to make that happen. Obviously if there were thirty students, I would know much more about them. Then I would be teaching alone. So I would say that doubling this number and giving two instructors does not create the same environment that one with thirty would do. I think if I had a choice I would think of a smaller class. But I'm not ready to give up on the idea that true collaboration with a larger group would work very well, at least on this level in the higher education level."

Learning Experience

To the question if the presence of two instructors in the classroom as a counterbalance to a doubled number of students influenced students' learning experience, Dr. Eggland's response was unwavering, "No, not much, not much. For some purposes it might work. I don't think it helps much. It doesn't do what I would like them to do, which is undress them academically, intellectually, and get them to carefully look at who they are and what they think, and force them into some critical thinking. So far I don't think it has happened. I've not seen evidence of that in the papers that I've read."

Academic Individualism

"The attitude that is conveyed is that if you achieve something with somebody, you only achieved half as much," noted Dr. Eggland, "A perfect example is a co-authored article in the professional journal. Oh you co-authored that's not as good, or if you co-authored and you are the second author that's even worse, or if you have three authors or four authors that's just totally worthless almost. But if you are a single author sole author that's meritorious, and so we have been taught we have been reinforced to work as individuals and nobody has ever re-taught us how to collaborate." Mr. Armstrong, however, did not perceive academic culture overly individualistic, at least to the degree that could hurt their collaboration. He explained, "Democracy encompasses individualism within parameters. Working independently is almost unheard of any more. In democracy, sure we want you to develop your skills, but you also have to develop your skills within the parameters or how those skills are going to work in the democratic society. If anything, my background has prepared me for collaborative rather than individual, because I found that two people working collaboratively can accomplish more than twice as much as two people working independently." He then related his experience to the years spent as a school principal, "The environment affected my perception. When you have a large group such as I had at Lincoln East High School, I'm not going to stand up there and lecture to people who teach. I'm a generalist and they are experts in their particular fields. So why would I not call them as experts to address certain issues within the larger context."

Shared Leadership

"I think you need to orchestrate so well if you are going to be on equal terms. I mean introducing new ideas and the actual delivery. I think you really have to orchestrate that," noted Mr. Armstrong, "Whereas the one takes the lead, the other supports. The true collaboration comes through planning as I understood the collaboration and that's an equal thing. But I still think there has to be somebody to say: 'Okay we are going to start!' and somebody who follows fills out all the blank spots. But as far as planning is concerned, totally equal on that." Referring directly to his collaboration with Dr. Eggland, Mr. Armstrong was clear on what had happened, "As far as sharing the leadership, it seemed to be that I was always the one who introduced the topic, and then he supported that topic with what he knew. I had the ultimate responsibility for making it happen, and he was there to make sure that it happened."

Role Identification

"When I look back I wonder if the whole process rather than having two equal collaborators had one lead teacher and an assistant or associate. I'd like to try to see if we can identify roles more clearly," noted Mr. Armstrong, "I don't think we did a very good job with identifying our roles. We didn't spend enough time before class started at the beginning of the semester to identify strengths and areas that may need help." Mr. Armstrong believed also that if that had happened, he would have understood better Dr. Eggland's style better and also his own, "We'd have a better handle on what we are trying to accomplish as far as teaching itself is concerned. I think that the real danger of collaborative teaching is that it turns into 'turn teaching.' And that's why I wonder if we wouldn't be better to have a lead teacher with an associate who is committed to be there all the time. I just think it's absolutely essential that both or three, depending on the size of the class teachers be there every time."

Final Advice

While trying to offer practical recommendations for future collaborators on the basis of his experience with collaborative teaching, Dr. Eggland illuminated the topic by instructing, "I would carve out more time out of my week to spend on it. I would figure out the way to adjust my schedule. I would know that I was going to do it far enough in advance, so I wasn't traveling in meetings or doing other administrative stuff. I would probably spend more time with Gene on planning. We really spent minimum amount of time in this whole period. We haven't spent more than a total of four hours actually sitting by the table and talking, maybe five and that's inadequate." However, Dr. Eggland did not look for scapegoats, "I take most of the blame for that. That's something I would change. I would somehow try to make the class smaller, at least this one. It's just too many people to meet the objectives that we had."

Descriptive Data

This part of the research analysis is based on the students' anonymous final course evaluations made available to the researcher upon completion of the course. Although none of the questions in the evaluation form dealt directly with the concept of collaborative teaching, eight out of the seventy-five students who completed the course expressed their opinions and shared their feelings on that issue. One student noted, "The dual teaching was good." The remaining seven, however, did not appear that generous and indicated their preference for one instructor due mainly to frequent absences of Dr. Eggland–whose frequent absence only made students "confused" and caused feelings of "frustration." In one of the reports, a student confided, "Either have one professor or two that would be there daily." In another evaluation, a student expressed a strong predilection for a single instructor, "I also feel very strongly that Mr. Armstrong should teach the class alone." Although only five percent of students mentioned the topic of collaborative teaching in their evaluations, it confirmed some of the observations provided by the collaborating instructors in the preceding interviews. Had the question of collaboration been posed in the evaluation forms, more elaborate conclusions could be drawn from that crucial source of information. It is clear from students' reports, as well as the instructors' insights, that the collaboration of Mr. Armstrong and Dr. Eggland was not a success. It is apparent that the course was not taught in the fully collaborative form as originally intended. The course resembled, using Mr. Armstrong's analogy a "tag team" or "turn teaching" of two instructors occasionally meeting in the classroom. It was also evident that Dr. Eggland was overwhelmed by the feeling of guilt for not being able to properly fulfill his duties. He blamed his lack of involvement in the classroom affairs on the overwhelming amount of administrative duties imposed on him by the college administration during the semester and the lack of control over the design of the course. He felt his role was reduced to a mere "guest speaker." Teamwork, however, became the ultimate pedagogical highlight of the class. All students assessed positively interactive nature of group activities opening each session. They enjoyed working with fellow students, making new friends, and learning from their experiences. One of the students reported, "I loved the group work. I quickly became friends [w/] my fellow group members. It made me excited to come to class. I learned a great deal from working in groups, active learning, cooperation, teamwork." Another student reported the therapeutic nature of social interactions foisted upon students during classroom activities. A student's psychological well-being was deeply and positively affected by constant exposure to teamwork. To the extent that he or she became quite adept at dealing with social interactions that previously constituted an uncomfortable and awkward relationship development barrier, "The interaction amongst all groups was very helpful. The interaction helped me out and also the class. I am now eager to speak instead of being shy. I think that getting together in the groups put all our ideas into one idea. It was teamwork that helped everyone." Not everybody shared those perceptions. Some students thought there were too few group activities and wished to see more teamwork being used during class. One of the students wrote, "Decrease the amount of large group discussions." Another evaluator alluded to the same issue but blamed the decreased effectiveness of large group discussions on the size of the class. A sentiment shared by. Dr. Eggland. To the contrary, one student thought that involvement of students in the class discussions was high in spite of the class size, "I thought the involvement of students was very good considering the size of group it was. I felt that the active involvement reinforced what was being discussed in the lecture." A sentiment shared by Mr. Armstrong. Another reported, "Large group discussions were more difficult because of the class size, but the groups represented a diverse microcosm of the larger class." Overall, however, students perceived group activities as a success and credited Mr. Armstrong for implementing them effectively during classes. One of the students commented on Mr. Armstrong's concept of "constructing the knowledge" together in the classroom, "I loved the theory behind talking-constructing, not instructing–very effective, especially for this subject matter." Most students were satisfied with all that happened in the class, "I don't think that I would change anything. I feel that this class was very informative." The overall evaluation of the class was very positive, "I have been in this university for five years and this ranks in the top five most useful classes. It wasn't a typical college class, but it was useful because it taught many different things in different ways." There were those who felt the class was too easy, "It was fun and interesting. I would make it a little harder. We didn't have to think or do too much and many of the ideas presented were common sense things. It was exciting and was instructed in an effective method of teaching. The instructors were very supportive and helpful and knowledgeable."

CHAPTER 8

PROCESS OF COLLABORATIVE TEACHING <u>ANALYSIS</u>

CASE STUDY #3

In this section, the researcher intends to answer the following questions that guide this journey into the complex world of collaboration: 1) What is the process of collaborative teaching? 2) What are the issues related to collaborative teaching? The researcher will also provide readers with an illuminating description of the context in which collaborative teaching took place and the profound benefits and consequences.

Entry vignette

For the majority of academic faculty members collaborative teaching is a concept far removed from diurnal reality of their work routines. Professors in highly specialized fields of study may find it difficult to collaborate with each other effectively. Even though educators' primary fields of interest include such disciplines as pedagogy and andragogy, they also heavily rely and derive their knowledge from rather eclectic disciplines of sociology, psychology, anthropology, math, sciences, philosophy, law etc. Consequently faculty members, the generalists that they tend to be, might find it somewhat easier to communicate and collaborate with each other professionals on a daily basis. This may in part explain more interest in collaborative teaching in higher education. The observations presented here will give insights into the nature of collaborative teaching in the academic environment.

The City and the Campus

University of Nebraska–Lincoln is the state's largest most comprehensive university offering quality education for well over a century. The institution has become one of the greatest Midwestern universities offering one hundred forty-eight undergraduate majors and one hundred nineteen graduate programs. Although ninety percent of the twenty-four thousand students enrolled this year [1999] come from Nebraska, students from every state and over ninety countries choose it as their intellectual destination. Lincoln, state's capital and its second largest city surrounds the campus. Over 200,000 people live in this city and projections forecast that within ten years population will double. The University of Nebraska–Lincoln, chartered by the Legislature in 1869, is part of the larger system that serves both the land-grant and the comprehensive public university for the State of Nebraska. University of Nebraska–Lincoln has three primary objectives: teaching, research, and service.

Collaborating Instructors

Coach, teacher, minister, administrator, collaborator! Gene Armstrong was born in a small town of four thousand located in the North-Central Nebraska. His childhood memories focus around the small place somewhere in the fields of the very heart of the American continent. Small town, small elementary and then high school allowed him to be involved in many activities. It also taught him many good lessons for life, "I took advantage of about everything offered in high school." Gene participated in everything from athletics to art. Upon high school graduation, Mr. Armstrong left his home town for Kearney State College, Nebraska. That was a growing experience for a still teenage boy, "So here I was, an eighteen-year-old-high school graduate participating with twenty five and twenty-six-year-old Korean vets." That experience, as he later recalled, made a big impression on him. It was then that Mr. Armstrong considered the career of a Methodist pastor. That idea however was never realized as right after college graduation, at the age of twenty-four, Mr. Armstrong entered the connubial bliss with a woman of his choice and began his life-long career in education. He started as a teacher of physical education and biological science. He was also a football and basketball coach, then a school administrator. Mr. Armstrong stayed loyal to the state of Nebraska, never leaving it for any professional position. Mr. Armstrong's life was quite seminal in more than one way. His most precious possessions include the heritage of four married kids with eight grandchildren and five dogs. At the time of the research study, Mr. Armstrong, at sixty-two years of age, was a graduate assistant pursuing a doctorate degree in the Department of Educational Administration at the University of Nebraska–Lincoln, teaching graduate as well as undergraduate courses.

First Class B female superintendent in Nebraska! Dr. Jody Isernhagen was born in Petersberg, Virginia, "I lived on the East Coast all of my childhood and a good part of my adult life. During my years growing up, I was in a family of five kids which in and of itself means that a lot of cooperation had to occur at home." Both of her parents had a high school education with a strong work ethic. Although she was second in birth order, in many ways she felt she was treated as a first-born, "This kind and warm full of love environment played a big role in building cooperative relationships with others," she reminisced. Dr. Isernhagen was awarded an undergraduate degree from Madison College with a teaching certificate in elementary education. She then moved around and lived in several states, mainly Alabama and North Carolina, working as an elementary remedial reading teacher, physical education teacher, and a track coach. The biggest part of her teaching career however took place in Virginia where she spent fifteen years of her life. In addition to her teaching experience, Dr. Isernhagen was an assistant principal, building principal, and elementary education supervisor–managing thirty five elementary schools. She received her Masters' degree in Curriculum and Instruction from Virginia Tech in 1978. Ten years later, she completed a doctorate in Educational Administration from the same institution. Dr. Isernhagen spent one year in Seoul, Korea teaching English. She greatly cherished that experience, "I've been overseas, so my experiences vary and that helps me to have insights as far as the needs of kids and people. Because I've been in lots of different settings that give me some understanding of various cultures I believe."

Dr. Isernhagen arrived in Nebraska in 1988. It was a time of big changes in her life. She received her doctoral degree and got married to a man with two teenage sons. She spent two years as a principal of a small elementary school in Hastings, Nebraska. Two years later she became the first female superintendent in a Class B school in the history of Nebraska. The newspaper headlines read, "Not in modern history has there been

145

a female superintendent of a Class A or B public school." It was always her goal to become a superintendent and it finally happened. During the research study, while starting as a faculty member at the University of Nebraska–Lincoln in the Department of Educational Administration, she still had two weeks to superintendent tenure to complete. The aspects that Dr. Isernhagen appreciated most in Nebraska were traditionally strong educational system and a solid work ethic, "The Nebraska educational system is very strong. It ranks fourth as far as test scores in the United States. There is a very strong work ethic here." Although she still misses the Virginia's ocean and the beaches, she came to like Nebraska, "I still love to go home. That's where we go for vacations, because I can't live without going to the ocean each year."

Teacher, principal, researcher, collaborator! Dr. Miles Bryant was born in Vermont in 1941, "I grew up in Vermont, a very rural state in those years, war years. My father was a military man," recalled Dr. Bryant. All of his early school education took place in Vermont. His college major was literature. He always wanted to be a teacher and that's what he did for a few years after graduation from Teachers' College, "I taught high school English all through private and public schools and moved into curriculum, supervision, and administration as I was doing that." At some point in his career, Dr. Bryant became a private school administrator and director of admissions, "Somewhere along in there I decided that I wanted to drop from work, not nearly to make a career change but just to learn more about school administration." As a result, Dr. Bryant moved along with his wife to California to begin his graduate studies at prestigious Stanford University. He elected a renowned Administrative Policies Social Science program that included economics, politics, sociology, and research methodology, "While going through the program, I took the job of a headmaster of a private school in San Francisco, California and did that for a while. I had a very miserable experience there with the board of trustees." He left the job without particular excitement about going back to school administration. That experience led him to consider other career opportunities. Following the advice of friends and family, Dr. Bryant decided to look for a job in academia, "So I sort of looked around and found positions opened at Texas, North Carolina, Iowa, and Nebraska. I ended up liking this one best, in part because of the match of what they wanted me to teach and what I wanted to teach." Paradoxically even though Dr. Bryant never intended to live in the Midwest, he ended up living here anyway and living quite comfortably. He has been a faculty member at the University of Nebraska–Lincoln, Department of Educational Administration since 1985 teaching organizational and administrative theory. He traveled extensively both within and outside the country. He visited Europe, China. For a while, he even taught in Israel. At the time of the research study, Dr. Bryant lived with his wife, an artist, raising two teenage boys one in high school and one in college. He and his wife often traveled to Colorado to fly fishing, which next to gardening and some odd house restorations was his favorite hobby.

Course History

The course EDAD 800 Schooling and Administration was initiated over three decades ago, "When I first started teaching this class, it was team taught with two other professors and began in the late sixties," reminisced Dr. Bryant. "That was the first time it was conceived. Then the course was extended to be worth six credit hours. When I started teaching the class it was very heavily infused with assessment philosophy. It was a very competitive class. At the time the class was constructed around simulations which were based on a K-12 school district with community data, teacher data, salary data, and school-board policies. Students had to role play the roles of a principal, superintendent, and curriculum director. The competitiveness of the class was further enhanced by the grading of students on a ranking system. No matter how good a student did, they were still ranked according to the curve the normal distribution. However students did not like the system and many complained about the course as a result. Students some of them had been teachers for many years and really found it very irritating to be graded in this fashion. I didn't like the system either. In the early nineties, the class was seriously reorganized to better meet the needs of the students." Dr. Larry Dlugosh, Educational Administration Department Chair, and Dr. Miles Bryant were the primary re-designers of the course. Looking at the history, Dr. Bryant while of the course retrospectively commented, "I think of this as two different classes. I taught the old class four times and the new version seven times. We all taught: Dr. Dlugosh, Dr. Isernhagen, and me. So we produced the change, but it still has a lot of similarities." At the heart of the new philosophy was the creation of the learning environment in which students were expected to feel free to express their opinions and develop critical thinking skills through elaborate discussions and argumentations. "We realized that people involved in school administration almost never have time to think and reflect on what they do because they are so bloody busy," commiserated Dr. Bryant. During the first five-week session of the summer of 1999, Dr. Miles Bryant, Dr. Jody Isernhagen, and for the first time Mr. Gene Armstrong were collaboratively teaching EDAD 800 Schooling and Administration.

Course Objectives

EDAD 800 Schooling and Administration was a graduate course designed to introduce students to many complex issues of schooling and administration that confront educators in contemporary schools. From a broader perspective, students were asked to examine the purposes of schooling, the degree to which schools were organized to achieve those purposes, and alternative ways that schools could be organized in order to achieve those purposes to better serve the needs of children and the goals of society. The course was designed to facilitate learning of the professionals well-versed in schooling and to provide them with an opportunity to test their experience against emergent knowledge. The course required one comprehensive project in which instructors asked students to develop strategies for improving instruction and learning in a technology supported simulated setting. Although instructors realized that some students may not prefer working in teams, they nonetheless decided to ask them to work collaboratively on the assignment. They made that decision because educational leaders are expected to work in groups and teams with other fellow educators. EDAD 800 Schooling and Administration was offered for six credits. The course had the following stated outcomes to achieve:

1. To develop promising ideas for school instructional and learning improvement compatible with the needs of children, parents, and society. In cases where those needs were in conflict, course participants were to develop ways to constructively use these conflicts to achieve desired objectives.
2. To articulate strategies and initiatives that held promise to improve instruction and learning for all students.
3. To articulate a personal statement about general purposes of public education in America.

4. To demonstrate an improved understanding of how to better relate interpersonally to others.

5. To expand one's knowledge and confidence of one's self as an educator and educational leader.

6. To develop personal skills in the following areas: a) oral communications, b) written communication, c) analytical ability, d) reflective skills, e) group facilitation skills, f) skills in technology use.

As a way of documenting their learning, each student was asked to prepare a notebook and portfolio containing information on the following topics:

1. Reflections on their own learning.
2. Promising ideas about instructional improvement.
3. Strategies and initiatives that held promise for all students.
4. Goals for the improvement of students' interpersonal skills.
5. Resources and information that students had acquired during the class.

Narrative Description
First Meeting

March 22, 1999, was the first day when three collaborating instructors met for the first time in an official manner to plan the future of the course. The meeting took place in the departmental library placed on the first floor of Seaton Hall, where Department of Educational Administration was housed. Small library was filled with doctoral dissertations and theses placed on the shelves on the right side of the room. Since the sky was clouded on that day, only two out of five windows were covered with opaque shades leaving plenty of natural light filling the room. Four tables arranged in the rectangular shape resembled the shape of the room itself. Dr. Jody Isernhagen was seated at the very center of the room. She was wearing gray pants, a green jacket and a brown scarf swirling around her neck completed this creative ensemble. On the contrary, Mr. Gene Armstrong was dressed rather casually wearing blue checkered sweater matched by white khaki pants and brown shoes. Dr. Bryant Miles, also rather casual, sported a light blue shirt and blue jeans. For easier communication, their seating arrangement reminded a triangle. The meeting which lasted almost two hours started at 10 a.m. sharp. Since both Dr. Miles and Dr. Isernhagen were faculty members at the Department of Educational Administration where Mr. Armstrong attempted to complete his doctoral studies, there was no need for official introductions. Dr. Miles and Dr. Isernhagen, who taught this class collaboratively for the last five years, introduced Mr. Armstrong to the major aspects of their experience with the course. The main objective of their meeting was to collaboratively identify the sequence of topics, reading materials, and assignments to be utilized in the course. The meeting was dominated by brainstorming ideas to establish the direction and philosophy to be applied in the course. Myriad of concepts emerged which included: newspaper articles, peer evaluations, personal writing, and reflective papers. Reflective papers found strongest support among collaborating instructors. The choice of reading materials and the style of instruction was another issue to be resolved during the meeting. The use of small groups and active learning was decided to be the main vehicle of classroom activities. In general, the meeting atmosphere was casual but serious and to the point. Everybody attempted to reach a consensus on the discussed subjects in a professional manner. Somewhere in the middle of the meeting Dr. Isernhagen raised the issue of the utilization of technology during the course. That suggestion animated Dr. Bryant who suggested use of teleconferencing as an alternative source of communication. The use of reading materials emerged as another urgent task. Dr. Isernhagen turned to both colleagues putting forward a few books she thought might be useful for the course. Although no decisions were finalized, instructors agreed to look at the suggested literature and delay final decision for the next meeting. Toward the end of the meeting, Dr. Bryant informed Mr. Armstrong about the application of various activities utilized in the course that Drs. Isernhagen and Bryant found useful in building team spirit while teaching the course for the last five years of their collaborative experience. The final fifteen minutes of the meeting was devoted to scheduling first week of the course by dividing loads and responsibilities among each other. They agreed to meet the following week to continue their preparation.

Second Meeting

March 29, 1999, was a beautiful sunny Monday with temperature in the 60s. The meeting started at 9:30 a.m. and took place in the departmental library located on the first floor of Seaton Hall. The room looked very much the same it did during the prior meeting except for the windows widely open to allow sunlight and gentle vernal breeze to fill up the entire room with warm invitation. Dr. Isernhagen started the meeting with a brief explanation of the major simulation that would run throughout the entire duration of the course. The web-based simulation, referred to as The Information Environment for School Leader Preparation (IESLP), was grounded in inductive and problem-based learning (PBL). The project by using technology as the mode of delivery placed the learner in the role of a doer as close as possible to the real situation. While Dr. Isernhagen was explaining the operational aspects of the project, Mr. Armstrong and Dr. Bryant jotted down pieces of information generating questions they would later address with Dr. Paddy Chance, a technology expert whom they arranged to speak to at 10:30 a.m. this morning. The following period of approximately thirty minutes was filled with brainstorming of ideas and topics they saw pertinent to this project. Dr. Paddy Chance, who had extensive experience with IESLP system, shared her knowledge and experiences with the collaborating instructors and clarify questions that may arise in the process. The reading material for the course was next on the agenda. Dr. Isernhagen presented a book on leadership that she thought would be an excellent addition to the materials already accepted by the instructors. "This is an excellent book," concluded Dr. Bryant after a few minutes of browsing. "Yeah, that's my kind of book," concurred Mr. Armstrong. The following ten minutes centered on how individual parts of the book should be utilized. After a short but focused discussion, the collaborating instructors agreed to include the book as part of the required readings. Right then Dr. Bryant proposed enriching the class by the panel of qualified guest speakers, "but not necessarily intellectuals or academicians." The idea was noted and postponed for the revision later on. At 10:30 a.m., the focus of the meeting shifted conceptually as well as geographically. Professors left the departmental library and briskly moved into the office of one of the professors in the department placed on the right side of the long corridor where offices of the departmental faculty were located. The office was a small square-shaped room full of books, papers, and documents of all sorts dispersed randomly all around the desks and shelves. An ample gray armchair placed at the very center of the room took majority of the available space. The walls were covered with pictures depicting various historical events that further added to the overwhelming impression of crowdedness in this tiny room. The conversation between collaborating instructors and Dr. Paddy Chance took place via the speaker phone. Instructors gathered around the phone. Dr. Isernhagen was closest to the microphone and led the conversation. She started with introducing her colleagues. The communication was dominated by Dr. Chance who summarized the nature of the IESLP project and shared her experiences with it. She was infrequently interrupted by questions and clarifications. The whole event went very smoothly with clear communication. The professors assiduously wrote down all the information provided to them. A few minutes after 11:30 a.m., the constructive meeting ended.

Third Meeting

On April 14, 1999, the meeting started at 9:40 in the morning. The departmental library at Seaton Hall was the place of choice. Dr. Bryant and Mr. Armstrong dressed rather casually took seats from across each other. Dr. Isernhagen wearing black and red checkered dress was seated to the left of Mr. Armstrong. Dr. Bryant, browsing through the files in his laptop, started the meeting by announcing, "Okay among other things I think we should talk about data." The initial quarter of an hour was occupied by discussion on the amount and kind of data that should be provided to students in the planned simulation. Since the project was to be a corner stone of the entire course, it was an important decision to make. This part of the conversation took place primarily between Dr. Bryant and Dr. Isernhagen with the latter occasionally walking around the tables to approach Dr. Bryant's laptop in an effort to clarify some application minutia. Dr. Isernhagen and Mr. Armstrong decided to contact individuals responsible for technology training as future resources for instructors and students. Next Dr. Isernhagen touched upon scheduling activities for the first week of classes. While Dr. Isernhagen brainstormed her ideas, Dr. Bryant took notes. The monologue soon segued smoothly to a key question raised by Dr. Bryant, "What skills do we want to develop? We know we want to develop oral and reflective skills. Are there any other we want to develop?" The question was followed by a prolonged discussion ignited by Mr. Armstrong's suggestion, "How about critical thinking and team development?!" At the initiative of Dr. Bryant conversation shifted somewhat from the tactical topic of technology use for decision making purposes to a strategic esoteric consideration for effects of politics on school dynamics, "In schools, we use politics rather than data!" This seemingly innocent statement opened a flood of new ideas on how to conduct a class to best equip students with relevant skills. Heated arguments concluded with accepting Dr. Bryant's idea, "So the task will be to create a 'new school' on the basis of students' scores!" Instructors finalized their statements of course objectives which Dr. Bryant scrupulously typed in his laptop. At about eleven o'clock, Dr. Bryant abruptly left the room due to other commitments. The meeting between Dr. Isenrnhagen and Mr. Armstrong lasted another thirty minutes and ended precisely at 11:30 a.m.

Fourth Meeting

Mr. Armstrong was absent on that day. Dr. Isernhagen was busily browsing through a revised description of the course provided by Dr. Bryant. April 23, 1999, was a cloudy and cold day but the forecasted rain for that morning did not come into fruition. The first twenty minutes of the meeting were filled with brainstorming, re-wording, and changing the initial draft of the course description. Final version was finally agreed upon, "So, those are the things that we've got so far." Next Dr. Isernhagen introduced the topic of students' portfolios. What exactly should it be? What title should it have? What should be the nature of the assignment? Instructors struggled with the questions for about twenty minutes when final agreement was finally reached. "Now the project," directed Dr. Bryant. Dr. Isernhagen dictated the list of objectives with Dr. Bryant jotting them down scrupulously in his laptop occasionally pausing for clarifications. After approximately sixty minutes, during which Dr. Isernhagen continuously took sips of soda from a medium-size cup with the big inscription from a popular Nebraska fast food restaurant "RUNZA" on it, Dr. Bryant kept charging forward, "Next what I'd like to do is to look at the daily schedule." In the customary fashion, the instructors went page by page through every day of the schedule suggesting changes, improvements, sometimes coming up with the entirely new ideas. After objectives for the course were crystalized, Dr. Bryant concluded, "Good progress here." Eventually instructors shifted their attention back to the students' main project. The computer simulated project would run throughout the course and both projects and presentations would be completed in a formal and professional manner. Right when instructors were ready to end the meeting, Dr. Isernhagen exclaimed, "Maybe Gene could do something from the perspective of a principal and use his expertise?" "Excellent idea," responded Dr. Bryant, "We can do that!" When left alone at a quarter to three Dr. Bryant pointed to the newly constructed course description and jokingly exclaimed, "I'm going to type it all now."

Fifth Meeting

It was a busy time for the Department of Educational Administration. The entire school was scheduled to move out from Seaton Hall to nearby Nebraska Hall. On the eve of the move, both professors and staff alike hectically scrambled to and fro packing and carrying their effects. The pile of brown boxes full of theses and dissertations filled up departmental library. That's exactly where collaborating instructors decided to meet again to review their progress. May 6, 1999 was unseasonably cold and rainy for a Nebraska spring. Moldy piles of stacked up boxes exuded a pungent and noisome odor. Since instructors did not complain, the overall ambience must have been tolerable. Mr. Armstrong and Dr. Bryant sat next to each other on the right side directly facing Dr. Isernhagen. At the very outset of the meeting, Drs. Isernhagen and Bryant informed Mr. Armstrong of the progress they have made thus far. After suggesting a few modifications to the schedule, Dr. Isernhagen remarked, "I think we are pushing a lot of information within the first few days." Dr. Bryant agreed and immediately suggested a few changes. Throughout the meeting, Mr. Armstrong sat quietly perusing handed to him schedule making only occasional suggestions. Dr. Isernhagen asked Mr. Armstrong to lead one of the classes. The topic would build on his experience as a school principal. He willingly agreed. "It's getting pretty formalized here Miles," noted Dr. Isernhagen, shuffling through the sheaf of papers piled up in front of her. Dr. Bryant responded with a smile, "We will change the schedule within the first twenty minutes of the class." "Yes we must be flexible," replied Dr. Isernhagen. In the latter part of this ninety-minute meeting, Dr. Bryant emphasized team effort as the defining element of this course. He also made it very clear to all present that he expected to see Mr. Armstrong working as an "equal," fully contributing to the course. In the final minutes of the meeting Dr. Isernhagen read aloud the final schedule. At 11:30 a.m., the spirited meeting ended.

Sixth Meeting

It had been two busy weeks since the Department of Educational Administration moved to its new location. Nebraska Hall was located on the southern side of the City Campus. In the past, this huge monstrosity served as a warehouse. It was surrounded by an imposing dormitory from the south and an expansive soccer field from the north. As expected from a former warehouse, the interior design of Nebraska Hall was composed of a massive industrial complex filled with long curvy corridors leading to faculty offices and utilitarian classrooms. On June 2, 1999, the collaborating instructors met for the last time before the official start of the course to review the status of their readiness. At 10 a. m., they entered one of the average-sized classrooms on the fifth floor. The entire building was spotted with offices and rooms, many without windows. The room where collaborators met was one of those windowless spaces that never saw the light of day. The beautiful sunny weather outside did not stand a chance. It could not permeate heavy walls of the fortress. Every wall in this room was accoutered with a door providing limited view of the adjacent rooms. Shining floor and walls however made the rooms seemed slightly more capacious than they really were. That relieved the somewhat claustrophobic surroundings in which collaborators met today. The room was furnished with three tables surrounded by all kinds of mismatched gray and blue chairs. Instructors chose the biggest table and sat next to each other almost in a straight line. Surrounded by papers and books, the collaborating instructors began their final preparations meeting. The hundred-minute long meeting focused almost exclusively on the revision of the course description which was being continuously twisted around for the last three months. The first few minutes were entirely devoted to the linguistic review of the material achieved by marking spelling errors, suggesting minor diction modifications etc. At one point, Mr. Armstrong announced he would not be able to attend one of the classes. "It's okay. You don't have to be there all the time," noted Dr. Bryant. Soon after Dr. Isernhagen distributed the textbooks she intended to use in the course. Upon a brief examination, all agreed and Dr. Bryant interpolated the titles into the syllabus. Dr. Bryant began a brief summary of the planned activities for the first day of the course. The discussion that followed transitioned toward discussion about students' project. Drs. Isernhagen and Bryant insisted on adding some "complicating" elements into the project to enhance the critical thinking component of the learning experience. Consequently, the colleagues attempted further rewording of the schedule and interjected new words into the syllabus in an effort to fine tune the objectives of the course. The instructors tediously worked over plans for every day of the five-week-course schedule, modifying the names and nature of activities to best reflect the intentions of the designers. The meeting, which was crammed with tedious activities of revisions, corrections, and modifications, was over at about twenty minutes before noon. Dr. Isernhagen summarized tasks to be attended to before the course began the following week. The meeting ended by Dr. Bryant stating, "It looks good to me. I think we are set."

First Class

The first day of the week on June 7, 1999, welcomed students with heat and humidity. The classroom where the session was scheduled to take place was located on the first floor of Nebraska Hall. Since long somewhat spooky looking corridors of the former warehouse led to the classroom, instructors placed arrows along the way to make finding the classroom possible. The square-shaped room with a big no. 130W painted on the door contained four narrow windows built in allowing precious little flow of sunlight through. Collaborating instructors arrived twenty minutes before the scheduled starting time of class at 8:30 a.m. in the morning. They seated themselves behind the long table facing students directly. Both Mr. Armstrong and Dr. Bryant were dressed rather casually on that day. Mr. Armstrong was characteristically the more casual of the two, wearing light khaki pants matched, while Dr. Bryant wore a slightly dressier long-sleeved shirt with a black vest. Dr. Isernhagen, on the other hand, showed up quite dressed up for the occasion displaying a fashionable long black dress. At exactly 8:30 a.m., Dr. Bryant stepped into the center of the classroom proclaiming loudly, "It's time to begin!" After a brief introduction, students embarked on their first task of rearranging tables to facilitate the collaborative learning style expected throughout the entire course both from the students and, in this case, instructors as well. Soon after, Dr. Bryant introduced students to the main objectives of the class. In the meantime Dr. Isernhagen and Mr. Armstrong distributed earlier prepared learning materials to the students. For the next hour or so, Drs. Isernhagen and Bryant took turns addressing various aspects of the course including their expectations from the students. The class consisted of twenty-five to thirty years old students, typically practicing school administrators and teachers from the neighboring areas. Male students were in the strong majority. Out of twenty-five students, only four were females. The class departed for their first break at 10:00 a.m. Forty minutes later students returned and started by filling out one-page long pre-instructional questionnaire prepared by the instructors. The time until the noon-break was filled with in-depth explanation of the syllabus, performed alternately by Dr. Bryant and Dr. Isernhagen. Students' questions followed. Not surprisingly most of the inquiries dealt with the assignments to which instructors responded thoroughly by taking turns. At noon the class was dismissed for an hour-long lunch break. At a few minutes after 1:00 p.m., the majority of students reconvened back in the classroom and immediately received materials for the exercise titled "goal activity" in which students based on the available information were expected to identify and then prioritize primary goals of schools and education. Students were divided into six groups with three to four individuals on each team. Since space in the building was not an issue, groups were asked to move to two adjacent classrooms to conduct discussions. One set of three groups moved to the neighboring classroom to the left–no. 129W, the second set of three groups moved to the classroom on the right with–no. 131W. Although both classrooms had the same generic architecture, the latter one possessed a slightly different quality to it. It was brightly light and, in lieu of long cumbersome tables, students enjoyed bright yellow chairs with small desks. Instructors meandered from one room to another looking pleased to see students engaging in animated conversations. After forty minutes, while students were still working, instructors met in the center classroom to review procedure they intended to use during individual group presentations. Soon after students joined instructors in the original class to present their insights to the entire class. Hour-long discussion developed in which students attempted to define learning and the roles schools should play in its execution. While Dr. Isernhangen initiated the discussion, Mr. Armstrong took upon himself to challenge students' assumptions and stimulate their critical thinking with novel ideas. At 3:00 p.m., Dr. Isernhagen stepped into the center of the classroom and congratulated students on the successful day of active participation and dismissed the class for the day.

Second Class

On June 8, 1999, at 8:30 a.m., students poured into classroom no.130W still a little drowsy. Almost all students wore shorts and T-shirts. The priests taking the class were the exception, easily distinguishable from the crowd by wearing black pants and short-sleeved clerical shirts with white collars clearly distinguishing their vocation. Instructors as well in their traditionally casual attire began the class with Dr. Bryant summarizing briefly the upcoming Thursday afternoon activity, scheduled to take place at Doane College, Nebraska. At the same time, Dr. Isernhagen jotted down relevant information on the board so that to avoid any misunderstandings. The remainder of the morning was filled with an overview of the book presented to students a day before. Mr. Armstrong contributed to the discussion by confronting students with his new ideas and simply sharing his practical experiences. At 11:40 a.m. the class departed for a short break. Half an hour later all students returned for an hour-long revision of the computer simulation, the primary team project students were scheduled to work on throughout the course. Dr. Bryant made an introductory review of the simulation emphasizing its goals and expectations. Dr. Isernhagen served a supportive role in this case by distributing list of suggested questions to which students were expected to find correct quantitative responses. Mr. Armstrong posed a few questions to Dr. Bryant to further clarify the emerging concerns. As this part of the class ended at 11:40 a.m., Dr. Bryant announced that two computer labs would be available to students who want to practice the simulation after the lunch break. At 1:00 p.m. sharp, students arrived at one of the labs and began testing the system. Five of them chose to practice in the computer lab located on the fifth floor of the Nebraska Hall. A relatively spacious room was filled with eighteen computers arranged in four even rows. Dr. Isernhagen facilitated the process by assisting practicing students who chose that lab for their practice. Most of the students, however, gathered in the Design Center located in Henzlik Hall which was a short five-minute walk from Nebraska Hall. The computer lab was located at the very back of a huge hall divided into several sections. The area equipped with thirty computers was quiet and very conducive to focused reflective study. Dr. Bryant and Mr. Armstrong seated at the very front and the very back of the room respectively served as facilitators to students coming in and out during the two-hour period. At 3:00 p.m., the last couple of students departed for the day.

Third Class

The classroom was assembled ahead of the class start on June 9, 1998. Dr. Bryant arrived at 130W Nebraska Hall at 8:00 a.m. to set up his power point presentation. Mr. Armstrong also arrived somewhat earlier than usual. Both were seated in the back of the room facing the front of the classroom as students slowly filled the space with the cacophony of noise and conversations. Dr. Isernhagen arrived last that morning. She immediately placed her papers on the table next to Mr. Armstrong and turned toward the students with a loud, "Good morning!" Dr. Bryant's presentation introduced students to multiple philosophies and theories of alternative approaches to school administration. The content, engaging as it was, provoked a thirty-minute highly animated discussion in which not only students challenged the merits of presented arguments but also collaborating instructors—who frequently disagreed with each other—further stimulating the heated debate. A brief video presentation filled the class time up to the first break. The class resumed at 10:50 a.m. with Dr. Bryant continuing his lecture on the theory of administration. After a short reflection, students kept charging with an onslaught of questions until the topic of the day appeared somewhat exhausted. Dr. Isernhagen, less frequently Mr. Armstrong, interjected their ideas into the discussion. After a long hour of highly esoteric intellectual back and forth Dr. Bryant requested that representatives from every group meet with the instructors to discuss the progress of their group projects. Students met with their respective teams to work on the projects at noon. Half an hour later, six group's representatives met with the instructors again on the fifth floor of Nebraska Hall in the same room where the collaborators had met for their planning session a week earlier. Since it was a lunch time and the room was adjacent to the kitchen the atmosphere was quite jovial with people coming in and out eating and drinking heartily. The entire class felt more like a party. Some time passed when both instructors and students gathered around two large tables. The primary purpose of the meeting was to elaborate on the group projects. The meeting took about thirty minutes. Dr. Bryant outlined the projects' main objectives and students followed up with clarifying questions. Dr. Isernhagen and Mr. Armstrong responded to the questions, sometimes asking each other to gain more clarity on the purpose and the objectives of particular segments of the project. At 1:30 p.m., the purposeful meeting adjourned.

Fourth Class

On June 10, 1999, entire class was wearing athletic attire in preparation for this afternoon team building exercises at Doane College, Nebraska. Even Dr. Isernhagen, who always made it a point to dress up for teaching, was wearing blue jeans and a red short-sleeved shirt on that day. One of the priests gave up his black attire for the sake of exercises as well (or perhaps just lost his faith...I didn't ask). Unfortunately, June 10 was a surprisingly cloudy day. Frankly, it looked like it was going to rain. All three instructors were readily lined up by the board waiting for the students to arrive. At 8:30 a.m., Dr. Isernhagen took charge by commencing a debriefing on the status of group projects. Everybody got so involved in discussions they barely noticed time had arrived for the first morning break. After the break at 10:15 a.m., Mr. Armstrong took over the leadership of the classroom and within forty minutes introduced students to the concept of change and creativity. He used a number of teaching methods including magic tricks, which apparently connected well with students who laughed heartily at the presented examples or I should say tricks. Dr. Bryant and Dr. Isernhagen sat together by the board at the time. Their gentle whispers and barely audible susurration could be hardly detected from a distance so as not to disrupt the class. The activities seemed to achieve the desired effect and stimulated students thinking "out of the box," in the words of Mr. Armstrong. The entire event could only be construed as a success, since a long discussion followed with students and instructors generating ideas and sharing experiences with each other. Throughout the entire time, Drs. Bryant and Isernhagen observed the audience interactions without really commenting much at all. Due to weather complications and impending rain, the scheduled trip to Doane College, a private college also located in Nebraska, was cancelled. Instead, students were invited to the Department of Educational Administration which recently relocated to the fifth floor of Nebraska Hall. The primary purpose was to introduce students to the staff and, most importantly, the departmental chair Dr. Larry Dlugosh. Shortly before noon, all students gathered in a large well-lit room capable of accommodating large audiences. Students sat in a circle behind tiny desks with instructors seated at the very back of the room. Dr. Dlugosh entered the circle and thanked students for choosing their program and outlined a very optimistic picture of the future work opportunities for educators with administrative degrees. After that short but informative speech, Dr. Isernhagen encouraged students to meet in groups to continue their work on the projects and wished students a nice weekend.

Fifth Class

The weekend passed and three days later on June 14, 1999, the students arrived back in the classroom refreshed to conquer the second week of that intensive five-week course. Although the day was sunny, it was not humid at all and classroom temperature was low enough to make everyone comfortable. Dr. Isernhagen stepped into the center of the class and in her usually energetic fashion stated, "Good morning!" After a brief outline of the intended schedule for the day, she referred to the first group responsible for so called "morning meeting" in which groups alternated with short introductory presentations relevant to the topic of the day. Meanwhile, Mr. Armstrong ensconced comfortably by Dr. Isernhagen sat behind the desk at the front of the classroom directly facing the students who briskly stepped into the center of the classroom and initiated their presentation. Approximately forty minutes later, Dr. Bryant arrived quietly and took a seat nearby his colleagues. By 9:45 a.m. both the presentations and the following discussion were over. Dr. Bryant invited students to "grab a bagel and a drink" and slowly get moving to the Beedle Center where the presentation of a film on issues facing teachers and administrators in poverty stricken districts would take place. The Beedle Center was nestled in a lush green setting one mile south from Nebraska Hall. The class met in a high tech auditorium of the newly built science building. The center was a capacious polygon-shaped capacious room with fifteen rows of red seats neatly arranged one behind the other. Auditorium did remind a traditional movie theater. All students, as if magically attracted to each other, chose to congregate at its very center. That arrangement however made the following discussion easier to facilitate–perhaps mature graduate students understood that intuitively. At 10:15 a.m., Dr. Bryant started the computer-controlled projector and the "show" began. The lights were dimmed and the subdued murmuring slowly died away and the room filled with silent expectation of the advertised event. Collaborating instructors chose to sit on the opposite ends of the room and by doing so strategically surrounded the students. About sixty minutes into the projection, Dr. Bryant approached Dr. Isernhagen, who was seated far to the left at the front of the auditorium. They exchanged a few thoughts and after approximately seventy minutes Dr. Bryant approached the switchboard and turned off the projector. After the lights came back on, Dr. Bryant students were asked the students for reactions. Apparently each student took something else from the film since almost everybody seemed to have a different opinion, including the instructors. Over time, however, Mr. Armstrong began to detect patterns of issues that surfaced most fervidly. After an additional fifteen minutes of sharing, Dr. Bryant ended the meeting with his concluding commentary and a few minutes before noon all participants egressed the auditorium for an hour-long break. After the lunch at 1:00 p.m., students were welcomed by the guest speaker who presented the topic of students' multifaceted personalities and their respective applications for the work of teachers and administrators. The presentation was informative as well as interactive with all present involved in the discussion in some way. During the activities, the instructors mingled with students in all three classes to their disposal, occasionally taking seats for a more in-depth conversation with more engaging students. At 3:30 p.m. Dr. Bryant customarily thanked the speaker for the presentation and, after a short outline of the activities for the following day, class was dismissed.

Sixth Class

On June 15, 1999 early in the morning, students appeared in the class still a little drowsy. One was trying to wake up by yawning secretly. Others used more proven methods of sipping freshly brewed coffee. The remainder chatted with their peers. Soon after 8:30 a.m., Dr. Bryant requested group numbers to take charge of the "morning meeting." For today's occasion, the scheduled presenters chose to focus on vouchers and school finances. Mr. Armstrong hidden somewhat at the back of the classroom observed the presentation. At about 9:00 a.m., Dr. Isernhagen arrived and stealthily snuck into the classroom so as not to disturb the students. The disquisition of sort was followed up by a short discussion which began rather slowly but, over time, it evolved into quite a whirlwind of heated argumentations when issues became more defined and opinions polarized. When appropriate, Dr. Isernhagen and Mr. Armstrong contributed their own remarks which, due to their practical nature, brought students' high-winded ideas down to earth. Dr. Bryant, on the other hand, as the most experienced academic with highly theoretical inclinations of his mind elevated the discussion to higher levels of abstruse theories and esoteric models. The activities that followed dispersed students around the floor sending groups to either room 130W or the adjacent 129W. The instructors strolled between the classrooms inspecting students' work and delivering succor when needed. And indeed the opportunities for aid arose frequently. After each group presented their conclusions to the entire audience, the class took a break at 10:50 a.m. and reconvened fifteen minutes later as usual in room 130W. Within the next hour, students focused analyzing hypothetical examples prepared by instructors. The task was to select the best candidate for the administrative job and provide appropriate rationale for the decision. Based on students' performance this far in the course, the instructors met in close proximity to each other to identify most optimal "complicator" to increase the level of task difficulty and enrich students' learning experience in the process. Thirty minutes passed when Dr. Isernhagen provided students with a clearly defined "complicator" that instructors agreed on in the meantime. Sauntering from room to room, the instructors continued to interact with the students. At noon, all groups assembled in room 130W. Dr. Bryant initiated the descant over the freshly completed simulation. Soon after, Dr. Isernhagen took over leading the discourse throughout the entire session. On a rare occasion Mr. Armstrong enriched the discussion with his own commentary. Thus far, that was the only function he fulfilled in this session. Class ended at 1:00 p.m. Students continued their work on group simulations till late afternoon.

Seventh Class

On June 16, 1999, the electricity in a large part of the city went out leaving best part of Lincoln's population stranded at homes. A number of students fell victim to this unprecedented inconvenience and 'conveniently' did not show up for class. Lack of access to hot water and malfunctioning traffic lights made commute too onerous for too many, especially those with small children who could not make it to schools on their own. Even though the class may have lacked the quorum, Dr. Isernhagen nevertheless asked a scheduled team to begin their introductory presentation. Today's subject explored "leadership styles." Students got engaged in their diurnal group activities customarily by now some staying in class no. 130W others migrating to the adjacent room no. 129W. Instructors ambled between the classrooms providing feedback when needed. Perhaps affected by the blackout Dr. Bryant arrived slightly later this morning at 9:00 a.m. quietly slipping into the classroom. When gathered together, the instructors updated each other on the raised in the morning topics and the most pressing issues facing students today. Shortly before 10:00 a.m., Dr. Bryant praised students leading the task for the productive morning warm-up and swiftly delineated schedule for the remaining part of the day. This time each student was asked to record thirty-second long speech which were later to be watched and analyzed by the entire audience. Almost instantaneously the buzz of justifiably anxious conversations erupted. Instructors helped to set up cameras in two neighboring rooms. Despite palpable jitters and apprehension accompanying any speech, all students completed the task successfully. Nobody passed out! Soon after, the relieved students walked obediently to the designated destination of the Design Center at Henzlik Hall where a guest speaker was ready to instruct students on the use of computerized spreadsheets. All participants arrived on time visible anxious to face yet another course obstacle–spreadsheets! How much stress can a person take during one day? Students seemed to ask themselves. Nonetheless they seated themselves behind computers filling most of the available spaces. One of the students introduced the guest speaker who agreed to share her knowledge and experience with the new tool. Dr. Bryant and Dr. Isernhagen mingled with students, or I should say ran from one student to another trying to extinguish fires that exploded among distressed and frustrated students. Mr. Armstrong sat at the back of the class seemingly supervising everybody else. Three to four other students with prior Excel knowledge and experience joined instructors helping struggling peers to avert all-out panic. The activity took approximately two hours and ended at the scheduled 3:00 p.m.

Eighth Class

On June 17, 1999, shortly before 8:30 in the morning, Dr. Bryant and Mr. Armstrong arrived in the classroom taking seats behind the front table. Since Dr Isernhagen left for a conference, for the first time students faced two collaborators only. Dr. Bryant began the class with a brief outline of the activities scheduled for the day and invited scheduled students to initiate a morning presentation. Revisions of individual video samples recorded a day before followed soon after. Upon careful review, Dr. Bryant applauded students for their work and turned to Mr. Armstrong with a declarative statement, "I think it's time for you to take it up!" Instantaneously Mr. Armstrong stood up approached the board switched on an overhead projector and began the presentation on educational leadership. A method Mr. Armstrong chose to convey his knowledge was a lecture and material presented appeared very dry factual and research driven. That put a little stumper on otherwise lively and engaging morning. Students however looked interested in the presented material with some taking detailed notes while others simply listened attentively. In general a presentation continued almost uninterruptedly with students infrequently interjecting questions. A few minutes before noon, Dr. Bryant applauded students for the quality participation sending them off to continue work on their simulation projects.

Ninth Class

On June 21, 1999, students slowly poured into the classroom. For the first time, Dr. Bryant was alone when the class began at 8:30 a.m. He was sitting behind the front table talking to a couple students occupying front row seats. A few minutes later, one of the assigned groups began the class with their presentation. Most of the class activities on that day took place in groups and as routinely students migrated between neighboring classrooms. Dr. Bryant allowed students complete freedom to lead the discussion. Mr. Armstrong arrived at the very end of the presentation sneaking in imperceptibly through the back door. Ten minutes later, Dr. Bryant asked students to assemble in Beedle Center where a documentary would be presented on developing public speaking skills. Slightly prior to 10:00 a.m., morning activities ended and students moved to the Beedle Center as instructed. It was the same auditorium where students watched another documentary a week before. Dr. Bryant was already sitting in the first row when first students arrived. Again students converged in the middle of the auditorium conversing vociferously when the projection began. Gradually the susurration died away with students seemingly turning into zombies enthralled by the allure of the silver screen. Soon upon completion of the film, which took about thirty minutes, Dr. Bryant turned to the audience for the commentaries. Students didn't disappoint and provided instructors and each other with a lively exchange of ideas frequently penetrating observations. The class was dismissed at 11:00 a.m. only to rejoin two hours later back in Nebraska Hall. The remaining two hours of the class were dedicated to career-related opportunities. The presentation was delivered by the guest speaker arranged for that day by Mr. Armstrong. At 3:00 p.m., the rewarding class ended.

Tenth Class

In the latter part of the course, cohesion among collaborating instructors began to break loose. A hundred percent classroom presence of all three instructors started to crumble. The variety of academic pressures and departmental demands began to exert pressure on the team. The following day, on June 22, 1999, class was led exclusively by Dr. Bryant. After a quick outline of the activities scheduled for the rest of the week, he swiftly moved to the diurnal introductory group presentation. The team introduced the concept of leadership. Considering the number of questions Dr. Bryant asked the students, it was quite apparent leadership theory was one of his favorite topics. Indeed his command of the topic was impressive. At about 10:00 a.m., Dr. Bryant released students for a short fifteen-minute break. At precisely 10:15 a.m., Dr. Bryant started his disquisition on the collection and analysis of quantitative research data. The class paused at 11:40 a.m. for a short break upon which students reconvened to continue work on the simulation projects.

Eleventh Class

On June 23, 1999, the class met at 128 Mabel Lee at 8:30 a.m. The building was located at the north side of the City Campus nearby Nebraska Hall crunched between the Recreational Center and Henzlik Hall. Small rectangular room in which students met was specifically outfitted to accommodate technical requirements of long distance education. It was equipped with three TV sets, two computer monitors for the leading instructors, two cameras, and a number of black microphones hanging from the ceiling. Dr. Bryant and Dr. Isernhagen sat next to each other in the first row, while Mr. Armstrong mingled with students at the back of the class. One of the enrolled in the course student who happened to be involved in long-distance education took upon himself to make an hour-long overview of the topic. Based on their own limited experience with the delivery of long-distance education, Dr. Bryant and Dr. Isernhagen pitched in with occasional remarks. The presentation wrapped up at 9:50

a.m. After quickly recapitulating major highlights of the freshly acquired knowledge, Dr. Bryant announced that rest of the day would be marked by each group meeting individually with collaborating professors to provide update on the simulation progress. Students dutifully marched back to Nebraska Hall and at 10:30 a.m. first group faced the instructors in the conference room. Drs. Bryant and Isernhagen sat next to each other. Mr. Armstrong, on the other hand, distanced himself visible them by taking a seat at the other side of the table. By the time the second group arrived, Dr. Bryant turned to Mr. Armstrong with a request, "Sit closer to us." Mr. Armstrong happily obliged moving his chair closer to the center. That welcoming gesture seemed to encourage Mr. Armstrong who took a visibly more active role in the review by asking more questions and contributing follow-up suggestions on how to improve the groups' performance. The first group arrived at precisely 10:30 a.m. and presented the results of their simulation. Each group began with a brief description of the results followed by instructors asking probing questions to make sure they fully understood the rationale for each decision made. Closing arguments focused on hypothetical scenarios and brainstorming potential decisions to address the problem. While hypothesizing and prognosticating, instructors made direct references to a number of theories and models introduced throughout the course. The remaining groups followed the same pattern. The last group was released at 1:30 p.m.

Twelfth Class

At 8:30 in the morning, on June 24, 1999, the three collaborating instructors were sitting in silence facing students. Soon after, when a group of students began their preparation for the morning presentation atmosphere turned rather hectic. In the meantime, Dr. Bryant outlined organizational issues for the day. Not to waste any time, Dr. Isernhagen distributed bulletins and questionnaires among the students. "Education as a privilege" was the leading theme of the opening discussion. Throughout the entire presentation, all three instructors sat together occasionally asking questions and elaborating on the debated ideas. Watching students arguing and generating (or as Mr. Armstrong would have it "constructing") novel concepts along with instructors was a truly learning in the making. After a brief ten-minute break at 10:30 a.m., students returned to the scheduled activities with alacrity. Dr. Bryant immediately stepped into the center of the class to elicit students' feedback on their learning experience thus far in the course. The overall feedback was quite positive. One student said, "What makes this class great is the fact that all three teachers present to me a different perspective. Jody says the sky is blue. Miles says no, it isn't. And Gene gives the perspective of a practitioner. And that's what makes the learning experience great." Another student also volunteered her perspective, "I think it's a really good team. I appreciate the different personalities." Soon after 1:00 p.m. Dr. Isernhagen introduced a guest speaker slated to talk about "Option II Paper" (an equivalent of a Master's thesis for a professional Master of Education degree). While Mr. Armstrong sat at the back of the classroom, Dr. Isernhagen and Dr. Bryant help to set up power point equipment for the presenter. Soon after Dr. Bryant joined Mr. Armstrong at the back of the classroom. Lights went off and the show began. Well into the middle of the presentation, Dr. Bryant asked students for a minute of reflection requesting a short recapitulation of the main points presented. Ten minutes before 3:00 p.m., Dr. Isernhagen and Dr. Bryant wrapped up the presentation by providing final advice of their own. At 3:00 p.m., Dr. Bryant expressed gratitude for the quest speaker's valuable contribution and wished students a nice weekend.

Thirteenth Class

June 28, 1999, welcomed students with a rainy Monday morning. At 8:30 a.m. from inside the classroom, the surroundings outside seemed almost pitched dark, as if those inside were looking into a dark void. As if trying to lift the spirits of the assembled group, instructors as well as students conversed vigorously. One of the students turned to the priest who just entered the classroom with a sardonic comment, "You look half awake." Mr. Armstrong, on the other hand, looked habitually cheerful. That was undoubtedly his most defining quality. In fact, his cheerful disposition was always quite contagious. Even his dress code–black pants with a fresh well pressed white shirt– reflected neat optimism during that otherwise gloomy morning. Dr. Bryant started the class with a quick announcement that the quest speaker scheduled for that day for reasons outside her control would not appear in class as scheduled. Dr. Bryant elicited feedback on the "chat activity" that students worked on during the weekend. Being an originator of the task, Dr. Isernhagen was heavily involved in the discussion. Fifteen minutes into the session, one of the groups took the lead of the daily presentation which for a change focused on the generational differences and their implications for educators. Students presented the topic, which generated a heated discussion which involved both students and instructors. At 10:20 a.m., Dr. Bryant announced the class was over for the day and students as usual headed for a group meeting.

Fourteenth Class

Right before 8:30 in the morning, on June 29, 1999, Dr. Isernhagen and Mr. Armstrong sat behind the front desk conversing quietly in an almost empty classroom. Five minutes later the buzz of entering students filled the entire classroom so much so that instructors had to move their chairs closer to each other to continue their conversation. Like the day before, the world outside the classroom looked ominously dark and cloudy. Just when Dr. Bryant arrived, Dr. Isernhagen displayed a list of assigned groups scheduled for the following activity. The students' task was to select a variety of pictures that, in their opinions, best presented the situation in the studied school district. Dr. Isernhagen and Mr. Armstrong joined groups in classroom 130 W, while Dr. Bryant worked with the teams occupying classroom 129W. After approximately twenty minutes, all students reconvened back in 130W to interpret the images, their meanings, and applications. Interestingly enough, one of the students commented on the image identified by Dr. Isernhangen, "That picture presents to me three professors who present to us in this course different perspectives: principal, professor, and superintendent. While students exchanged their ideas, Mr. Armstrong stood up to collect the visual aids used in the activity. After the discussion reached its climax and students' enthusiasm started to wane, Dr. Isernhagen distributed a sign-up list for groups to decide on the dates of the final project presentations. At 10:00 a.m., Dr. Bryant stood up and announced they were not going to meet in the afternoon, except for those students who were scheduled to participate in the chat-rooms. He briefly outlined the schedule for the following day and ended the class for the day.

Fifteenth Class

Right before 8:30 in the morning, on June 30, 1999, a guest speaker–Dr. Larry Dlugosh (chair of the Department of Educational Administration) accompanied Mr. Armstrong and Dr. Isernhagen. The classroom was filled with buzz of students discussing their final projects. A few minutes later Dr. Bryant joined the faculty and officially introduced the guest. The group's morning presentation attempted to differentiate the concept of "virtue" and "value". This very philosophical topic stirred lots of argumentation among the audience. A number of alternative explanations were raised in the process. Dr. Isernhagen rather passionately wrote down most of the presented material in her notebook. After a short break at 10:00 a.m., students returned to the classroom and Dr. Dlugosh took over. The thesis of his disquisition was based on the reviewed literature dealing with current issues facing educators in the technologically and culturally changing society. Collaborating instructors positioned themselves on opposite sides of the classroom, de facto surrounding the students. Dr. Isernhagen, who assiduously wrote down the presented ideas, was situated closely by the door at the front of the classroom. Dr. Bryant on the other hand stood by the window on the right with Mr. Armstrong seated leisurely at the back of the classroom. Upon concluding his presentation and shortly entertaining a brief Q & A session, Dr. Bryant left the classroom leaving faculty and students still arguing the merits of the presented material. The class ended thirty minutes before noon. Dr. Isernhagen invited scheduled students for their "chat-rooms" at 2:00 in the afternoon.

Sixteenth Class

After torrential rain and a tornado warning issued across Lincoln metro area a day before, the weather of July 1, 1999 welcomed students with a beautiful sun and a mild breeze. At 8:30 in the morning, all the surroundings seemed orderly and the class ready to begin. All instructors were present on that day. Dr. Isernhagen and Mr. Armstrong conversed lightly right by the entrance door. Dr. Bryant, stationed in his favorite place by the window, chatted with a few students who approached him a few minutes earlier. When the time arrived, Mr. Armstrong stepped into the center of the classroom with a robust, "Okay, the bell has rung!" He quickly presented students with a quote of the day, provided a brief commentary, and quietly receded to the back of the classroom. Dr. Isernhagen took his place and introduced students to the topic of the day. Since yesterday's subject introduced by students a day before spurred a lot of controversies and polemics, the instructors adjusted the plan and decided to continue the subject of virtues and values. However, this time decision was made to focus the content on school leadership alone. While engaged students passionately applied the knowledge to the environments in their own school districts, instructors met together at the front of the classroom to fill out some past due paperwork. Except for a few occasional exchanges, each focused on his or her own task. It did not take more than forty minutes when Dr. Isernhagen in a characteristically energetic fashion began discussion that filled the rest of the morning. Although the debate itself was heated, the temperature in the classroom was quite chilly—so much so that one of the students commented to his friend, "It's kind of cold here!" While Dr. Bryant and Dr. Isernhagen stimulated discussion with comments and suggestions, Mr. Armstrong withdrew toward the back of the class providing one or two comments only. Once again, probably not by design or even intentionally instructors surrounded students from all sides. A few minutes before noon, Dr. Isernhagen recapitulated major points of the day and stated, "We are going to end the session with Gene's quote." She allowed students thirty seconds to ponder over the statement. Then, without further notice, class was dismissed at noon sharp. At 2:00 p.m., Dr. Isernhagen invited students for their individual "chat-rooms" as usual.

Seventeenth Class

The final week was almost exclusively filled with students' presentations. On July 6, 1999, all collaborating instructors were seated at the very back of the classroom with Drs. Bryant and Isernhagen close to each other and Mr. Armstrong slightly removed to the right. The entire session was divided into three equal parts, approximately two-hours long, during which individual groups presented the results of their simulations. Groups varied in styles of submission. Some used technology such as power points, others traditional transparencies only. The dress code also differed from very professional to semi-professional. None of the students, however, wore shorts on that day. In terms of the process, all groups followed the same generic pattern. Upon the conclusion of each presentation, instructors provided brief commentaries occasionally submitting questions to vitalize audience and further prompt the classroom conversations putting final critical thinking touches. Dr. Bryant and Dr. Isernhagen developed an interesting dynamics. When Dr. Isernhagen posed a question, Dr. Bryant almost immediately reinforced the point with his additional comment adding another dimension to the developing almost seamlessly constructed knowledge based on students' research findings. Mr. Armstrong limited his commentaries to what an independent observer might construe as a consultancy of sort, not quite in synch with the other two collaborating instructors. That phenomenon, however, was a well-entrenched pattern throughout the duration of the course. After the third group finished their presentation and the short discussion ended at 3:00 p.m., class was dismissed.

Eighteenth Class

July 7, 1999 was another day of presentations. This time groups four through six took the challenge of entertaining the remainder of the audience. Presentations took exact same steps established a day prior each lasting approximately two hours and immediately followed by a brief discussion facilitated by the instructors. Collaborators compared and contrasted presented material among the groups emphasizing each group's strengths but most importantly reinforcing learning points most relevant to the course. Groups completed their presentations at 3:00 p.m., upon which Dr. Bryant thanked students for their "wonderful work."

Nineteenth Class

Since July 8, 1999, was the course's last day, many students must have felt compelled to make a statement by arriving late. The entire morning was busy filling out administrative paperwork such as final course evaluations, assessment sheets prepared by instructors for their own use etc. They spoke to students and each other to gain as much feedback as possible. Not only timing but also dress code for that day was very informal. All students as well as instructors wore shorts and T-shirts. Even the priests always dressed in black wore shorts and T-shirts as well, which made recognizing them from the rest of the group unusually difficult on that day. There was, however, a reason for this extremely relaxed dress code. The "ropes activities" in Doane College, planned earlier but postponed because of the inclement weather conditions, were rescheduled for the last day. A few minutes before noon Dr. Isernhagen distributed directions on how to get to Crete–small city in Nebraska where Doane College is located approximately thirty miles west of Lincoln. The certified instructor scheduled to supervise the activities led the group to a small forest nearby Doane College. The first two activities had a purpose of developing teamwork skills–most prominently trust. They were relatively easy to conduct and therefore involved everybody present. The latter activity presented more of a challenge and consumed ninety percent of time spent in the field. The purpose of the activity was to conquer the fear by climbing over the ropes installed forty feet above the ground, switch the gear in mid-air and finally slide down on the secured line at the other end of the structure. Three female students could not break their fear factors and decided to opt out. Surprisingly, despite a considerate challenge and evident apprehension on the part of participants, students and instructors alike completed the challenge. They not only completed it, but took extreme pride in it. Three female students looked somewhat dejected, perhaps regretting the road not taken. The entire session was over at 5:00 p.m. with all students and instructors rewarding themselves with beer in the local bar.

Development of Issues

In this section, the researcher intends to answer the second of the sub-questions: What are the issues related to collaborative teaching?

Collaboration Defined

"I've got something in my mind that tells me that collaborative teaching means constructing, designing, implementing, delivering, and evaluating–all those things," admitted Dr. Bryant, "I mean you can work with another person where you do a piece of curriculum content and then another person does another piece of curriculum content. You can call that teaming when one person is talking and another is just sitting not participating in any way in any part of the experience. I wouldn't call it a collaborative work, but plenty of people would. So my definition of collaboration involves almost a seamless kind of partnership that is going on where individuals are involved." For Dr. Bryant being together all the time is the collaborative priority, "We don't have specialized roles. We are there all the time. When we are planning we are there together. So we do the work in unison. We don't specialize. You take this piece. I will take this piece." According to Dr. Bryant, a sense of mutuality amongst all collaborating team members especially in the classroom constitutes the essence of a collaborative effort, "So I think the way we've defined collaboration is that there is very much of mutuality so that we hold in class together." For Mr. Armstrong, "Collaboration meant a cooperative effort to plan, to perform whatever the task is, and evaluate together with equal input from all participants." Dr. Isernhagen agreed with Mr. Armstrong almost verbatim, "It is a cooperative activity involving parties from different backgrounds, experiences, walks of life, and focused on the attainment of a set of goals, or series of goals, or a specific outcome that you would like to accomplish." Dr. Isernhagen did not believe a collaborative effort required a particular set of personalities, abilities, or philosophies. It is the "process" itself that makes the collaborative teaching successful, "Sometimes you can have people of very similar abilities and be a winning team. Sometimes you can have people of very different abilities and be a winning team. Sometimes you can have people that lack certain skills and build a winning team. It is the way you frame and go about doing the activity that makes you a winning team."

Relationship Building

While trying to identify first stage in the process of collaborative teaching, Dr. Isernhagen noted, "I would say the very first stage comes in relationship building. And when I say relationship building, I'm talking about things from understanding philosophically and knowing where a person is coming from. Sensitivity to individuals when you are planning, when you are talking, when you are documenting, when you are interacting because that is one of the interrelationship building factors that can set you back." Dr. Isernhagen compared the choice of collaborating partners to selecting a dance partner, "It's almost like choosing a dance partner and making your dance steps all match, and every time somebody steps out it throws the dance off. In a way, it's almost like a marriage. You have to carry out the daily activities and sometimes there is fighting and daily activities that can raise suspicions, they can raise dissatisfaction, they can raise wonderful challenges and wonderful results. I would say relationships, relationships, relationships is probably one of the most key pieces, and then the philosophy that you develop amongst yourselves and then how you carry it out." Dr. Bryant concurred that for successful collaboration "relationships are critical," but he did not think "It has to be a good friend relationship. I think you have to like each other and certainly I think you have to want your colleagues to be successful. First of all, we are not close personal friends. Being good friends creates efficiencies because there are now a lot of things we can know through casual conversations when we know quickly what's on the other persons' mind. We don't have to do a lot of preparatory work. The reason that this course has worked well for those of us who have taught it is that in many ways we are very task-oriented. We have consensus about what we want to accomplish, and we don't let our individualities get in the way of accomplishing that." Although Dr. Bryant believed that this strong task orientation of all collaborating instructors was a guide that kept them from damaging their work, he also acknowledged that "the relationship part is incredibly important. And some of it is just having fun being engaged. And I guess you can't really be engaged with people you don't really have relationships with. In order to collaborate, in order to do the kind of teaching we are doing, you have to spend time constructing and designing. And before you can do that you have to know each other reasonably well." Mr. Armstrong's view on importance of building relationships for the success of collaborative effort didn't diverge much from that of his colleagues, "I think it might be the number one condition. And I don't know whether we will ever have the luxury of having these relationships pretty much solidified before we present, or before we instruct, or construct. If I had to prioritize the importance of relationships, I would say it would be either at or near the very top. I have to know where they are coming from. I have to know where they are strong, where they can use support. And I can only do that by developing a relationship with them. If you are involved in something like we are involved in, then I think relationships come first. Again what I've observed among the few of the groups in our class is that the task isn't completed because the relationships aren't there. So if it's a task that you know you have certain amount of time to complete and it's not a crisis, then the relationships are the most important. Because of the amount of communication and type of communication required in this type of relationship are so important. The mutual respect for one another has to be there. If the respect is there, the communication is there and so is the completion of the task. So again I would have to say that relationships are the highest priority."

Teaching/Learning Philosophy

"If the relationship building that occurs does not simulate how you really are as a person. If you're just being a nice person here and that's not how you really operate, then your teaching philosophies could end up being very different," noted Dr. Isernhagen. Consequently, "The relationship may not stick together. The team teaching may not succeed simply because philosophically you are from different points of view. They all overlap. The relationships are always here. Then the planning phase may be here. Then the implementation phase may be here. Then the evaluation may be here. And permeating the whole thing is your philosophy. One thing that I have found in education is that it is very rarely that you see arrows in models. It's just not the way we operate. Education is just a relationship human humanistic kind of base. It's very difficult for those circles in the models not to overlap each other. There is an interdependence that grows. It never goes away." Dr. Bryant concurred that "Pedagogically speaking, it's important for all collaborating instructors to be on the same plane. However in terms of content, I think it's almost important that there will be differences. Because that way we can give, we can represent different viewpoints for students. We want students to construct their own understandings. It's important that we have differences. I think in this context having different beliefs about educational standards and what schools should look like and that sort of thing, I think it's important that we have differences in beliefs." Commenting on the same issue, Mr. Armstrong noted, "It makes it a lot easier and I think effective if everybody agrees to just a few basic tenets. One of them is learners learn best when they are actively involved. So especially in our environment, we are in a Teachers' College, which means we better have some consistencies in philosophy if we are going to send teachers out who are going to teach the way we think. And the research says it's the best way to teach."

Planning

Considerate of accurately reflecting individual stages involved in collaborative teaching Dr. Isernhagen stated, "Once you get through that relationship building which ties into the planning aspect for me which I think is definitely another stage of collaborative teaching, you get through the planning stage when you are trying to implement your plan with the students. You move into another phase because then Miles take a piece of the class I take a piece of the class. You see us trying to provide balance in the class so everybody has a voice in the class." Mr. Armstrong, on the other hand, struggled with identifying planning as a stage in the process whatsoever, "I can't say that it's a stage. Probably there is more planning in the forming stage, but there is planning through the performing stage. It's kind of ready fire and aim philosophy. You make sure where the target is so you can take aim, but eventually you've got to correct as your job is off course because the target keeps moving. So again I would say the major planning is done during the forming stage but you plan through all four stages." To me said Dr. Bryant, "The planning process is when all of us have an idea of what we will talk about and we decide whether or not to incorporate that into the course. The planning is really from when you start to think creatively about what's the learning experience going to look like—whether we want to hang on to or whether we want to get rid of. We have ideas and we discard them. We have ideas and we accept them. I'm sure we'll make some changes. I doubt we'll use the same textbooks next year for example. We'll do something different."

Course Design

When asked about the importance of their involvement in the design part of the course, Dr. Bryant responded decisively, "I think it's essential. It's one of the most important things about this class. I think if you don't participate in the design of the course and if you don't have any ownership in the class, your work in the class would be passive rather than driven by a real sense of mission and intrinsic motivation." Trying to relate his current experience with collaborative teaching to that in the past Dr. Bryant reminisced, "It's never been, this course has never been that one individual laid-it-all-out. Other people came and participated. It's been a collaborative process in constructing the experience. We change it every year. At the end of the course, we will spend time talking about what we would do differently." As an example, Dr. Bryant alluded to the computer simulation (IESLP) introduced this summer for the first time a response to students' need for acquiring data-driven decision-making skills, "That was done in the characteristic way of how we work together. Jody learned a lot about this case. She got signed up so that she could do it. Mr. Armstrong's participation in the course design was practically nonexistent and consequently so was his ownership in it." "A lot was done before I stepped into the scene," concurred Mr. Armstrong, "The design was already there. By the time I stepped on the scene, they pretty much had an idea. Because of this and lack of knowledge of how the class was run, I wasn't able to contribute a whole lot." He did not however blame his collaborators, "I'm not saying they have exempted me from the design. In fact, they tried to get me involved in the design of it."

Selecting Partners

The experiences with collaborative teaching convinced Dr. Isernhagen that carefully selecting right individuals to have the collaborative relationship with is a crucial decision, "You can match up people from here to sundown and not pick the right people and when put together they could be very discouraged. You almost have to have a sense that this person or these people you are going to work with are on the same wave-link or processing as you are. I think we innately pick partners that we know we can get along with, and that's where you have to start." Proper conscious choice of collaborating partners also found its way to the top of Mr. Armstrong's list, "I think it's probably near the top as far as importance goes." Unfortunately in the case of this collaboration, Mr. Armstrong did not have that choice, "Jody and Miles came to me and invited me to be part of their team. But only after they had become well acquainted with me and how I operate had they decided this guy can fit into the team. I had no voice in the selection of my partners. I may have a voice next semester, but bottom line is I think it's vitally important." Dr. Bryant shared analogous perception, "I think you have to have people you like to work with. If I had a choice, I would choose someone I like more to work with. You can easily get sidetracked as a teacher or professor if all of the sudden you are fighting interpersonal battles with your colleagues. So you know somebody who has some sort of a particular issue that they want to teach students and I happen to think that it doesn't fit in here very well. In fact, if I don't like that other person, then I've got problems talking to that other person who knows why but there will be a sense of reluctance. If you like people, it's much easier to have conversations with them. There is much more trust. And I suppose that trust is the word that is the key. I think that trust is very much the glue that holds the three of us together as a teaching team."

Partnering vs. True Collaboration

Participation in designing the course was crucial for Dr. Isernhagen for at least two reasons,

"Number one it added to the relationship, and number two it increased the feeling of ownership. Where you build the relationship is over the design. And if you don't have opportunity to do that and somebody delivers it to you, then I think you don't feel the ownership for it. If a person owns the change or owns the event they are more likely to be a committed partner to it. I think it's really pretty critical. I think you are partnering when you do something that's somebody has already set up. A true collaboration is when people get together they analyze, synthesize, and decide, and come up together here is our plan. Partnership here is the plan. How do we carry it out with two people is different." To illustrate the notion, Dr. Bryant used a comparison, "It would be like comparing of what you would find in a sort of product development business. Our work is to try to be inventive very analytical."

Professional Development

Dr. Isernhagen expressed a profound conviction that the collaboration she just experienced contributed greatly to her professional development, "The Collaborative setting creates an atmosphere conducive to learning and that creative environment is difficult to create in traditional settings. Sometimes there is a discomfort in going and observing other professionals and seeing what they do. This way, when you work in a collaborative setting you work so closely together that you are able to see them, able to demonstrate skills without putting them in the spotlight where they are uncomfortable. In a collaborative setting, people begin to be very comfortable in sharing things that they would not share otherwise in a professional setting. Not many people just go out and observe somebody. I think there is much greater self-growth when you work in collaboration. You get into the viewpoints of three different individuals. You rally around each other's viewpoints or you say different things. So I think you gain greater insight because of that. Because of that background and experience that all of those people bring to the table everybody goes away with everybody else's experience and modeling. And that modeling is a wonderful thing. It is what you don't get if you do this by yourself or you just go and talk about it or watch somebody else. Without actually being inside their head and doing the planning and that kind of thing, it is difficult to obtain what you get in a collaborative relationship. So I think it's worth it." Content sharing was not the only aspect of what Dr. Isernhagen perceived to be a significant attribute of collaborative teaching, "The delivery, the interaction with students, what is acceptable, what's unacceptable, different styles of delivery of actual activities, how to get students to interact. For instance, Miles values people. He values relationship building. He is very intuitive as far as wanting to know what students are thinking by picking out points and tying together individual points of thinking. I'm not so intuitive yet because I haven't had that experience, but I'm very interested in that." By referring to Dr. Bryant's teaching style and experience, Dr. Isernhagen continued, "So his modeling is very good for me as an individual and I recognize that and value that. So he has something he has a skill almost that I'm interested in pursuing. I have the skill that he is very interested in too and that is I was a recent practitioner. So I have life experience with day to day operations that he knows and values. So there is this reciprocal kind of acceptance that I think has to exist in a team teaching situation. There is a learning piece that occurs between teacher and teacher, teacher to student, student to student and back from student to teacher. So I think all of that is the key piece in collaborative teaching." Although Dr. Bryant believed that as a consequence of this collaboration he also gained as a professional, he was unable to pinpoint precisely how, "My perception of that would be that this has been different because Larry Dlugosh [his previous collaborator] is not involved this time and I'm not sure if I can tell you how it's been different. There are some obvious things and that is that all of them bring experiences that I don't have. I learn from Gene just because he is a professional educator. One of the most important advantages of collaboratively designing the learning experience for twenty-two students is that with doing that with two other colleagues I've got the advantage of looking critically at something that we created." And that common experience is what Dr. Bryant valued most, "What makes me a better teacher is the commonality of the experience. If I take the time to look at that and try to understand how that is of value this summer, then I'll see something different than I saw previously." Dr. Bryant believed it is the process, not the content, from which he learns most, "I don't think it's so much that another professor another colleague teaches me something

It's more of an experience that we share is what teaches me something. Sometimes it happens but that's not the main thing that I see as growth." For Mr. Armstrong, professional development takes place anytime he is exposed to other professionals, "If you have any receptivity at all for their ideas. There are a lot of things I have yet to learn. And like Jody's background is in superintendency. For example, yesterday we were talking about budget–that was a growing experience for me to learn about it from the superintendent perspective." Toward the end of the course Mr. Armstrong was confident that he developed greatly as a professional. Aspects most emphasized included, "First of all I've learned that in higher education or in postsecondary education you can lean more toward laissez-faire, but I didn't think you could. As far as pedagogy of a learner, as far as delivering instruction by other instructors, I've gained some professional knowledge perhaps some skill. It's been great. I've really enjoyed it because I've learned so much about how to teach, how to help kids learn, about topics in education that there is research, the kinds of questions that you ask students to generate conversation." At the end of the course, Dr. Isernhagen, as if summarizing that issue, quoted Dr. Bryant who said, "We've learned so much and we are all learners in this class and every year that I've done this we've been learners. And I think that's what unique. When you are with somebody else, you can be a learner."

Leadership

"Even though I've been here for five years, I look to Miles to being a lead person because he's taught this class for years and years and years. So experience plays a part in that relationship building process," noted Dr. Isernhagen. When describing Mr. Armstrong's role in the collaborative effort she presented quite a different assessment, "And then I look at Gene and he is new to the process and I know he has the level of discomfort just because he is new. So his discomfort is more than mine. And Miles is probably the most comfortable." While speaking of leadership in the context of their team, Dr. Isernhagen noticed, "I think leadership rotates. I don't think it's always the same. I think we just kind of saw Miles as a leader when we first sat down with the group because he is the one with the most tenure. He is the one with the most experience. When we were dealing with the practicality–how the things are going to be carried out–Miles already had it on his computer so he volunteered to do that to keep that updated and to keep that going. When we dealt with ISLEP because I was doing the data testing, they kind of looked at me to get that set up, to get the e-mail addresses." According to Dr. Isernhagen, the planning part was a different story, "When we looked at it, actually sitting down and planning, I think it was kind of leaderless group. Everybody had a voice and an equal voice. We kind of went leaderless. So the leadership rotates. I think we've gone to a leaderless style at some point where we all had equal voice. I think it was based on need at that point in time." Dr. Bryant on the other hand when addressing the concept of team leadership hoped that, "Everybody is in charge. We do different things. There is no particular person that is more important than another person. I would say that three of us, particularly Jody and I and I think Gene, is growing into this. The three of us do the leadership piece together and one thing is important that everybody be there and participates all the time. This joint kind of leadership we created could not take place if somebody disappears and is not present. When decisions need to be made then you have to have a hierarchy. I guess at some point." Perhaps for understandable reasons, Mr. Armstrong's perception differed significantly on that issue, "I still have not seen an example of true collaboration in a sense that everybody is on an equal plane. There is always somebody that is a leader in this case. In my perception Miles is a leader because he's got the experience and expertise. Jody has taught it for several years, but I see her as close to collaboratively on equal with him as anybody. I see myself as another tier below those two. I said to them you've done the planning years and years. I can give suggestions and support, but I still feel like it's a hierarchical set up."

Trust

"In the absence of any kind of hierarchy, another type of glue that holds people together is trust. So there has to be that element of trust," noted Dr. Bryant, "Before you can do this kind of collaborative teaching we are doing is really dependent upon trust." In the same manner Dr. Isernhagen acknowledged trust to be a huge part of relationship building process absolutely necessary to succeed in collaborative teaching, "The degree of trust that's established amongst the parties that are working together. There is almost a code of unwritten rules and how you operate in collaborative building, meaning how you treat each other. I think trust is involved in that. I think communication, conversation is involved in that, and sensitivity are what make the winning team, and the degree to which members have that or can produce that in the collaborative setting." Mr. Armstrong could not agree more with both of them, "And again there is the word of trust that comes to the top–flexibility and trust. If Miles were to take a lead on something and he didn't follow through, then that would affect not only two of us remaining but also twenty-two or three in the class."

Division of Roles

Although personality or aptitude tests were not applied prior to the course, Dr. Bryant believed that each of the collaborators "knew that some of us were good at things and some of us were good at other things. And we sort of let our talents take us into different areas of responsibilities for the course." Dr. Isernhagen observed that their team roles were distributed according to individual strengths and noted that in the collaborative teaching, "Everybody has to feel that they are pulling their own weight. In some team teaching situations, people tend to want to sit back and not to take an active role in that. If one person does all the work that builds animosity, and because of that I think it will eventually come across to the students." Dr. Bryant when reflecting upon the roles individual instructors played on their team stated clearly, "We try not to create a hierarchy. In the case of Gene, he is taking a little bit of a back seat because he does not see himself as equal and it is fine. If he wants to that's fine with me." It was clear from observations that Mr. Armstrong did indeed experience a number of awkward situations that may have led to developing certain inhibitions on his part to see himself as equal vis-à-vis other team members, "My perception is that they perceive me as the one who's been through the experience, practical experience part of it but not academic. And I have difficulty accepting that as a way to make myself equal. I still don't feel like I'm on the same plane as they are with their degrees and their experiences on higher levels." Indeed during the initial stages of collaboration it did seem that most difficult task for Mr. Armstrong was to identify his place and role on the team, "My major role in this situation was to identify where in this situation I fit. Two of them have taught this course many times. It was new to me. I have not only ever taught it, I never took it. So it was new to me." He then noted, "So I saw my role that of filling in some little blank spots. They have the general picture they knew the direction the class needed to go, and I saw my role to support their efforts. They allowed me to interject the ideas, but for the most part the syllabus had already been established. It was just the case of finding out how we are going to implement it. Now when the class started, I continued to support and supplement what they were doing. They have given me some opportunities for leadership that I accepted happily. I guess my job is to identify those moments to take leadership and then to step back when it's time for me to support." According to Mr. Armstrong, one of the positive outcomes of working together as a team was the variety of ways in which instruction delivery was conducted, "Miles uses video his computer, while Jody uses participants with the textbook to present it in a different way. She didn't tell them she allowed students to do that. So I think it's a team that complements itself very well using a variety of styles but each very effective." Mr. Armstrong saw the division of roles being evolutionary in nature, "I see an evolution of roles. Again Jody and Miles know each other very well. The two of them don't know me very well. So there is an evolution of roles as we go on. We discover each other's strengths. We usually look for little strengths. So if somebody has a strength in a certain area this one takes a lead."

Flexibility

"Some of the plans have to be very tentative in team teaching. You write them down and you are trying to go by them, but the conversations that occur in this class are as important as the plan," acknowledged Dr. Isernhagen, "Conversations can get very deep. Threads that leap from conversation about society to education and back, opposing viewpoints within the class that's what the class is about–having people sort out in their minds which pieces they want to pull." Dr. Bryant's view in that regard was quite similar, "If you propose something and the other members of the team say no, well then: What's your reaction to that rejection? How do you deal with that?" I think if the environment in which you design the work as a collaborative professor is that you expect that some ideas may work some may not work then you are not personally insulted by that. In our context it's critical. Since we don't know what students are going to do or what the needs of the groups will be until they unfold before us, you have to be flexible. So flexibility is extremely important." Similarly Mr. Armstrong noted, "Flexibility–absolutely! I don't know how anybody can teach collaboratively without being flexible, and I see a great deal of that in the two with whom I'm working. When you work on your own, there is only person you affect. When there are three of you, it impacts all three of you. If one of the three has caused a need for flexibility, the other two have to go along and support or modify."

Training & Development

"I've never had any formal training. I learned how to collaborate by getting together," began Dr. Isernhagen, "I have gone to formal trainings since we started collaborating, because it gives me insights into what we must do to build effective collaboration. If people are interested in collaboration, one of the best ways to learn is to sit down with others who are interested in collaboration and talk about what it is that we want to do together." At the same time, Dr. Isernhagen was not quite sure if formal training would have a lot of meaning before instructors actually get together and start dealing with real issues, "I think until you have done it I'm not sure that training is going to be so meaningful. But if you are in trying to build collaboration and you are working with people and you are going to training. I think it would be very helpful, because it kind of helps to sort the pieces." To some extent, she was apprehensive that training professors in this area before they actually embark on any collaborative work may unnecessarily scare some of them, "It's tough if people think that something's going to be a lot of work, they often won't even embark on it. So to do it right before you go in if you knew you were going to do it collaboratively and if you knew the steps and the stages, it may be like the stages of change–you know what the steps are. I'm not sure that helps you to go through the change. Because if people don't interact and don't want to be collaborative in nature anyway, if they don't have a desire to share with one another across the table before the planning of any class comes about, then I say again there is a difference between partnering and collaborating." Dr. Bryant, on the other hand, expressed some level of discomfort with the expression "training." He stated, "Well I don't know about training. I'm a little bit uncomfortable with the word training. I guess that is probably because of my experience as a teacher. So you become a teacher and then you learn to modify what you do. There are other ways of teaching. And I think at that point in your career learning to do collaborative work is probably important. So I wouldn't see a pre-service training, probably in-service program would allow people to experiment and try things out." Dr. Bryant was convinced that collaborative teaching should be reserved for more experienced faculty, "I still believe that the teacher needs to have something to teach. That's the first stage that you need to go through—you need to master the field the discipline. Once you acquired the foundations of knowledge and expertise, you are able to teach to lecture to center on the kind of method you use. Once you accomplish that, then I think you can start to modify that and do other kind of teaching such as collaboration with other professors." However, according to Mr. Armstrong teaching teachers how to collaborate beforehand is a valuable experience, "Because preparation would be done in the light of the fact that collaborators would know some of the techniques of collaboration. Right now, it appears to me that we learn collaboration by doing it, exposure to it. The necessity to get something done we collaborate in certain ways. We really want collaborative teaching, but I think the reason that most people don't is because they don't understand it. Techniques of collaboration would be wonderful to be taught. There are techniques of collaboration that you just don't walk and understand."

Time Commitment

According to Mr. Armstrong, collaborative teaching, as compared to traditional individual approach, takes more time at the beginning only with savings accruing later in the process, "I think it takes more time at the beginning, less time later. I think if you do it by yourself, you plan as much as you can early but as you go on you are responsible for keeping these things going on. It takes more time in the middle and the end—I mean the individual, collaboratively it takes less." Mr. Armstrong learnt that planning part of collaborative teaching takes and moreover should take most of the time, "With collaborative planning, I think it should take more time because you need to determine who needs to do what and that can be done during the planning period. Mr. Armstrong gave a lot of credit to his colleagues for the planning part of the course, "Miles put tons of time because he did all the paperwork. He got it done in hard copy. Jody helped and I helped too." According to Dr. Isernhagen, "Only the first stage of building relationships is time consuming, all other stages that follow rest on this foundation. You have to be willing to dedicate time to the process of collaboration and sometimes I think once you get into a collaborative relationship and you build the relationship, everything works so smoothly and so fast." Dr. Bryant concurred, "Well the collaboration requires the way we've done this spending a lot of time together to negotiate and come to agreement. We all have different ideas and when we all come together and talk about it, well we shall do that or not." Dr. Bryant further agreed that over the years of working with Dr. Isernhagen, they spent a lot of time together introducing ideas, accepting and sometimes discarding them, "That's going on as we have taken the time to come together and make proposals." To the question if overall collaborative teaching takes more time than individual teaching, Mr. Armstrong responded "No, I think not. What I think is important is that the three of us know whose shoulders a particular responsibility will fall on. And once that happens, the two of us trust that this task will get done." Dr. Bryant on the other hand thought collaborative teaching does take more time, "Oh it takes a lot more time. To do a really good job with any class takes a lot of preparation time. But the difference here is that we spend so much time in class together. But we treat it as an opportunity rather than a problem. If we didn't spend that time together that would be a very different collaboration." Dr. Bryant shared a piece of advice with those who intend to teach collaboratively, "If I were to give some advice to somebody who is thinking about doing this, I would say well the first thing you have to do is to make sure that you can commit the time planning and delivery."

Need for Collaboration

Attempting to formulate rationale for which academic instructors would want to collaborate, Dr. Bryant identified two basic reasons, "One is the need for some sort of instructional delivery that is best served by collaboration. There are times when people do collaboration for collaboration sake, just because they think that's the thing to do. So they do it not because there is a need for collaboration, but because they are committed to collaboration ideologically and philosophically. This course began because there was a need for collaboration. Historically, this course had a high number of students and simply that fact alone always required that there would be a number of people assigned to do it. So the model always was a number of professors teaching it." Although the enrollment in this particular course dropped down over the years from seventy to present twenty, for Dr. Bryant, "Numbers are not driving the need for multiple professors in this case. We saw that each of us had different strengths and different weaknesses, and that if we utilize those in an integrative way in this sort of constructivist philosophy, we could probably design pretty good things for students." Mr. Armstrong agreed, "Philosophically, I feel that two maybe three people can accomplish more than two people separately, mainly because you have different perspectives on the same subject. In true collaboration, you have as many perspectives as there are participants." Mr. Armstrong frequently asked himself this question: Can three people working collaboratively accomplish more than three people working separately with thirty-three students? "I'm inclined to think yes. Mainly because there can be one person presenting the material, and two people can be observing or supporting students and maybe will see things that one person who is presenting doesn't see. I even think with seventy to a hundred students you can give more honest legitimate feedback than you can give by yourself." For Dr. Isernhagen, the primary reason for multiple instructors was "So that students get a more defined and rounded philosophy of education, a more balanced approach to administrative leadership. What Miles might see he sees through his perceptions and his eyes and his experiences. Likewise, I do the same and Gene does the same." Dr. Isernhagen pointed to other differences she found relevant, "It just happens that I'm elementary based, Gene is very high school based, and Miles had private school experience; and I think it comes through when you start talking about administrative leadership." Dr. Isernhagen, however, made it clear she didn't see that to be the only reason for which academic teachers might want to collaborate, "I think other reasons that people teach collaboratively is because they learn new ideas from the people that they work with. It's an opportunity to bounce off new techniques and have somebody else who can say you know I've tried that one time before and here is what happens, maybe if I had done this and so. It's a frame that gives an opportunity to share and try with others new ideas, have other people to sit and look at it and see why it worked or why it didn't work. Collaborative teaching is a way to have a dialogue about your own teaching, about students that you encounter on a daily basis. We touched on the students, we touched on a teacher, we touched on the content itself. I think people can bring in the actual content from their own perspective through their readings that they've had and the research that they've had. Miles quotes somebody who is an expert researcher. I quote somebody who is a staff developer. So I think it gives a whole different set up of readings and ways to analyze the literature, so even content is being impacted." According to Dr. Isernhagen the size of the class should dictate the need for increased number of instructors, "I think that the larger the group of students the more collaborative teaching could be used to your advantage. Number one, you can break them into smaller groups when you get to certain stages, and then reverse it back when you want to present general information. Gene is going to take one person and talk with him and I'm going to take somebody else and talk with her based on our own styles." To support her viewpoint. Dr. Isernhagen provided a concrete example, "There was a student that I know is not going to respond to a female. Just from being in the room and listening and hearing, it would be much better if the information came from a male. So I think this is in and of itself another reason for collaborative teaching. We don't like to think about it, but I think it's true. I think there are some people that relate better and are more comfortable with certain types of individuals, especially when you are talking about something that might be sensitive to them."

Objectivity

When devising most equitable method of assessing students' work Dr. Bryant proposed that, "We each will read students' journal and pass them around. So I think we focus on somebody's learning and we do that as sort of a team. It would be like a team of doctors working with a patient. What's the best thing for this person. We get three sets of bias." Dr. Isernhagen saw collaborative teaching as a conduit to increase objectivity and opportunity to better meet students' needs, "When you have more than one point of view about an individual student and what their needs are, you are more likely to meet the individual needs of the students. It's that verification on a daily basis from someone else."

Risk Taking

Dr. Bryant believed that because there are several persons on a team, it would be easier to make certain drastic changes in the way the course is to be conducted, "We made a decision a long time ago not to grade students, and that's a risk in the university environment. And we have been criticized for that. We have been criticized by colleagues for giving away a grade." However, Dr. Bryant defended his position, "Because there are several of us doing that, that's easier to do than if we were teaching on ourselves." Dr. Isernhagen indicated she agreed with Dr. Bryant, "I think you are probably more likely to be a risk taker only because you know there is somebody else there that can monitor that somewhat. In this environment it can go two ways. If I'm comfortable with my team members, I may be more of a risk taker simply because I have them to rely on. That way if something doesn't get across correctly, they are going to straighten it out. On the other hand if I'm not comfortable with my team members, I may take a lower sense of risk in the classroom. So I think the comfort level would play a big role in that." Dr. Isernhagen also pointed to differences between the members of their team, "I think with Miles and I we are very comfortable. Gene is still more tentative, but I think he is becoming more comfortable as we go along and as he gets to feel comfortable, he's much more likely to interject and add ideas now than he was at the beginning." Surprisingly, Mr. Armstrong expressed a completely different take on the proclivity for risk-taking in the context of the collaborative effort, "If I wouldn't have to answer to anybody if I were just one, but if you are in collaborative situation you've got two people watching. It is not a calculated risk. In other words, it is one that has a reasonable chance of succeeding. And I'm not sure it's all bad, because I think you need feedback just like the students need feedback. I would probably tend to take more chances if I were there by myself." In conclusion, Dr. Bryant made a note about his perception of students' awareness that three sets of eyes were watching them, "We read their journals each of us reads their journals, and we all respond to those. So we are watching all the time. I think students understand that we are watching."

Modeling

"There are three of us because we hope we model every day the kind of activity that we want them to be able to see what happens in the Socratic kind of setting when there is a lot of the dialogue," noted Dr. Bryant, "However, not all of them really noticed the difference. Some students comment on that. For some, it's really important and they see that and value it and they pick up cues on how it can be done. Some students don't think about that at all. To them we are just there." Nonetheless, "Through collaboration we model different approaches to education. It models the type of approach to education which is different it makes them think and gives them sort of philosophical values or lets them develop some philosophical understandings that gives them confidence to become leaders." For Mr. Armstrong, the ability to present the same problem from three entirely different angles is of paramount import, "I see three strengths based on background. Miles bring his higher education perspective. So we really have three circles out here all focusing on the same thing all very accepting of each other's ideas and perceptions. I still quote, 'I can't hear what you are saying because what you are keeps ringing in my ears.' My own upbringing my religious training says to do more by what you do than by what you say. So I'm pretty much stuck into that." In the same spirit, Dr. Isernhagen argued that teaching students vicariously through direct observation is probably the most fundamental part of the teaching profession best exemplified through collaborative teaching "I think walking the talk is really important to students. I think that's critical to the whole concept of leadership. I think modeling is probably the biggest part of the teaching that there is. I think that's important to anybody that you are trying to work with or talk with. But the modeling piece what you believe about leadership and then demonstrating that is regardless of where you are if that's with students, it's out in a school setting, in your department. I think that's really important."

Personality

"In what we are doing all of us need to be engaged intellectually as well as emotionally and psychologically," reflected Dr. Bryant, "So does it take a strong personality? It doesn't take a domineering one, that wouldn't work. Somebody has to be the person upfront." Mr. Armstrong agreed that indeed it does take a certain personality to work on a team and not everybody has it. He remarked that an effective collaborator needs to be ready to relinquish some of his or her power, "I think you gain power you gain control by giving it up appropriately. Miles says 'Meet wherever you want, do whatever you want. There is a trust level there that he has established with this type of students that says they are going to get there so I don't have to control everything they do." "When you think of a strong psyche," Dr. Isernhagen interjected, "if you are talking type A personality where they have to do everything themselves or they overtake the group constantly, then I think it will show up in other elements of the collaboration, and it won't be a very strong collaborative." She recognized that somebody who is going to "dominate the conversation and be very domineering and 'I'm not doing this unless we are doing this'. That's not being collaborative at all anyway. And I would say that they may not be a good collaborative partner." However, she believed that if managed properly collaborators with a domineering personality may be of value to a team, "If it's domineering in everything, then it can be a downfall to a collaborative. If it's a strength which we can play to and utilize in a collaborative and you have team members that know how to handle that, I think it could be valuable. Somebody who has a weak personality style and is not very trusting and is not very confident would have as big of a problem as the domineering person because they may wait for everybody to direct what they should do and how we should carry this out and not offer any suggestions or ideas. So I think it may be as detrimental. No, I don't think everybody is built to do collaborative teaching and I don't think you can just go out there and dictate we are going to do everything collaboratively. I think you have to find partners that sort of are interested in working together. So I think that collaborations must be carefully designed, and if it looks easy it doesn't happen like that all the time."

Team Size

When asked about the most desirable size for the team of collaborating instructors, Dr. Bryant could not come up with any concrete figure but did offer instead a piece of advice, "I guess if we had a hundred students, I would want to have a team of five to six people. We have twenty-two students in this semester and three people are plenty. I'm sure there is a point where collaboration becomes difficult to organize. Getting everybody on the same page, getting people into meetings, interacting with each other. So I don't know what the exact number is but I'm sure it reaches the point where those relationships cannot be sustained because of size. I'm certain that after a certain number you couldn't build the relational ties that are necessary." For Mr. Armstrong, how collaborators organize work between each other was more important than the number of persons on a team. As a case in point he brought up a recent example, "I was gone this morning. Jody's been gone on Thursday and today. So much of the time from here on is going to be just two people. There is going to be somebody gone part of the time anyway. So knowing that, perhaps three is the way to start with the idea that we wouldn't finish this class collaboratively." According to Mr.

Armstrong, having several people on a team increases assessment depth and amount of feedback available to students, "For instance, I took half of the journals Miles took the other half and we had them corrected and back to them today. So it makes it possible to dig deeper into the journals than if I had to do them all by myself." For Dr. Isernhagen, the number of collaborating teachers on a team was heavily dependent on the nature of the task to be completed and the number of students enrolled, "When you get into collaboration in teaching, I would say this is a pretty nice size for what we are doing. I think if you've got four, five, or six in a room trying to come up with a plan I think it would be very difficult. I think it's based on the activity and based on the number of participants that you influence affecting it in some way." Dr. Isernhagen listed three basic reasons for which involvement of a larger number of teachers would be undesirable, "Number one, I think students would be overwhelmed by the number of people that are there and they would think why does it take so many people to teach this many students? Number two, it's costly. Number three, just getting together takes longer. Every time you add a voice it's going to take that much longer in the conversation to make everybody feel comfortable." When speaking of the current team, Dr. Isernhagen agreed that "We've got a pretty good number with three. I'm very comfortable. With two instructors, we could do it. But I think it's very nice that we have the balance of elementary, high school, and private because it gives a really complete picture." Although she believed that together with Dr. Bryant alone they could do a pretty good job, the presence of Mr. Armstrong was valuable for all involved, "Miles and I could teach this class. We've taught it and we sort of know, but I think Gene adds another whole dimension to it, and I would hate for us to lose that dimension. So I think you look at the task that you have, you assess what it is that we have to do here, and then you say who are the stakeholders that have a voice in this task or should have a voice in this task?'"

Conflict

Dr. Bryant credited collaborating instructors investing in building trust as the primary cause for relatively nonexistent conflict during their collaborative process, "Lack of conflict of any kind was because we did a lot of building of trust earlier on." Similarly, Mr. Armstrong detected no conflict whatsoever during the five-week period of working together,

"I haven't heard any strong words by anybody to anybody in terms of I flat out disagree with you on this." Upon a brief reflection, however, he qualified that statement slightly, "Obviously we each have our own perspectives but I don't see that as a conflict. I see that as a strengthening." Dr. Isernhagen observed similar dynamics, "I don't see any conflict. I don't feel any at all. I don't know maybe I'm not uncomfortable. I've dealt with a lot of conflict in my life though. Being a superintendent is a position where we deal with conflict all the time. So come here and do this there is no conflict as far as I'm concerned. I am sure that there are times that I will say something and Miles would think where did that come from? And that would generate conflict in his thoughts about what should be in the class. I'm sure it's the same for Gene. It is for me also. Sometimes I hear things and I want to run out and grab something and say you know I don't think we all see it that way! I think maybe I see it from this point of view and you almost want to clarify to see if you heard what was said. So I think conflict in thinking and thoughts always happens and I think it happens for students and people who are doing the teaching. We would not be doing our job if that didn't exist because I think that's the reason why you put the collaborative together. It is important to have an open conflict because then you kind of come to some agreement either to disagree or to agree or to say that you didn't have the same common language and now when the language is clear you understand. Conflict is something that offers us the opportunity to clarify what we mean and to tell what we think is important. A lot of times in conflict we all grow. So yes I think it's important. I don't think however it's necessary to go out and create conflict if it's not there."

Reflection/Feedback

"Reflection is rare although badly needed in higher education," noted Mr. Armstrong," The structure especially in high school setting you get feedback, but in higher education the only feedback is when you ask for it. You do what you think is best and you ask students to give you feedback, but you don't have to share it with anybody. I think everybody needs feedback. I can't imagine performing at the optimal level without feedback and feedback from my contemporaries, especially in collaborative teaching. I would welcome feedback from the other two and I would hope they would welcome feedback from any of the rest of us." Very infrequently, Mr. Armstrong commented on his colleagues' performance and when he did he felt very extremely uncomfortable doing so, "There are things that I would love to say but because of my level here I'm not comfortable to say. You know, if you do this you would do it better. I think there is an opportunity of higher education to give feedback to one another without fear of losing a job but I don't know if we do a very good job with that." Dr. Bryant found collaborative setting conducive to reflection, "Sometimes it happens when we sit down formally sometimes it's just casual conversations. That might be just passing by Jody's door and she asks something and we might go onto a different conversation, and all of a sudden we build new understandings together." For Dr. Isernhagen, feedback from peer collaborators was of paramount import, "It's important and it's important especially to me because I'm new. I think it allows me to say to Miles: Do you think this is of any value? And that gives me then some carryover to my other classes and how I handle myself in other classes." Dr. Isernhagen theorized that the collaborative setting might be especially useful for those in need of external feedback, "So it may be that the people who need external feedback to improve what they are doing may be well served in collaborative relationships."

Stages in Collaborative Teaching

During the fourth week of this condensed five-week course, Mr. Armstrong referred to a well-established in management literature pattern of group development. Tuckman (1965) hypothesized that groups go through four basic stages of development: forming, storming, norming, and performing, "I observed a lot of storming during the last week. But I guess the significant thing that I discovered is that just like other groups we are going through these stages as well. I don't think we have reached the norming phase yet. I think the two of them because they are experienced in teaching this course pretty much know the direction we are headed. Being the new person on a team, I find myself having to determine where my niche is on this team." To the question of how he would define the norming stage, Mr. Armstrong responded, "The norming stage would be when confusion begins to subside and you begin to fall into the pattern of how you do things. The storming stage on the other hand is when you've got all this data, you've got all these things, and probably it's not organized in the way that you really understand what's going on. However, more and more I see us norming. For example, Jody and I were talking about how we could have done a better job preparing students for the technology part and we decided how we can do that. So I see us norming more and more than I have in the past." At the same time, Mr. Armstrong perceived the performing period as evolutionary in nature, "For us, performing was a steady evolution. They gave me certain responsibilities right at the beginning so I understood those right away and I could prepare for those, but it's the unwritten things that I'm learning as I go along. Eventually, once I've got through the cycle once I do it again I think I'll be much more comfortable making suggestions and contributing."

Listening Skills

Perhaps the biggest challenge of collaborative teaching according to Dr. Bryant is the ability to listen to your collaborators, "You have to learn how to listen to other professors, that's difficult. We don't listen very well to each other. You have to be willing to construct either the learning experience or curriculum anew, and not begin with what you've done in the past and assume that your own cannon is the cannon that will be used in the class. So you begin anew. You have to start fresh."

Environment

"To create an academic environment in which creativity flourishes appropriate climate needs to be provided by the university," argued Dr. Bryant, "I think if you want to have people doing creative work whether inventing something new they have to feel safe and as I said the model of faculty member is to get between that safe haven and anything that disrupts that. I feel quite comfortable with the autonomy that I'm provided. However there is certain pressure there is pressure to produce quality of learning experience that students don't complain about. There is certainly this kind of pressure. There is pressure to do a good job. There is pressure that we want the feedback. Larry Dlugosh [departmental chair] wants it to be positive. To some degree we compete against ourselves. Each year we organize the experience that each year it works. Then that forces us to achieve at least a comfortable amount of success." Dr. Isernhagen defined external environment in which her work is embedded as the one filled with students, "We all have responsibilities regardless of the freedom that we have. We have responsibilities to our students. The freedom is more about the topics and what you can and cannot discuss in a class setting. I feel that there is very little that we can't talk about that we have that freedom, but you are bound by the fact that people are paying money for the class and they are expecting to learn how to be quality principals." She further defined her environment in terms of ethics and ethical obligations toward students, "Ethically, regardless of whether you have academic freedom or not that's what you are supposed to be teaching. So I feel like it's not really how I do things just because we have academic freedom."

Evolutionary Nature of Collaborative Teaching

Dr. Isernhagen defined collaborative teaching "as a very open-ended process. It's a developing process. I think you can have certain stages where you are relationship building, you are planning, you are implementing, you are evaluating. But even as you are implementing you are constantly evaluating and you are assessing whether to go back and change something in your plan or do it the way it was. So I think a lot of the stages overlap and I think it's very hard to put it in a linear fashion, but then I don't think teaching is a linear fashion either. Sure you have an introduction to your class, you have a syllabus, there are some things that may make it look like it's a linear process, but if you are really assessing what students need and meeting the needs of students, it's not linear." Dr. Isernhagen found the evolutionary aspect of collaboration wrapped around in a continuous dialogue among teachers as part of a bigger concept of the approach to education in general which is by nature emerging and developing, "I don't think any good teaching goes exactly by its plan and there is always re-direction, re-guidance and that sort of thing." When asked the same question, Dr. Bryant concurred without a trace of ambiguity, "It's not linear. You know life in the academic department where you grow you go into this collaborative mode and then you exit from it and then you go back into it and then you exit from it. It's not linear."

Final Assessment of the Collaborative Effort

All collaborating instructors identified the review of the teaching experience by collaborating instructors immediately following students' final course evaluations to be the last stage of the collaborative process, "Evaluation of what was successful, what wasn't. Was it successful because we did a great job? Was it a student's group? Was it the personalities? Was it the material we chose? Was it the style we used? What made it successful?" Dr. Isernhagen noted, "Students' final assessment of teaching would be my last stage. The students' evaluation would come before that because we have to assign grades." When asked about the last component of the collaborative process immediately following termination of the course Dr. Bryant concluded, "Well we haven't done the last part of it yet because we have to look at what students learned from the class, evaluations, we haven't done that. So since it's an ongoing experience, it doesn't end."

Descriptive Data

This section is based on the students' final course evaluations made available to the researcher upon completion of the course. At the request of the researcher, the collaborating instructors agreed to add an additional question specifically addressing students' reactions to the presence of multiple instructors in the classroom into the final course evaluation form. The analyzed data confirmed a number of issues identified by the researcher during the interviews, personal observations, and participants' observations. Literally, all evaluating students expressed their overwhelmingly positive assessment of the collaborative setting provided by the collaborating instructors. One of the students stated, "Having three instructors was extremely educational. We were allowed to observe three different personalities, three different teaching styles, and different experiences. The interaction between you guys was helpful–a learning experience within itself." One of the students emphasized, "Mutually complementary and reinforcing nature of the collaborative experience. I found it helpful since three instructors were able to bring out the strengths of the other two. Three instructors made for a balanced presentation." Another student found the presence of multiple instructors in the classroom less intimidating, "It provided balance to the classroom instruction. Each teacher had her or his own viewpoints and ideas which were brought to the classroom. This was less intimidating than having one teacher who had his or her one viewpoint." In the same way, two other students found atmosphere created by a number of instructors in the classroom more inviting, "It was good to have three different perspectives and special areas of experience and expertise. The three instructors were able to diffuse potential personality conflicts thus making the atmosphere much more inviting and open." One of the students wished to see collaborative setting in every class, "This was very helpful because we always could receive three different points of view: principal, superintendent, professor. I would like to see this happen all the time." Another evaluator pointed to leadership in the collaborative team, "The three instructors did not have equal or the same roles. I noticed a definite leader-follower aspect and it was evident that plans had been made to include all of the instructors in some kind of instructional activity. I believe the three instructors played off of each other well and gave a richer learning experience than a single could." One of the students noticed mixed gender within collaborating team, "Wonderful, three different perspectives: former principal, former superintendent, college professor/researcher, one female, two male[s]." Almost all students were expressing their gratitude for having opportunity of being exposed to three different perspectives and three kinds of expertise. One observation was most representative of them all, "I don't think the course would have been nearly as effective without the three styles and experiences. Yes anyone of the three could have taught the course but not as well."

CHAPTER 9

PROCESS OF COLLABORATIVE TEACHING CROSS-CASE ANALYSIS

INTRODUCTION

The purpose of this study was to explore and gain in-depth understanding of the process of collaborative teaching conducted by two teams of two and one team of three faculty members teaching in a major Midwestern research university. The study was designed to answer the Grand Tour question: What is the process of collaborative teaching conducted by three teams of academic faculty members at higher education of a Midwestern university? and identify issues involved in the process. Seven academic instructors participated as case study informants. The narrative description was placed in the first section of each case study. After completing each case study, several key issues emerged related to the grand tour question. The identification of the issues came during the writing of the second section of each case study. During readings of the transcripts from each of the interviews, the researcher coded the most significant issues that emerged from the text. Finally, after re-reading the narrative description and considering the issues identified in the original transcripts, seventy-four issues emerged. The following issues were identified in individual case studies:

Case Study #1

Choosing Partners
Teaching/Learning Philosophy
Joy of Working with Others
Professional Development
Knowledge Construction
Diversity
Active Learning
Real World
Collaboration Beyond the Classroom
Consensus Building
Mutual Facilitation
Division of Labor

Case Study #2

Course Design
Tag Team
In/Out of the Classroom
Feeling of guilt
Getting Acquainted
Teaching Styles
Roles Division
Divergent Experiences
Convergent Experiences
Learning
Complementation
Mutual Feedback
Supervisor's Feedback
Reflection
Conflict
Freedom from Isolation
Status Differentiation
Trust
Confidence
Collaboration is the Future
Modeling Collaboration

Learning Community
Assessment
Commitment to Collaboration
Time Commitment
Collaboration as Evolution
Course Design
Personal versus Professional
Class Size
Learning Experience
Academic Individualism
Shared Leadership
Role Identification
Final Advice

Case Study #3

Collaboration Defined
Relationship Building
Teaching/Learning Philosophy
Planning
Course design
Selecting Partners
Partnering versus True Collaboration"
Professional Development
Leadership
Trust
Division of Roles
Flexibility
Training & Development
Time commitment
Need for Collaboration
Objectivity
Risk taking
Modeling
Personality
Team Size
Conflict
Reflection/Feedback

Stages of Collaborative Teaching
Listening Skills
Environment
Evolutionary Nature of Collaborative Teaching
Final Assessment of the Collaborative Effort

The identified issues were combined and categorized using two distinctive methods. In the first method, the issues were grouped by individual case studies. During the process of examining the issues of individual cases, and even earlier during the writing process, it became clear that some issues had become repetitive, which was indicative of their central and essential value to the case studies. Some issues, however, were clearly unique to a specific case study and because of that difficult to group into larger themes. In the second method, after a series of sorting and reductions, the researcher, through cross-analysis, lumped together emerged issues into six themes, which are indicated by the numbers immediately on the left side of the listed issues. Issues within the same larger theme have the same number, which allows readers to determine the frequency with which an issue occurs. For example, issues like the number of students in the classroom ("class size"), the need for teachers to serve as role models of collaboration ("teachers as role models"), the opportunity to reflect on the teaching while working with other faculty members ("reflection"), breaking the isolation of faculty members ("instructors' isolation"), providing various, often contradictory, perspectives on issues ("variety of perspectives"), a more realistic picture of the reality ("objectivity") created basis for the first cross-case theme–"need for collaboration." The other five themes were created by the researcher following the same logic. However, after the final list had been established, some issues still remained tangential to the bigger themes identified by the researcher. Numerically identified individual case study issues and cross-case themes, along with their definitions, are listed below:

Individually Labeled Case Issues

(4) Selecting Partners
(3) Teaching/Learning Philosophy
(2) Joy of Working with Others
(5) Reflection/Feedback

(1) Learning

(5) Knowledge Construction

(5) Diversity

(3) Active Learning

(1) Real world

(2) Collaboration beyond the Classroom

(4) Consensus Building

(5) Mutual Feedback

(4) Division of Labor

(4) Course Design

(4) Tag Team

(2) Collaboration beyond the Classroom

(2) Getting Acquainted

(3) Teaching Styles

(4) Roles Division

(1) Divergent Experiences

(1) Convergent Experiences

(5) Mutual Feedback

(1) Shared Leadership

(5) Mutual Feedback

(2) Conflict

(1) Freedom from Isolation

(2) Status Differentiation

(2) Trust

(2) Confidence

(1) Collaboration is the Future

(1) Modeling Collaboration

(5) Learning

(4) Commitment to Collaboration

(4) Time Commitment

(6) Evolutionary Nature of Collaborative Teaching

(4) Course Design

(2) Personal versus Professional

(1) Class Size

(5) Supervisor's Feedback

(1) Academic Individualism

(4) Shared Leadership

(4) Role Identification

(1) Final Advice
(6) Collaboration Defined
(2) Relationship Building
(3) Teaching/Learning Philosophy
(4) Course Design
(4) Selecting Partners
(4) Partnering versus True Collaboration"
(5) Learning Experience
(4) Leadership
(2) Trust
(4) Division of Roles
(4) Flexibility
(5) Training & development
(4) Time Commitment
(1) Objectivity
(5) Risk Taking
(1) Modeling
(2) Personality
(4) Team Size
(2) Conflict
(5) Reflection/Feedback
(4) Stages in Collaborative Teaching
(4) Listening Skills
(6) Evolutionary Nature of Collaborative Teaching
(4) Final Assessment of the Collaborative Effort

Cross-Case Themes

(1) Need for collaboration

Rationales for which academic professors and administrators decide to create teams to teach in collaborative settings

(2) Relationship Building

The interpersonal dimension of collaborative work during which professors interact as well as get acquainted with one another on the personal level

(3) Teaching/Learning Philosophy

Variety of teaching styles and learning philosophies represented by individual professors

(4) Task Completion

Aspects of collaborative work that directly relate to accomplishing course objectives

(5) Professional Development

Aspects of collaboration that add to the professional development of collaborating professors

(6) Evolutionary Nature of Collaboration

Collaborative teaching defined as cyclical, evolving, emerging, and developing over time process

Cross-Case Theme #1

Need for Collaboration

The need for collaboration theme was heavily imbued in all three cases. The theme was defined by the researcher as the rationales for which academic professors and administrators decide to create teams to teach in collaborative settings. The theme emerged from a large number of emerging issues that played an important role in defining the reason for which academic faculty may want to experiment with teams of collaborating instructors. Closer review of data indicated the existence of two bifurcated dimensions on which the need for collaboration should be considered. The first dimension had to do with faculty–instruction deliverers, the other students–instruction recipients. Enhanced quality of knowledge acquired from the collaborating instructors was perhaps the most salient benefit of collaborative teaching. Having the mission of educating students to the best of their abilities at the helm, most of the collaborating instructors almost instinctively talked about the need for collaboration as a tool for enriching students' learning experience. Presenting various perspectives to students on the same issues contributed immensely to the development of students' critical thinking skills.

In their research, Wilson and Martin (1998) noted:

> The students also benefit from experiencing two perspectives on complex issues. Often we agree, sometimes we disagree. It becomes apparent to students that there is often no one 'right' answer, only the opportunity to discuss the pros and cons of each alternative, to question reasons for a specific position, and to decide for oneself how the issue should be addressed or the problem solved. (p. 11)

The ability to model what instructors attempted to teach represented another inherent advantage of collaborative teaching. According to research participants, it was important to "walk the talk." In the judgment of the informant, "Students learned as much by listening to teachers as we did by watching them."

Robinson and Schaible (1995) argued that:

> Collaborative pedagogy holds much promise, but only if faculty members themselves can learn to become better collaborators.... Both our classroom research and literature on learning indicate that students learn from the behavior we model—whether we are mindful of it or not. If we preach collaboration but practice isolation, or team-teach with inadequate preparation, students get a confused message. Through learning to 'walk the talk,' we can reap the double advantage of improving our teaching as well as students' learning. At the same time, we will contribute to the rebuilding of a sense of community in higher education. (p. 59)

> When we're short a copy, or when the masking tape that is usually in the classroom has walked away, we are available to handle the logistics without unduly disrupting the flow of the class. One of us is always available to give extra attention to individual students or groups. (p. 5)

The presence of other colleagues united in pursuing the same goal can have tremendous benefits in terms of learning opportunities. None could have occurred has the faculty been exposed to a traditional, isolated form of teaching. Guarasci and Cornwell (1997) regarded academic teams to be the cornerstones of learning communities, "Learning communities are conscious curricular structures that link two or more disciplines around the exploration of a common theme" (p. 109). Wilson and Martin (1998) reflected, "Good team teaching necessarily results in a more reflective approach to teaching (p. 10)....and as critics, we hold the mirror of serious reflection for each other, assuring that our failures are examined and improved, we are assured that our triumphs will be celebrated" (p. 5). Similarly Mayo and Gilliland (1979) observed that "During collaboration faculty must teach under the scrutiny of their peers from other disciplines" (p. 67). Most research participants in the described in this book study observed that breaking the isolation in which academic professors work releases instructors' crave for some kind of feedback from their peers. Robinson and Schaible (1995) provide similar confession, "Collaborative teaching can help us overcome the frequent sense of isolation felt by many faculty members" (p. 59).

Cross-Case Theme #2

Relationship Building

The relationship building theme has been present in all three cases. The researcher defined the theme as the interpersonal dimension of collaborative work during which professors interact as well as get acquainted with one another on the personal level. The development of trusting relationships among the team members constituted the glue keeping together all other aspects of team's work. Properly managed relationships from the very outset of the collaborative endeavor to a great measure predetermined its success. The informants found the ability to relate to their team members on "friendly" terms having significant impact on task-related issues such as planning, curriculum development, and everyday management of the course. The research participants agreed that not everybody can be an effective team member. Effective collaborators need to be comfortable with each other and should possess certain characteristics including: flexibility, communication skills, and likeability.

Griggs and Stewart (1996) point out that key aspect of effective classroom collaboration is the ability to communicate, which many a time is a serious problem among academics, "Frequently members of academe have difficulty sharing with each other common problems" (p. 2). Wilson and Martin (1998) agree that "A team teacher must be flexible; both time and intended coverage of subject matter must be adjusted to accommodate the other team member" (p. 8). The feeling of ownership of the course in all of its dimensions: choice of collaborating partners, curriculum delivery, collaborative assessment of their work together have been observed by the researcher to be the single most important aspect of successful collaboration. According to Dr. Isernhagen, "People tend to support what they created." The spirit of that insight has permeated the entire process of collaborative teaching and was shared by all informants. Owning the course and the ability to readily relate to one another, preferably on personal level, significantly affected the work of collaborating instructors. Quotidian situations such as formal and informal phone calls to each other, adventitious encounters in the halls had implications on what was then happening in the classroom. Quite consistently, research subjects found it difficult to separate personal lives from their professional identities as collaborators. Consequently, the ability to communicate with each other openly with trust, camaraderie, and unconditional support when needed was the key component of successful collaboration.

Wilson and Martin (1998) found collaborators' role as "cheerleaders" an essential ability each team member had to possess, "As cheerleaders for each other, we counter the often-deadening isolation of the classroom. It is comforting to have an understanding colleague to say, 'Some days are diamonds, some days are stones' (p. 5).... Just as trust develops slowly between students and teachers, it must be actively cultivated in the relationship between co-teachers" (p. 58).

Interpersonal conflict among collaborating instructors was almost nonexistent in all three cases. Some informants believed it to be the consequence of "Midwestern socialization which conditions people to avoid conflict at all costs." Others ascribed lack of conflict to selecting right partners. Most of the informants, however, agreed that content-related conflict could be very useful for collaboration, "Content-related conflict, if handled properly, could increase the quality of the work for all involved, both instructors and students." This kind of conflict was regarded as a "contributor to developing critical thinking skills for all involved, including collaborating instructors." Academic status differentiation among collaborating instructors has been found an important catalyst moderating the nature of relationship the instructors experienced while working together. Although, according to research participants, there were conscious efforts to minimize the hierarchy within the teams' leadership structure, the graduate assistant status of one team member in case no. 2 and case no.3 appeared to seriously impede the intrinsic equilibrium of power within those teams. Frequently, according to the informants, Mr. Armstrong–graduate assistant–elected not to comment or speak up on a number of important issues both within and outside the classroom. He admittedly "did not feel comfortable enough to challenge other faculty members. In fact, I probably avoided it more than I should have."

Cross-Case Theme #3

Teaching/Learning Philosophy

The teaching/learning philosophy theme appeared consistently in all three cases. The researcher defined the theme as the variety of teaching styles and learning philosophies represented by individual professors. The research subjects sent contrary messages within the framework of that concept, which made the analysis of this theme somewhat of a challenge. Closer review of collected data indicated a bifurcate approach of informants to that theme. Collaborating instructors have come from two opposing philosophical positions on how to teach to best achieve course learning objectives. Some informants argued for a uniform teaching/learning philosophy shared by all collaborators as a necessary ingredient of successful collaboration. Others, on the contrary, saw divergent teaching/learning philosophies as the most valuable tool available to collaborators to boost efficacy of the learning processes. Regardless of the approach, however, a cornucopia of evidence indicated the team members' deep-seated belief in flexibility to be an important characteristic of a successful collaborator. This trait was found extremely relevant to the discussed theme. Informants claimed that "collaborating instructors need to be able to adjust to the teaching styles of their teammates."

Wilson and Martin (1998) reasoned it takes a great amount of discipline not to overstep and infringe upon the peer collaborator. In the same token, material covered by one instructor should not be "rehashed" by another collaborator, "A team teacher must be flexible. Both time and intended coverage of subject matter must be adjusted to accommodate the other team member" (p. 8). Some informants believed that differences in certain aspects of teaching/learning philosophies and the ability to adjust to one another's style lies at the very heart of successful collaboration. Indeed, it is what collaboration is all about, "Collaborative teaching by nature calls for the clash of divergent opinions and different point of views, because that, in consequence, will develop critical thinking skills among both students and instructors. Therefore, students' exposure to variety of teaching styles will be positive in the long run." One research subject, however, did not share that view and believed that as "Teachers' College's faculty members, they have obligation to present to students a relatively cohesive teaching philosophy, consistent with the sound research findings." According to the Educational Testing Service (1992), team teaching cannot be successful if teachers differ significantly in terms of their approach to students' learning processes. Similarly, in the opinion of Wilson and Martin (1998), "If the philosophies are shared, differences in the other elements-experience, background, and approaches only enrich the team-teaching experience for both teachers and students" (p. 8).

Cross-Case Theme #4

Task Completion

The task completion theme was found present in all three studied cases. The researcher defined the theme as the aspects of collaborative work that directly relate to accomplishing course objectives. Since all of the studied cases were strongly task-oriented, it did not come as a surprise that a large number of emerging issues related to that aspect of the collaboration. Since research participants found difficulties in listing "phases" of collaboration, the researcher decided to use a word "dimensions" instead, finding the word's connotation more reflective of the studied reality. Even though collaborative teaching cannot be conceptualized in a strict linear fashion, closer review of the collected data did indicate the existence of some sort of order. The researcher identified six task dimensions which could be construed as the abstract framework of the collaborative process. First task-related dimension dealt with *choosing collaborating partners*. In case study no. 2, and to some extent also in case study no. 3, instructors were assigned to work with each other. That arrangement according to the informants sabotaged their commitment to the team. Similarly, lack of influence on course design was hugely detrimental to instructors' "buying" into the project. For that reason, the researcher dubbed *course design* as the second dimension. Similarly, lack of ownership in the course was found to be a significant administrative disadvantage with a potential of seriously undermining the effectiveness of a collaborative effort. *Planning and preparation* dimension was also found significant. Time spent together before the onset of the classroom activities was especially important as it allows collaborators to bond and forge personal relationships that will bear fruits where it truly matter—the classroom. The below-referenced quote reflects best the overall agreement on the importance of team members' involvement in defining the task as an inherent part of effective "collaboration":

> Not all activity that involves a group of individuals can be deemed collaboration. Maienschein (1993) provides the example of museum collection development, where collectors who work together to build the museum's collection co-labor, but as they do not participate in defining the task, the activity cannot be considered 'collaboration.' Thus, to be considered a collaborator, one must, at some point in the activity, 'participate in articulating the goal' (Maienschein, 1993, p. 170). (Gunawardena et al., 2010, p. 212)

Although this dimension is time consuming, if handled properly, it may release a significant amount of time to deal with other key dimensions of collaboration such as *instruction delivery* and *students' evaluations* later on in the process. According to the informants, if the first three dimensions are handled appropriately, the following dimensions are much easier to implement successfully. Collaborators emphasized the need for flexibility on the part of the collaborators during the entire period of collaboration. *Self-assessment* of the collaborative effort was identified as the last of the six dimensions. The researcher did not have an opportunity to observe this part of the collaborative process. In case study no. 1 & 2, collaborators never met (although collaborators in case no. 2 did express the wishes to do that). In case study no. 3, collaborators met to assess their results and reflect on the experience weeks after completion of the course.

According to Austin and Baldwin (1991):

Although small-group models might label the steps in the collaborative process somewhat differently, each effective collaborative team must proceed through four basic stages: (1) choosing colleagues or team members, (2) dividing the labor, (3) establishing work guidelines, and (4) terminating a collaboration. (p. 6)

Wilson and Martin (1998) in their research article based on four-semester long of collaborative teaching at the college level course, identified three basic areas of integration, "1) coordination of course content among the three disciplines, 2) team teaching of strategies common to all disciplines, and 3) coordination of integrated course assignments" (p. 3).

Cross-Case Theme #5

Professional Development

The theme of professional development was present in all three cases. The researcher defined the theme as the aspects of collaboration that add to the professional development of collaborating professors. The theme was supported by a solid amount of data indicating the importance of collaborative teaching as a tool for academic instructors' growth and development.

Professional development meant something else to each individual instructor, indicating the variety of channels through which collaborative teaching could be utilized to improve the process in the long run.

Team learning can be a key success factor for surviving in turbulent environments and it shows the importance of facilitating team learning as a valuable corporate asset that may drive learning across all networks within the organization. The challenge is to expose the system, organization or teams to as much chaos as possible, while balancing far away from equilibrium. It is on the edge of chaos where self-organizing and emergent behavior will arise. One may gather that in the current economic turmoil, this should not be too difficult to achieve. (Fisser et al., 2010, p. 67)

One of the research participants bemoaned lack of respect for collaborative research that decreased drastically along with the number of names associated with a particular research article. According to Gunawardena et al. (2010) negative associations with multiple authored research articles has changed over the past three decades,

> Across the various scientific disciplines, the average number of authors per paper steadily increased from 1980-1998 (Glanzel, 2002). In science and engineering, including the social sciences, scientists are working together even more, with the proportion of single author works dropping by half from 1975 to 2005 (Jones, et al., 2008). Similarly, the field of LIS has seen a corresponding increase in multidisciplinary scholarship, with Odell and Gabbard (2008) showing a 14% increase in other fields' citations of LIS journals in the period 1996-2004 when compared to 1974-1996.... This change in research paradigm is influencing LIS education, shifting the focus from discipline-based to problem-based education (Druin et al., 2009; Lørring, 2007; Moss & Ross 2007; Ribiero, 2007). While LIS has a predisposition for interdisciplinarity, it has not always had the best integration within its own diverse scholarly communities (Saracevic, 1999). (Gunawardena et al., 2010, p. 211)

For most informants, professional development meant learning from each other and constructing knowledge together. For others, it meant exposure to broadly understood diversity of backgrounds, experiences, novel perspectives, and information. Still others understood professional development as highly desirable feedback from a colleague.

Wilson and Martin (1998) recalled their own experiences in that context:

> We spend a great amount of time—often over lunch—discussing the course activities and reflecting on those strategies that seem to work and on those that do not work as well. Insights from the observing (as opposed to the actively teaching) partner often result in better adaptations of strategies to meet student needs and preferences. Immediate feedback from a peer is gratifying, especially when the class is less than demonstrative. (p. 10)

Some informants defined professional development as commonality of experience, or simply having fun together. Learning new teaching techniques and activities, or simply having a helper in the classroom was also of value.

In case of Wilson and Martin (1998), the role of muse was highly appreciated:

> Our many and varied experiences in all kinds of educational settings mean a collective wealth of creative ideas. Lack of inspiration by one of us is nearly always countered by a useful—and sometimes brilliant—suggestion by the other. This role, too, has changed as we become more experienced with working together. In our early weeks of team teaching, we looked for help primarily during planning. Now we feel free to interject ideas as the lesson is progressing, often prompting stories of insights that we know the other one has in her repertoire. (p. 5)

Cross-Case Theme #6

Evolutionary Nature of Collaboration

Although the evolutionary nature of the collaboration theme emerged only in case no. 2 and case no. 3 but not in pilot case no. 1 (which was based on very limited amount of data), the researcher found it too significant to ignore in the cross-case analysis. Indeed, the theme appeared at the very heart of the collaborative teaching process and was consequently placed at the center of the model developed by the researcher to visualize the process of collaborative teaching (Figure 1). The researcher worded the theme as collaborative teaching defined as cyclical, evolving, emerging, and developing over time process. All informants agreed that collaborative teaching is far from a linear sequential process in which one phase ends and another begins. In fact, one of the research subjects, while alluding to collaborative teaching dimensions, vehemently steered away from models with simple arrows and boxes. A thorough review of collected data clearly indicated collaborative teaching as an emerging evolving fluid process, accompanied by features and dimensions unique to each team. Collected observations did not, however, indicate chaos, confusion, or disarray. Task-related aspects of the collaborative work in particular seemed arranged in a logical order, in which respective dimensions overlapped and complemented each other. The evolutionary nature of the collaborative teaching process in higher education has been reaffirmed by a large amount of available research (Ramirez, 1983, Gray, 1989, Austin and Baldwin, 1991).

CHAPTER 10

The Process of Collaborative Teaching <u>Synthesis</u>

CONCLUSIONS

Focus on increased integration, both in teaching and learning, can provide students with a well-rounded education and prepare students for success in an increasingly collaborative and interdisciplinary world. Success in collaborative teaching does not come easy; co-teaching a class can take almost as much effort as teaching it individually. It requires commitment on the part of all involved and institutional support. In both research and education, the benefits of interdisciplinarity will not come quickly. (Gunawardena et al., 2010, p. 219)

A review of cross-case analysis has led the researcher to some conclusions about the process of collaborative teaching in higher education. The conclusions are the result of examinations of triangulated data organized from interviews with collaborating instructors, observations of all available activities, participant observations, and written documents provided by the informants. The purpose of the study was to gain an in-depth understanding of the process of collaborative teaching in higher education and identify issues related to the process in studied cases. The Grand Tour question that guided the study was: What is the process of collaborative teaching conducted by three teams of academic faculty members at a Midwestern university? Research participants defined their collaboration as an emergent process that evolved throughout the course of working together. Ramirez (1983) defined collaborations as the arrangements among stakeholders that are emergent and developmental in nature. Austin and Baldwin (1991) observed the collaboration to be an emerging process "through which the roles of participants, their decision making processes, and their goals and agreements evolve over time" (p. 63).

The conducted research confirmed the existing research findings on small group development that two dominant areas collaborators deal with in the process of working together are dichotomized between relationship issues and task issues (Bennis & Shepard, 1956; Tuckman 1965; Schein, 1969; Tuckman & Jensen, 1977; Austin & Baldwin, 1991). Bennis and Shepard (1956) noted that the first phase of collaborative effort, labeled "dependence," is characterized by team members dealing with the leader's authority; and is followed by the second phase, "interdependence," in which team members deal with conflicts surrounding identity and intimacy. Schein (1969) formulated theory of group process development in which similar bifurcate distinction is made between interpersonal issues ("self-oriented behavior") and task issue ("task-oriented behavior") (p. 45). The correspondence between the "interpersonal realm" and the "task realm" prompted Tuckman and Jensen (1977) to define a five-stage model which include the following stages: "forming," "storming," "norming," "performing," and "adjourning." (p. 426). The "forming" stage is characterized by the efforts to get acquainted with other members of a team and the task itself. The "storming" stage is characterized by team members expressing a variety of negative feelings toward each other and resisting the task. Eventually, team members overcome mutual hostility and resistance to task becoming more open toward novel ideas—that stage is referred to as "norming." The "performing" stage crowns the collaborative process with team members focusing entirely on reaching goals and accomplishing task. During the "adjourning" stage team members conclude their work and deal with the issue of separation. Austin and Baldwin (1991), summarizing literature review on small group development, noted, "While each theory is distinctive, they share an emphasis on the dual challenges that confront collaborative groups, however: that is both interpersonal and task issues must be handled if collaboration is to be successful and productive" (p. 65).

The extant research emphasizes order of "phases" or "stages" through which teams progress during their development in some identifiable sequence. According to Bennis and Shepard (1956), task-related issues precede interpersonal aspects in the group development process, "The evolution from Phase I to Phase II represents not only a change in emphasis from power to affection, but also from role to personality" (p. 436). Similarly Schein (1969) identified task and interpersonal aspects of collaboration as the primary issues that collaborators must deal with in the collaborative process but in reverse. That means, Schein theorizes that members of the group will not move to the task issues, such as clarifying data, seeking opinions, and maintenance functions before resolving interpersonal issues first, "The problems which a person faces when he enters a new group stem from certain underlying emotional issues which must be resolved before he can feel comfortable in a new situation" (p. 32). Although research subjects in the studied cases identified "phases" of their collaboration, they found it difficult to clearly distinguish boundaries separating one stage from another. Thus to better visualize the process of collaborative teaching, the researcher decided to refer to identified phases as "dimensions," using a cyclical, in lieu of suggested by the majority of available research linear sequential models, "Early studies of organization were dominated by the 'scientific management' school of thought leading to an almost exclusive preoccupation with the 'structural' or static elements of organization" (Schein, 1969, p. 10). Consequently, in the model developed by the researcher (Figure 1), dimensions, although moving in a fairly organized order, overlap and intertwine with each other along the entire process. Although both interpersonal and task-related dimensions lie at the heart of the collaborative process identified in this research, the relationship building aspect of the collaboration has been found to play most fundamental role in studied cases, especially in the early stages of the collaborative process, affecting all other aspects of the collaborative effort. On the basis of the researcher's interviews, triangulated by observations, participant observations, and review of available documents, the researcher found it difficult to provide a reader with a carefully organized list of phases enumerated in an easy to remember fashion. The theoretical models of the collaborative process, identified in the literature on small group development, overwhelmingly illustrate phases of collaboration organized in a linear, sequential, cause and effect order. Although easy to read and remember, those models, in the opinion of the researcher, vastly oversimplify a much more complex reality and context in which academic teams exist. To better understand the collaborative process, readers must understand that people exist and function on multiple dimensions simultaneously. Dealing with task issues such as designing, planning, preparing, delivering instruction, evaluating students, and assessing the results never ends until collaborators keep working together. In the same manner, relationship building among collaborators is a never-ending journey that begins on the day collaborators first meet and ends only when the collaboration has been "adjourned." That comes to show how dynamic the process of collaborative teaching is and how flexible collaborators must be to successfully complete their work in a professionally satisfying fashion. At various points of the process, instructors stressed different aspects of work to be more important than others. At the outset of the collaboration, the emphasis weighed strongly on the need to build relationships with each other via learning about mutual interests, past experiences, and hobbies. With time, however, instructors shifted their focus onto the task itself. Nevertheless, the social fiber of the collaborative effort remained tremendously important permeating all other dimensions throughout the entire process of their collaboration. Consequently, it would be incorrect to conclude that once instructors shifted their focus to task-related day-to-day classroom management aspects of their work together, they all of a sudden stopped functioning as feeling individuals and become pure professionals instead. Collaborating instructors begin and end the collaboration facing similar issues, but confronting them on different levels. Although the planning aspect of the work might have been strongly present during the first few meetings of the collaborative process, it was also found heavily emphasized later on in the process as instructors "constructed" new knowledge and understanding of each other's strengths and weaknesses. In the same way, although collaborators moved to the instructional delivery dimension, they did not stop to plan, design, or redesign the course when a need arose. Although all studied teams were highly task-oriented from the very inception of their work together, the relationship building factor was an ongoing process tangible throughout the entire process. For that reason, the theory that the researcher felt most comfortable with in the context of studied cases was the model developed by Schutz (1958) which designates group interactions as cyclical, somewhat akin to changing a tire, where the bolts are tightened in sequence and then the sequence is repeated anew. In Schultz's (1958) view, the collaborative process consists of three phases: 1) the "inclusion phase," 2) the "control phase," 3) the "affection phase." During the "inclusion phase," group members focus on getting acquainted with one another by discussing smaller insignificant issues such as for instance their biographies, "Critical issues to be handled at this phase are interpersonal boundaries and members' commitment to the group" (p. 66). In the "control phase," teammates distribute power, control, and responsibilities among each other, "Elements of this task oriented phase are establishing rules and procedures, structuring decision making, discussing the group's orientation to its work" (p. 66). Finally, in the "affection phase," collaborators focus again on socio-emotional aspects of their work and the way they relate to the decisions made about the group's structure, decision making processes they created in control phase, "During this phase, group members might express hostility, jealousy, or positive feelings toward each other" (p. 66). After resolving those issues, the cycle gets repeated anew, "As these issues are resolved, the group cycles back to the concerns of the first phase" (p. 66). The research findings confirm also Day and Day's (1977) precepts of the "negotiated order theory," which transmuted the view of organizations from rigid predictable entities to supple plexiform networks of emotionally charged organisms, "Organizations are thus viewed as complex and highly fragile social constructions of reality which are subject to the numerous temporal, spatial, and situational events occurring both internally and externally" (p. 132). Although more in-depth study should address women's perspective of the importance of relationship building and its effect on the process of collaborative teaching, the researcher found that male collaborators valued relationship building in a comparable manner with that presented by the only female collaborator present in the study. That finding stands in contrast to some research claiming that women academics have a tendency toward more personalized interaction with colleagues (Simeone, 1987). Similarly, Austin and Baldwin (1991) claimed that "While men often interact with colleagues primarily on a professional basis, women tend to view their associates as colleague-friends. This pattern is evident even among highly research-oriented women professors" (p. 90). In the study conducted by the researcher, five out of six studied subjects were men, yet the issue of relationship building came up as a singularly most significant factor of successful collaboration. Thus, the researcher cannot confirm emphasized in the academic literature stereotype that female professors are more emotional (relationship-oriented) than their male counterparts. Even Srivastva, Obert, and Neilsen (1977), who dichotomized most critical dimensions of collaboration between those of relationship and task orientation, admitted its limitations to groups of a larger size that might be fraught with more nuances, "While the small group has been extensively studied, there is a theoretical gap which prevents this knowledge from being optimally useful to the field of organization development" (p. 84). Srivastva et al. (1977) acknowledges that although previously described theories focused on the critical dimensions of group life, they created a theoretical gap by not recognizing the group's external environment in which it is embedded, "Insufficient conceptual work has been done to describe the relationship between the small group and the larger organization that surrounds it, and thus, forms its immediate environment" (p. 84). Interviews with research subjects indicated their awareness of the external environment which in their opinions had less to do with the university administration, policies, or guidelines and more to do with intrinsically motivated reasons for which they became educators to begin with. The informants defined their external environment as ethical obligation to those they serve–the students, not university administration. Since academic freedom makes pursuit of truth possible in a way that is free from organizational constraints, the developmental dynamics of teams operating in other milieus might differ from that found in this study.

Gray (1989) formulated a three-stage model of group development, which by his own admission is applicable to any kind of collaboration, "While there is not a clearly prescribed pattern that characterizes every collaboration, there appear to be some common issues that crop up repeatedly" (p. 55). The model includes three major phases: 1) "problem setting," 2) "direction setting," and 3) "implementation." In the first setting, "Problem solving requires identification of stakeholders, mutual acknowledgment of the issues that join them, and building commitment to address these issues through face-to-face negotiations" (p. 56). Gray's (1989) first phase does not include identification and choice of collaborating partners as a separate distinguishable phase of the collaborative process. That was however identified as a key phase by research participants, weighing heavily on the successful completion of their collaboration. Research participants who were administratively assigned to the team were especially eager to admit that lack of control in that decision undermined their commitment to the collaborative effort. Similar sentiments were expressed by those research participants who did not have an opportunity to partake in the design phase of the course (Gray's phases 1 and 2). In those cases, instructors had the course-related materials and activities handed to them by administrators or other collaborators. Consequently, the pride of ownership was taken away right at the outset of their collaboration and their motivation gravely undermined. Research subjects found the ability to relate to teammates, on at least "friendly" level, absolutely crucial to successful collaboration. During one of the interviews, Dr. Bryant noted, "They don't have to be my friends, but I at least have to like them." Remaining subjects shared similar opinions. The ability to relate to one another on a friendly personal level was found crucial in all three studied cases. Private socialization of collaborating instructors had admittedly direct bearing on what transpired in the classroom. According to Dr. Eggland, "No matter where I meet with my friends, we always end up talking about 'professional stuff.' "

Professional development, consequent to collaborative teaching, has been found significant across all three studied cases. That finding is consistent with the extant research findings. Maeroff (1993) insisted on the need to develop academic faculty as much as students. Implicit in the team approach to educational change is a concept of professional development that orients faculty toward the continuous intellectual renewal, "A true learning community would be one in which all members, adults included, were constantly expanding themselves" (p. 12). Robinson and Schaible (1995), looking for alternative ways to professionally develop faculty, shifted attention from collaborative learning to collaborative teaching, "Research on collaborative learning indicates that its benefits for students include higher achievement, greater retention, improved interpersonal skills, and an increase in regard for positive interdependence. We find that collaborative teaching benefits us as well" (p. 58). According to research subjects, collaborative teaching, if handled properly can be a valuable tool contributing significantly to the growth of not only students but also collaborating instructors and the entire academic community. Learning opportunities, mutual feedback, and reflection are valuable benefits of collaborative setting. Some informants emphasized the opportunity of building departmental camaraderie as a result of working in teams. They learned that the collaborative setting stimulated risk taking and creativity among the collaborators, "Some things would not have happened had there been more than one teacher in the classroom," noted Dr. Isernhagen in one of the interviews. Robinson and Schaible (1995) reported, "We have found that the collaborative arrangement spurs each partner to locate, share, and experiment with fresh ideas for structuring class sessions, creating more effective writing assignments, and improving our skills at critiquing student papers" (p. 59). Wilson and Martin (1998) identified enhanced risk-taking as the welcome benefit of collaborative teaching:

> An unexpected benefit is the support for risk-taking that team teaching affords....We each feel that with the other's encouragement and professional insight we can try new strategies, knowing that the debriefing will be supportive and encouraging, and will result in improved future lessons. (p. 10)

Professional development meant something else for everybody involved in the study and was determined individual personalities, interests, or even needs at that particular point in time. One of the informants expressed his gratitude toward teammates because working with them opened his eyes on teaching techniques, methods, activities that he had never thought could work. Those with shorter teaching tenure appreciated feedback, reflection, commonality of experience, or simply having fun together. For Wilson and Martin (1998) "team teaching has been just plain fun. We both missed the company of other adults when we taught in the public schools and enjoy the camaraderie evident in our joint classroom" (p. 10).

According to the Educational Testing Service (1992), "Similar philosophies in terms of learning objectives are necessary factors that collaborating instructors must possess to successfully complete their collaboration (p. 118). The importance of cohesive teaching philosophies among collaborators was also emphasized by Robinson and Schaible (1995), "Early on, discuss your teaching philosophy and methods and present your honest–not your ideal self" (p. 57). The reviewed data made it difficult for the researcher to either confirm or disconfirm those statements. Some informants expressed opinions contrary to the above-referenced claims and opinions, others agreed with them. Some believed that cohesive philosophies of teaching and learning among collaborators are necessary for meaningful collaboration. Yet others regarded divergent styles of individual instructors as fortes rather than foibles. In spite of informants' claims that different styles added to the value of experienced education, observations of the researcher and review of students' evaluations did not confirm these statements. Let's take as an example case study no. 2, in which one instructor showed clear preference for the lecture and large group discussions and the other leaned toward active learning and small group activities. Both of them expressed deep conviction of the appropriateness of their teaching styles, adamantly defending their positions with sound rationales. That, in the opinion of the researcher, inhibited full utilization of the collaborative setting. Many a time this ideological clash led to open dissatisfaction of individual instructors, undermining commitment to collaboration. In its entirety, collected in this research data tends to support the existing findings that declare cohesive teaching styles of collaborating instructors more conducive to a fruitful collaboration. However, enhanced number of experiences, backgrounds, and perspectives, if utilized appropriately within the collaborative setting, can add to the quality of learning experience. Wilson and Martin (1998), go even farther by claiming that "If the philosophies are shared, differences in the other elements–experience, backgrounds, and approaches only enrich the team-teaching experience for both teachers and students" (p. 8). Robinson and Schaible (1995) argued that collaborative teaching encourages instructors to check their ingrained tendency to slip back into the style of teaching with the student as mere passive receptacle, "When teaching collaboratively, however, we can rely on each other to reinforce our new styles of teaching" (p. 59). The conducted research partially confirmed this claim. Some of the research participants, who before collaboration did not trust that certain teaching techniques could truly work, after the exposure to their colleagues' work in the classroom, converted and expressed willingness to utilize them in the future.

The study built its theoretical underpinnings on the existing models and theories of small group development. Due to the relative paucity of models of collaboration in higher education, the researcher utilized the available research conducted in business environment. The cyclical nature of the collaboration, as identified by the researcher in the conducted study, may be explained by a highly politicized milieu of academe. Finally, the fact that building relationships among faculty members has been found to be of paramount importance to the successful collaboration may point to the importance of the process over product in the academic environment.

RECOMMENDATIONS

The ability to choose relatable partners with compatible personalities has been single most consistent finding across all three cases. Trusting relationships among collaborators constitutes glue that keeps all other elements of the process together. Two, out of six, studied faculty members were assigned to collaborative teams administratively. It is recommended therefore that collaborating instructors have the ability to select the colleagues they feel most comfortable working with, rather than having administrators randomly assigning team members based on their availability.

The active participation of collaborating instructors in designing the course content has been strongly associated with the sense of ownership in the collaborative processes. The quote: "You are most committed to what you have created," was frequently repeated throughout the study. It is recommended therefore that collaborating instructors are made responsible for preparing course objectives, materials, and other related activities. Researcher's observations indicated that those collaborators who did not participate in designing the course showed less enthusiasm and commitment to collaboration, both within and outside of the classroom. Participation in collaborative design of the course has also been found to enhance interpersonal relationships between team members.

Enhancing awareness of the collaborative process among those who desire to teach collaboratively is strongly recommended. "Collaborative teaching does not just happen." The spirit of that statement, expressed by one of the research subjects, resonated strongly across all studied cases. Informants identified academic culture that glorifies and rewards individual faculty achievements as the culprit. According to research subjects, since teamwork in academe is counterintuitive yet desired, there is a need to educate academic faculty in collaborative processes, techniques, and methods. According to informants, many disappointments could have been avoided had the professors been educated in certain areas. Austin and Baldwin (1991) noted, "Successful collaborations involve a complex set of attributes and activities, each requiring careful attention from the parties involved. Faculty who wish to collaborate should be familiar with all aspects of this process" (p. 98). However, training in specific areas was suggested by the research subjects to be more valuable during the process of collaboration not before or after. It is recommended therefore that training on the effective use of collaborative teaching be applied generously but most importantly timely–during the collaborative process.

A review of data indicated that not all academic faculty members are suitable for the collaborative teaching. It should never be assumed by administrators that every professor on staff is a potential candidate for collaboration. Research subjects attributed certain personality traits of effective collaborators. Professors with a strong need for power and control or strongly domineering individuals may not be good candidates for collaborators. Faculty members need to express the intrinsic interest in teaching with peers and be ready to commit their time to work with them. Robinson and Schaible (1995), based on their six-year experience with collaborative teaching advised, "Look for a co-teacher with a healthy psyche. Choose a person who doesn't appear to have a strong need for power or control, who is comfortable with him- or herself, and who is not easily offended or put on the defensive" (p. 57). Wilson and Martin (1998), when discussing prerequisites for collaborative teaching, identified a strong "psyche" as one of the key elements of a suitable collaborator:

> Another prerequisite is a strong psyche. Team teachers share the stage in the classroom. One's teaching is constantly observed– and evaluated–by the other. The center of authority is constantly moving, with teachers being equal one moment and in a more or less dominant position the next. (p. 8)

It is recommended to include junior faculty on collaborative teams. The researcher observed that collaborative setting enabled less experienced faculty easier transition into the teaching profession. On one occasion, Mr. Armstrong acknowledged, "I still feel like I'm a learner….I've learned that I can do things I didn't think I could do before." As a consequence, the researcher recommends that collaborative teaching be used as a mentoring tool, introducing new faculty to the teaching profession more effectively.

It is recommended to promote collaboration in academe. Austin and Baldwin (1991) noted that, "Data on the outcomes of collaboration are not universally positive. Yet sufficient information supports the benefits of collaborative relationships to recommend them as a useful vehicle for extending academic resources and enriching academic life" (p. 97). The researcher found that teachers who collaborate grow professionally, learn from each other, reflect on their teaching, exude more creativity, strengthen bondages among departmental faculty, promote learning environment, create knowledge, and encourage risk-taking more willingly. Austin and Baldwin (1991) further reinforced their recommendation:

> Both empirical evidence and anecdotal reports testify to the value of collaborative relationships....Evidence also suggests that collaborators tend to be more creative and less averse to risk than those who work alone. Personal benefits, such as greater satisfaction with work and overall psychological well-being, are correlated with collaborative activities as well. (p. 97)

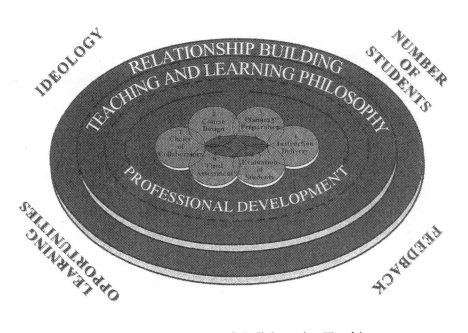

Figure1. The Process of Collaborative Teaching

WORKS CITED

Academic American Encyclopedia (Vols.1-21). (1996). Danbury: Grolier Incorporated.

Austin, A. E., & Baldwin, R. G. (1991). Faculty Collaboration: Enhancing the Quality of Scholarship and Teaching. (In ASHE-ERIC Higher Education Report no. 7). Washington, DC: George Washington University. (ERIC Document Reproduction Service No. ED 346 805).

Oxford Dictionary of Quotations, The. (1999). Oxford University Press.

Alter, S. (2006). Pitfalls in Analyzing Systems in Organizations. Journal of Information Systems Education. 17(3): 295-302.

Baer, L., Knodel, B., Quistgaard, J., & Weir I. (1993). Partners in Progress: An Integrative Approach to Educational Quality. In D. Hubbard (Ed.), Continuous Quality Environment (pp. 199-221). Maryville, MO: Prescott Publishing.

Banta, T. (1993). Is There Hope for TQM in the Academy? In D. L. Hubbard (Ed.), Continuous Quality Environment (pp. 142-158). Maryville, MO: Prescott Publishing.

Barr, R. & Tagg, J. (1995). From Teaching to Learning–A New Paradigm for Undergraduate Education. Change: 27, 13-25.

Bazerman, C. (2005). Practically Human: The Pragmatist Project of the Interdisciplinary Journal of Psychiatry. Linguistics and the Human Sciences, 1(2), 15-38.

Bazerman, C. (2008). Handbook of Research on Writing: History, Society, School, Individual, Text. London: Routledge.

Beard, R., Myhill, D., Riley, D., & Nystrand, M. (Eds.). (2009). The SAGE Handbook of Writing Development. London: SAGE.

Bennis, W., & Shepard, H. (1956). A Theory of Group Development. Human Relations, 9(4): 415-437.

Bensimon, E. (1993). Redesigning Collegiate Leadership: Teams and Teamwork in Higher Education. Baltimore, MD: The Johns Hopkins University Press.

Bergen, D. (1994). Developing the Art and Science of Team Teaching. Childhood Education: 70, 242-244.

Bertram, B. (1998). "Twenty-First Century Literacy." Online Posting. July, 7, 2003. <http://alexia.lis.uiuc.edu/~chip/pubs/21stcentury/>.

Betts, S. C. (2009). Hunches and Leaps of Faith: Intuition and Faith in Decision Making. Allied Academies International Conference. Academy of Organizational Culture, Communications and Conflict Proceedings. 14(2): 6-9.

Bocchino, R. & Bocchino, K. (1997). The Art of Presenting: Advanced Techniques and Strategies for Facilitating Transformational Learning. Conference Presented by the Ohio Department of Education. (Division of Federal Assistance. Deer Creek State Park, Ohio, June 2-3, 1997).

Bogdan, R. C. & Biklen, S. K. (1992). Qualitative Research for Education: An Introduction to Theory and Methods. Boston, MA: Allyn and Bacon.

Borrego, M & Newswander, L. K. (2010). Definitions of Interdisciplinary Research: Toward Graduate-Level Interdisciplinary Learning Outcomes. Review of Higher Education. 34 (1): 61-84.

Bowles, P. D. (1994). The Collaboration of Two Professors from Two Disparate Disciplines: What It Has Taught Us. Paper Presented at the Symposium "Collaboration Pays Off: An Advance Program for At-Risk College Freshmen Teaches a Few Lessons to the Students, Faculty, and the Institution," at the Annual Meeting of the National Reading Conference (San Diego, CA, November 30 - December 3). (ERIC Document Reproduction Service No. ED 386 744).

Braun, N. M. (2004). Critical Thinking in the Business Curriculum. Journal of Education for Business. 79 (4): 232-236.

Burchfield, J.D. (1990). Lord Kelvin and the Age of the Earth. University of Chicago Press.

Capra, F. (1996). The web of life. New York: Anchor Books.

Carothers, R. L. & Richmond, J. (1993). Faculty as Customers: Hard Lessons for Administrators. In D. L. Hubbard (Ed.), Continuous Quality Environment (pp. 180-199). Maryville, MO: Prescott Publishing.

Chang, H. (2004). Inventing Temperature: Measurement and Scientific Progress. Oxford University Press.

Choi, B. C., & Pak, A. W. (2006). Clinical and Investigative Medicine. 29 (6): 351-364

Claucius, R. (1850). On the Moving Force of Heat and the Laws of Heat which May Be Deduced Therefrom. Oxford University Press.

Clayton, C. M. & Eyring, H. J., (2011). The Innovative University: Changing the DNA of Higher Education from the Inside Out. San Fransisco, CA: Jossey-Bass Inc.

Cone, T. P., Werner, P., &. Cone, S. L. (2009). Interdisciplinary Elementary Physical Education Champaign, IL: Human Kinetics.

Cooper, H. M. (1984). The Integrative Research Review: A Systematic Approach. Beverly Hills, CA: Sage Publications.

Corben H. & Philip S. (1994). Classical Mechanics (Reprint of 1960 Second Ed.). Courier Dover Publications.

Coveney P. & Highfield R. (1992). The Arrow of Time : A Voyage Through Science to Solve Time's Greatest Mystery. Fawcett Books.

Creswell, J. W. (1994). Research Design: Qualitative and Quantitative Approaches. Thousand Oaks, CA: Sage Publications, Inc.

Creswell, J. W. (1998). Qualitative Inquiry and Research Design: Choosing Among Five Traditions. Thousand Oaks, CA: Sage Publications, Inc.

Davies, P. (1988). The Cosmic Blueprint. New York: Simon and Schuster.

Davis, J. R. (1995). Interdisciplinary Courses and Team Teaching. Phoenix, AZ: American Council on Education and the Oryx Press.

Day, R. & Day, J. (1977). A Review of the Current State of Negotiated Order Theory: An Appreciation and a Critique. The Sociological Quarterly, 18: 126-142.

Deming, W. E., (1996). Out of the Crisis. MIT. Cambridge, Massachusetts.

Deming W. E., (1995). The New Economics for Industry, Government, and Education. MIT. 1993 (Second Edition, 1995).

Denzin, N. K. (1970). The Research Act in Sociology: A Theoretical Introduction to Sociological Methods. Chicago, IL: Aldine Publishing Company.

Denzin, N. & Lincoln, Y. (1994). Research Design: Qualitative and Quantitative Approaches. Thousand Oaks, CA: Sage.

Denzin, N. K. & Lincoln, Y. S. (Eds.) (1994). Handbook of Qualitative Research. Thousand Oaks, CA: Sage Publications, Inc.

Dinur, A. R. (2011). Common and Un-Common Sense in Managerial Decision Making under Task Uncertainty. Management Decision. 49 (5): 694-709.

Donaldson, A. D. & Sanderson, D. R. (1996). Working Together in Schools: A Guide for Educators. Thousand Oaks, CA: Corwin Press, Inc.

Drexler, A. B. & Forester, R. (1998). Teamwork-Not Necessarily the Answer. Human Resource Magazine, 55-58.

Educational Testing Service, (1992). A Guide to the NTE Core Battery Tests. Princeton, NJ: Author.

Ellis, A. (1985). Overcoming Resistance. New York, NY: Springer Publishing Company.

Eisner, E. W. & Peshkin, A. (1990). Qualitative Inquiry in Education. New York, NY: Teachers College Press, Columbia University.

Erickson, R. (1986). Qualitative Methods in Research on Teaching. In M.C. Wittrock (Ed.), Handbook of Research on Teaching (pp. 119-162). New York, NY: Macmillan Publishing Company.

Ernst, M. (2005). One Long Argument: Charles Darwin and the Genesis of Modern Evolutionary Thought. Harvard University Press.

Fennel, M. & Sandefur, G. (1983). Structural Clarity of Interdisciplinary Teams: A Research Note. Journal of Applied Behavioral Science, 19(2): 193-202.

Fey, M. H. (1996). Transcending Boundaries of the Independent Scholar: The Role of Institutional Collaboration. Paper Presented at the Annual Meeting of the Conference on College Composition and Communication (Milwaukee, WI, March 27-30). (ERIC Document Reproduction Service No. ED 397 402).

Fisser, S. & Browaeys, M. J. (2010). Team Learning on the Edge of Chaos. The Learning Organization. 17 (1): 58-68.

Flower, L., Wallace, D. L., Norris, L., & Burnett R. E. (1994). Making Thinking Visible: Writing, Collaborative Planning, and Classroom Inquiry. Urbana, IL: National Council of Teachers of English.

Fox, M. & Faver, C. (July 1982). The Process of Collaboration in Scholarly Research. Scholarly Publishing, 13: 327-39.

Freed, J. E., Klugman M. R., & Fife J. D (1997). A Culture for Academic Excellence: Implementing the Quality Principles in Higher Education. Washington, DC: The George Washington University.

Gabor, A. (1990). The Man Who Discovered Quality. Random House, NY, 1990.

Geltner, B. B. (1994). The Power of Structural and Symbolic Redesign: Creating a Collaborative Learning Community in Higher Education. (ERIC Document Reproduction Service No. ED 374 757).

Gianfranco, M. (2007). Some New Theoretical Issues in Systems Thinking Relevant for Modelling Corporate Learning. The Learning Organization. 14 (6): 480-488.

Glaser, B. G. (1978). Advances in the Methodology of Grounded Theory: Theoretical Sensitivity. Mill Valley, CA: The Sociology Press.

Gray, B. (1989). Collaborating: Finding Common Ground to Multiparty Problems. San Francisco, CA: Jossey-Bass Inc.

Gray, H. (1980). Management in Education: Working Papers in the Social Psychology of Educational Institutions. Driffield, England: Nafferton Books.

Griggs, H. & Stewart, B. (1996). Community Building in Higher Education: To Bring Diverse Groups Together with Common Goals. Education, 117, 185-188.

Guarasci, R. & Cornwell, G. H. (1997). Democratic Education in an Age of Difference: Redefining Citizenship in Higher Education. San Francisco, CA: Jossey-Bass Publishers.

Guba, E. G. & Lincoln, Y. S. (Summer 1985). Fourth Generation Evaluation as an Alternative. Educational Horizons, 63, 139-141.

Guba, E. G. & Lincoln, Y. S. (1989). Fourth Generation Evaluation. Newbury Park, CA: Sage Publications, Inc.

Gunawardena, S., Rosina, W. & Agosto. D. E. (2010). Finding That Special Someone: Interdisciplinary Collaboration in an Academic Context. Journal of Education for Library and Information Science. 51 (4): 210-221.

Haber, M. W. (1991). Collaborative Teaching in Journalism. Paper Presented at the Southwest Education Council for Journalism and Mass Communications Symposium (Corpus Christi, TX, October 6, 1991). (ERIC Document Reproduction Service No. 341 053).

Hamel, J., Dufour, S., & Fortin, D. (1993). Case Study Methods. Newbury Park, CA: Sage Publications, Inc.

Hausman, C. R. (1979). Introduction: Disciplinarity or Interdisciplinarity. In J.J. Kockelmans (Ed.), Interdisciplinarity and Higher Education (pp. 1-11). University Park, PA: The Pensylvania State University Press.

Hess, J. D. & Bacigalupo, A. C. (2011). Enhancing Decisions and Decision-Making Processes through the Application of Emotional Intelligence Skills. Management Decision. 49 (5): 710-721.

Hewit, J. S. & Whittier, K. S. (1997). Teaching Methods for Today's Schools: Collaboration and Inclusion. Needham Heights, MA: Allyn & Bacon.

Howal-Zidon, M. M. (1994). Collaborative Teaching: A Case Study of an Alternative Method in Pre-service Education (Doctoral dissertation, The University of North Dakota, 1994). Dissertation Abstracts International, 55(12), 3815.

Hunter, J.D. (1991). Culture Wars: The Struggle to Define America. In J.H. Newman. The idea of a University (p. 322). New Haven: Yale University Press.

Incropera F. P., Dewit, D. P., Bergman, T. L., & Lavine, S. A. (2011). Fundamentals of Heat and Mass Transfer. John Wiley & Sons Inc.

Jurkovich, R. & Paelinck, J. H. P. (1984). Problems in Interdisciplinary Studies. Vermont, England: Gower Publishing Company.

Kast, F. E. & Rosenzweig, J. E. (1996). General Systems Theory: Applications for Organizations and Management. In M. T. Matteson & J. M. Ivancevich (Eds.), Management and organizational behavior classics (pp. 47-65). Chicago, IL: Irwin.

Klein, J. T. (1990). Interdisciplinarity: History, Theory, and Practice. Detroit, MI: Wayne State University Press.

Lane, M. E. (1993). Team-Based TQM: A Model for Post-Bureaucracy. In D. L. Hubbard (Ed.), Continuous quality environment (pp.33-50). Maryville, MO: Prescott Publishing.

Leaptrott, J & McDonald, J. M. (2008). Assessing Managerial Decision Using the Dual Systems Theory of Reasoning: Future Challenges for Management Researchers. Academy of Entrepreneurship Journal. 14 (1/2): 77-93.

Kilian C. S. (1992). The World of W. Edwards Deming. Second Edition, SPC Press Inc., Knoxville.

Klein, J. T. (2006). Resources for Interdisciplinary Studies. Change. 38 (2): 50-56.

Knowles, R.N. (2002). The Leadership Dance: Pathways to Extraordinary Organizational Effectiveness. ISBN 9780972120401.

Lane, D. A. & Down, M. (2010). The Art of Managing for the Future: Leadership of Turbulence. Management Decisions. 48 (4): 512-527.

Lewin, K. (1936). <u>Principles of Topological Psychology</u>. New York: McGraw-Hill.

Lewis, R. G. & Smith, D. H. (1994). <u>Total Quality in Higher Education</u>. Delray Beach, FL: St. Lucie Press.

Liening, A. (2013). The Breakdown of the Traditional Mechanistic Worldview: the Development of Complexity Sciences and the Pretense of Knowledge in Economics. <u>Modern Economy</u>. <u>4(4)</u>: 305-319

Locke, L. F., Spirduso, W. W., & Silverman, S. J. (1987). <u>Proposals that Work: A Guide for Planning Dissertations and Grant Proposals</u> (2nd edition). Newbury Park, CA: Sage.

Maeroff, G. I. (1993). <u>Team Building for School Change: Equipping Teachers for New Roles</u>. New York, NY: Teachers College Press.

Mayo, D. G. & Gilliland, B. E. (1979). <u>Learning and instructional improvement digest</u>. Memphis, TN: Memphis State University Press.

McLaren, P. G., Mills, A. J., & Durepos, G. (2009). Disseminating Drucker: Knowledge, tropes and the North American Management Textbook. <u>Journal of Management History</u>. <u>15 (5)</u>: 388-403.

McCarthy L. P. & Walvoord B. E. (1988). Models for Collaborative Research in Writing Across the Curriculum. In S. H. McLeod (Ed.), <u>Strengthening Programs for Writing Across the Curriculum</u> (pp. 77-91). San Francisko, CA: Jossey-Bass Inc., Publishers.

Merriam, S. B. (1988). <u>Case Study Research in Education: A Qualitative Approach</u>. San Francisco, CA: Jossey-Bass.

Merriam, S. B. (1991). <u>Case Study Research in Education: A Qualitative Approach</u>. San Francisco: Jossey-Bass.

Miller, S. (1994). New Discourse City: An Alternative Model for Collaboration. In S. B. Reagan, T. Fox, & D. Bleich (Eds.), <u>New</u>

Directions in Collaborative Teaching, Learning, and Research (pp. 283-300). Albany, NY: State University of New York Press.

Moran, M. J. & Shapiro, H. (2007). Fundamentals of Engineering Thermodynamics. John Wiley & Sons Inc.

Nelson, D. & Cox, M. (2004). Lehninger Principles of Biochemistry. Palgrave Macmillan

Neufeldt, V. (1994). Webster's New World Dictionary (7th ed., Vols. 1-20). New York, NY: Prentice Hall.

Newton, I. (1687). Principia, Book I, Scholium I, especially 15-16.

Neumann, K. (2013). Know Why' Thinking as a New Approach to Systems Thinking. Emergence: Complexity and Organization. 15 (3): 81-93.

Nobel, D. (1986). The Interaction of Task Type and Social Structure in Small Groups: An Analysis of Success in Interdisciplinary Research Teams. Ph.D. Dissertation, Stanford University.

Palaima, T. & Skarzauskiene, A. (2010). Systems Thinking as a Platform for Leadership Performance in a Complex World. Baltic Journal of Managemenet. 5(3): 330-355

Parker, G. (1990). Team Players and Teamwork. San Francisco, CA: Jossey Bass.

Parlett, M. & Hamilton, D. (1976). Evaluation as Illumination: A New Approach to the Study of Innovative Programmes. In G. Glass (Ed.), Evaluation Studies Review Annual, 1, 140-157.

Pellissier, R. (2012). A Proposed Frame of Reference for Complexity Management as Opposed to the Established Linear Management Strategies. International Journal of Organizational Innovation (Online). 5 (2): 6-67.

Pilarik, L. & Sarmany-Schuller, I. (2009). Emotional Intelligence and Decision-Making of Female Students of Social Work in the Iowa Gambling Task. Studia Psychologica. 51 (4): 319-328.

Pope, A. (1999). The Oxford Dictionary of Quotations. Oxford University Press.

Prigogine, I. & Fengers, I. (1984). Order Out of Chaos. New York: Bantam Books.

Ramirez, R. (1983). Action Learning: A Strategic Approach for Organizations Facing Turbulent Conditions. Human Relations, 36(8): 725-742.

Prince, M.J., and RM. Felder. (2006). Inductive Teaching and Learning Methods: Definitions, Comparisons, and Research Bases. Journal of Engineering Education, 95 (2): 123-38.

Robinson, B. & Schaible, R. M. (1995). Collaborative Teaching: Reaping the Benefits. College-Teaching, 43, 57-59.

Seaman, D. (1981). Working Effectively with Task Oriented Groups. New York, NY: McGraw Hill.

Schein, E. (1969). Process Consultation: Its Role in Organization Development. Reading, MA: Addison-Wasley Publishing Company.

Scherkenbach, W. (1991). Deming's Road to Continual Improvement. SPC Press, Knoxville, Tennessee. Competitive Thinking: Right or Wrong?

Seger, L. (2011). Agency Sales. 41 (6):41-42.

Senge, P. (1990). The Fifth Discipline: The Art and Practice of the Learning Organization. New York, NY: Doubleday Dell Publishing Group, Inc.

Shannon, C. & Weaver, W. (1949). The Mathematical Theory of Communication. Urbana, ILL: University of Illinois Press.

Simeone, A. (1987). <u>Academic Women: Working Towards Equality</u>. South Hadley, MA: Bergin and Garvey Publishers.

Simpson, J. A. & Weiner, E. S. (1989). <u>The Oxford English dictionary</u> (2nd ed.,Vols. 1-20). Oxford: Clarendon Press.

Sinclair, M. & Ashkanasy, N. M. (2005). Intuition: Myth or a Decision-Making Tool? <u>Management Learning</u>. <u>36 (3)</u>: 353-370.

Singh, H. & Singh A. (2002). Principles of Complexity and Chaos Theory in Project Execution: A New Approach to Management. <u>Cost Engineering</u>. <u>44 (12)</u>: 23-32.

Skarzauskiene, A. (2010). <u>Measuring Business Excellence</u>. <u>14 (4)</u>: 49-64). Bottom of FormSlavin, R. (1996). Research on Cooperative Learning and Achievement: What We Know. What We Need to Know. <u>Contemporary Educational Psychology</u>, <u>21</u>(1), 43-69.

Smith, K.A., S.D. Shepard, D.W. Johnson, & RT. Johnson. (2005). Pedagogies of Engagement: Classroom-Based Practices. <u>Journal of Engineering Education,</u> <u>94 (1)</u>: 87-101.

Smith, L. M. (1990). Ethics in Qualitative Field Research: An Individual Perspective. In E. W. Eisner & A. Peshkin (Eds.), <u>Qualitative Inquiry in Education: The Continuing Debate</u>. New York, NY: Teachers College Press, Columbia University.

Smith, S. C. & Scott, J. J. (1990). <u>The Collaborative School: A Work Environment for Effective Instruction</u>. Eugene, OR: Clearinghouse on Educational Management University of Oregon.

Soltis, J. F. (1990). The Ethics of Qualitative Research. In E. W. Eisner, & A. Peshkin (Eds.), <u>Qualitative inquiry in education</u>. New York, NY: Teachers College Press, Columbia University.

Sterman, J. D., (2000). <u>Business Dynamics: Systems Thinking and Modeling for a Complex World</u>. NY: McGraw-Hill Higher Education.

Sperling, M. (1994). Speaking of writing: When Teacher and Student Collaborate. In S. B. Reagan, T. Fox, & D. Bleich (Eds.), <u>New Directions in Collaborative Teaching, Learning, and Research</u> (pp. 213-227). Albany, NY: State University of New York Press.

Srivastva, S., Obert, S., & Neilsen, E. (1977). Organizational Analysis through Group Processes: A Theoretical Perspective for Organization Development. In C. Cooper (Ed.), <u>Organizational Development in the UK and USA: A Joint Evaluation</u>. London: The Macmillan Press LTD.

Stake, R. (1995). <u>The Art of Case Study Research</u>. Thousand Oaks, CA: Sage Publications, Inc.

Stanford, J., (2008). Lecture on Genetics and Entropy. Cornell University.

Stevenson, B. W. (2012). Application of Systemic and Complexity Thinking in Organizational Development.<u>Emergence: Complexity and Organization</u>. <u>14 (2)</u>: 86-99.

Strenski, E. (1988). Writing Across the Curriculum at Research Universities. In S. H. McLeod (Ed.), <u>Strengthening programs for writing across the curriculum</u> (pp. 31-43). San Francisko, CA: Jossey-Bass Inc., Publishers.

Swenson, R. (1997). Autocatakinetics, Evolution, and the Law of Maximum Entropy Production: A principled Foundation toward the Study of Human Ecology. <u>Advances in Human Ecology</u>, <u>6</u>, 1-46.

Swenson, R. & Turvey, M. (1991). Thermodynamic Reasons for Perception-Action Cycles. <u>Ecological Psychology</u>, <u>3(4)</u>, 317-348.

Thornton, B., Peltier, G., & Perreault, G. (2004). Systems Thinking: A Skill to Improve Student Achievement. <u>The Clearing House</u>. <u>77 (5)</u>: 222-227.

Trist, E. (1983). Referent Organizations and the Development of Interorganizational Domains. In R. Tannenbaum, R. Marguiles, and F. Massarik (Eds.), <u>Human systems development</u>. San Fransisco: Jossey-Bass, 1985.

Tuckman, B. (1965). Developmental Sequence in Small Groups. Psychological Bulletin, (63)6: 384-89.

Tuckman, B. & Jensen, M. (1977). Stages of Small Group Development Revisited. Group and Organization Studies, 2(4): 419-427.

Vance, C., Deone, Z., & Groves K. Considering Individual Linear/ Nonlinear Thinking Style and Innovative Corporate Culture. International. Journal of Organizational Analysis. 16 (4): 232-248.

VanDyke, P. (1995). The Culture for Quality: Effective Faculty Teams. Maryville, MO: Prescott Publishing.

von Bertalanffy, L. (1968). Organismic Psychology and Systems Theory. Worchester: Clark University Press.

von Bertalanffy, L. (1976). General System Theory: Foundations, Development, Applications. Publisher: George Braziller.

Watson, M. (1996). Teaching to Learn: WAC, Composition, and Engineering Classrooms. Paper Presented at the Annual Meeting of the Conference on College Composition and Communication (Milwaukee, WI, March 27-30). (ERIC Document Reproduction Service No. ED 398 587).

White, H. C. (2001). Markets from Networks: Socioeconomic Models of Production. Princeton, NJ: Princeton University Press.

Wiedmeyer, D. & Lehman, J. (Spring 1991). The "House Plan": Approach to Collaborative Teaching and Consultation. Teaching Exceptional Children, 6-10.

Wilson, V. A. & Martin, K. M. (1998). Practicing what We Preach: Team Teaching at the College Level. Paper Presented at the Annual Meeting of the Association of Teacher Educators (Dallas, TX, February 13-17, 1998). (ERIC Document Reproduction Service No. ED 417 172).

Woodside, A. G. (2006). Advancing Systems Thinking and Building Microworlds in Business and Industrial Marketing. The Journal of

Business & Industrial Marketing. 21 (1): 24-29. Advancing systems thinking and building microworlds in business and industrial marketing

Yeats, D.E. & Hyten, C. (1998). High-Performing Self-Managed Work Teams: A Comparison of Theory to Practice. Thousand Oaks, CA: Sage Publications, Inc.

Yin, R. K. (1989). Case Study Research: Design and Methods. Newbury Park, CA: Sage.

Yin, R. K. (1989a). Case Study Research: Design and Method (Revised Edition). Newbury Park, CA: Sage Publications Inc.

Zander, A. (1979). The Psychology of Group Processes. Annual Review of Psychology, 30: 417-51.

Zangwill, W. & Harry, R. V. (1993). Benchmarking outstanding leadership in higher education: Innovation today and tomorrow. Thousand Oaks, CA: Sage Publications, Inc.